ALLERTON PUBLIC LIBRARY
DO NOT MARK
IN THE BOOK

ALLERTON PUBLIC LIBRARY
P9-EIF-445
3 121

South Carolina

By Henry Leifermann
Revised by Jane O'Boyle
Photography by Eric Horan

COMPASS AMERICAN GUIDES
An imprint of Fodor's Travel Publications

Compass American Guides: South Carolina
Editor: Paul Eisenberg
Compass Editorial Director: Paul Eisenberg
Compass Creative Director: Fabrizio La Rocca
Editorial Production: David Downing
Photo Editor and Archival Researcher: Melanie Marin
Map Design: Mark Stroud, Moon Street Cartography
Cover Photo: Eric Horan

Copyright © 1995, 1998, 2000, 2006 Fodors LLC
Maps copyright © 1995, 1998, 2000, 2006 Fodors LLC

Compass American Guides and colophon are registered trademarks of Random House, Inc.
Fodor's is a registered trademark of Random House, Inc.
All rights reserved under International and Pan-American Copyright Conventions. Published in
the United States by Fodor's Travel Publications, a unit of Fodors LLC, a subsidiary of Random
House, Inc., and simultaneously in Canada by Random House of Canada Limited, Toronto.
Distributed by Random House, Inc., New York.
No maps, illustrations, or other portions of this book may be reproduced in any form without
written permission from the publisher.

Fourth Edition
ISBN 1–4000–1485–9
The details in this book are based on information supplied to us at press time, but changes
occur all the time, and the publisher cannot accept responsibility for facts that become outdated
or for inadvertent errors or omissions.

Compass American Guides, 1745 Broadway, New York, NY 10019

PRINTED IN CHINA
10 9 8 7 6 5 4 3 2 1

To the fine people of South Carolina.

CONTENTS

Topical Essays and Sidebars

Maps

Literary Extracts

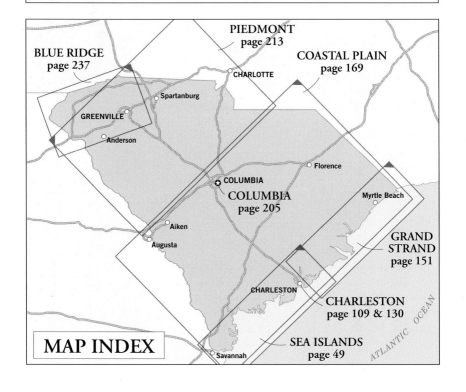

PIEDMONT
page 213

BLUE RIDGE
page 237

COASTAL PLAIN
page 169

CHARLOTTE

Spartanburg

GREENVILLE

Anderson

Florence

COLUMBIA

COLUMBIA
page 205

Myrtle Beach

Aiken

Augusta

**GRAND
STRAND**
page 151

CHARLESTON

CHARLESTON
page 109 & 130

SEA ISLANDS
page 49

Savannah

ATLANTIC OCEAN

MAP INDEX

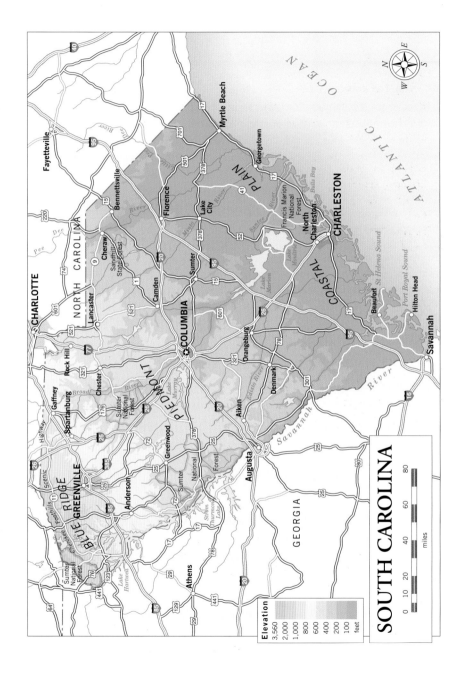

SOUTH CAROLINA

OVERVIEW

■ SEA ISLANDS

The Sea Islands comprise more than half of South Carolina's coastline and are separated from the mainland by sprawling estuaries and salt marshes. The sunny beaches of Hilton Head and Folly Beach are among the liveliest on the Atlantic, while the wetlands of Edisto and Hunting islands are among the most pristine. The natural beauty of this gentle coast and its sea-buried treasures of oysters, crab, and shrimp are as compelling as its historic sites, such as the graceful antebellum mansions in Beaufort and the Penn Center on St. Helena Island, where freed slaves first found schooling.

■ COASTAL PLANTATIONS

Scattered along the coast and nearby rivers are dozens of plantation manor houses, palatial keepsakes from the Old South. Among the most impressive are Drayton Hall, dating to the mid-1700s; Hampton Plantation, where the well-known Pinckney family greeted George Washington on the portico; and the magnificent gardens of Middleton Place.

■ CHARLESTON

More than a hundred years older than the United States itself, Charleston is the jewel of South Carolina. Its rich history is lovingly preserved throughout the city, from Revolutionary War–era cobblestone streets to elegant antebellum homes along the Battery and from the gracious new suspension bridge to Fort Sumter, where the first shot of the Civil War was fired.

■ MYRTLE BEACH AND GRAND STRAND

The Grand Strand beaches, broad expanses of white sand, stretch for over 60 miles, nearly all of which are covered with beach towels during summer months. Myrtle Beach, the largest town on the Strand, attracts thousands of visitors to its high-rise hotels, golf courses, restaurants, shopping outlets, and music theaters. Brookgreen Gardens, with its extensive collection of American sculpture, lies in quiet splendor at the south end of the Strand in Murrells Inlet, itself famous for its row of seafood restaurants.

Middleton Place, the nation's oldest landscaped gardens.

■ Coastal Plain

This region of varied terrain—swamps, pastures, farmland, and forest—encompasses two-thirds of the state, including the capital city. Cultured and historic Columbia offers a number of museums and restaurants as well as one of the nation's best zoos. Throughout the region are inviting small towns such as Camden and Sumter.

■ Piedmont

Once the region of hardscrabble farming, the Piedmont has become the manufacturing center of the state. The small town of Edgefield dates its cottage industry to 2500 BC, when the Catawba tribe crafted pottery from the region's distinctive soil; Edgefield potteries still thrive today. Abbeville's charms have less to do with industry than with the subtle elegance of its town square and redbrick thoroughfares. This region is also home to four significant Revolutionary War battle sites.

■ Blue Ridge

This northwest corner of South Carolina is a mountain wilderness. Found here are magnificent waterfalls, trout-filled lakes and streams, hiking trails through forests of hemlock, and gorges draped with moss. Running the Chattooga River is one of the most thrilling whitewater adventures in the country.

SOUTH CAROLINA FACTS
THE PALMETTO STATE

CAPITAL:
Columbia

STATE FLOWER:
Carolina (yellow) jessamine

STATE ANIMAL:
Whitetail deer

STATE BIRD:
Carolina wren

STATE TREE:
Palmetto

STATE FISH:
Striped bass

STATE REPTILE:
Loggerhead turtle

ENTERED UNION:
May 23, 1788, 8th in the United States

STATE MOTTO:
Dum Spiro Spero ("While I breathe, I hope")

POPULATION: 4,218,460 (2005)
White 63%
Black 28%
Hispanic 1.5%
Asian/Pacific 1%
Native American .3%
Mixed/Other 6.2%

FIVE LARGEST METROPOLITAN AREAS:

Columbia	664,229
Greenville	574,939
Charleston	562,665
Spartanburg	259,322
Myrtle Beach	206,039

ECONOMY:

Principal industries: tourism, agriculture, manufacturing
Principal manufactured goods: automobiles and aviation components, textiles, chemicals
Principal crops: soybeans, cotton, corn, peaches, hay, tobacco
Per capita income: $18,795 (38th highest)

Kayaking in the Lowcountry.

GEOGRAPHY:

Size: 30,111 square miles (40th largest)
Highest point: 3,560 feet (Sassafras Mountain)
Lowest point: sea level (Atlantic Ocean)

CLIMATE:

Highest Temp	Camden	111° F	July 28, 1985
Lowest Temp.	Caesar's Head	-19°F	Jan. 21, 1985
Driest Place	Columbia	41.95"	Ann. Rainfall
Wettest Place	Caesar's Head	81.16"	Ann. rainfall

FAMOUS SOUTH CAROLINIANS:

Lee Atwater   Bernard Baruch   Charles Bolden   James Brown
James Francis Byrnes   John C. Calhoun   Chubby Checker
Mary Boykin Chesnut   Pat Conroy   James Dickey   Dorothea Benton Frank
Leeza Gibbons   Dizzy Gillespie   Andrew Jackson   Jesse Jackson   Jasper Johns
Robert Jordan   Francis Marion   Andie McDowell   Mickey Spillane
Strom Thurmond   Vanna White

HISTORY AND CULTURE

South Carolina tumbles down from the southeast corner of the Blue Ridge Mountains, southeast through a rolling piedmont across a rich coastal plain and washes down toward the sea through massive river deltas, which form a spiderweb of magnificent tidal creeks and salt marshes. These low waters are protected from the Atlantic Ocean by a chain of countless barrier islands that span 187 miles of coastline. This is one of the smaller states of the union, at least in physical area. You can pick mountain blueberries along the churning Chattooga River in the morning and still drive across the state in time to watch an ocean sunset at Kiawah Island. Measured in terms of the human senses, however, South Carolina is probably the gentle giant of the continental United States.

Spanish moss drapes lazily from the gnarled, embracing limbs of incredible trees, the largest oaks this side of the continental divide, muffling the call of the chickadee and painted bunting. Peaches and pecan trees give shady respite from rolling fields of tobacco and tomatoes, which might radiate outward from a derelict manor house. So might a lane of rotting wooden shacks behind the kitchen house, which take your breath away in their collective simplicity and enduring silence. Sultry jasmine scents the winter walls of camellia while you pull a crab up from a "pluff mud" creek and a giant wood stork squawks through the heavy air toward a salt breeze.

Family members congregate under the same camellias their ancestors planted, because South Carolinians don't leave here, at least not for long. Bottle-nosed dolphins play beneath an ocean sunset where the Edisto River rushes out into the sea. The horizons are wide in the Lowcountry, the shrimp is sweet and the water is warm.

In South Carolina, the pace is slow and the voices soft because time stopped here a long time ago. Some mistake this for backwardness, but it is quite the opposite: it is the enduring quality of a culture closely connected to nature, for better or worse. As you sip a sweet tea and suck down a salty oyster, you will wonder why you never visited here before, and you will reason how to come back as often as possible.

Peaceful Dolphin Head, the northern shore of Hilton Head Island.

An engraving by Jacques le Moyne depicts the French expedition under René de Laudonnière entering Port Royal Sound in 1564.

The Palmetto State was a pivotal player in American history for two centuries, beginning when it was founded in 1670. During the 1920s, a black expatriate named Kelly Miller declared: "South Carolina is the stormy petrel of the Union. She arouses the nation's wrath and rides upon the storm. There is not a dull period in her history."

On the heels of this observation, however, dullness set in for more than 60 years. The Great Depression, emigration to the industrial north and west, disenfranchised civil rights advocates, and poor education systems did not draw a lot of industry or interest from the outside world. However, these tough times carried long-hidden benefits to the future of South Carolina. The lack of economic development enabled the cash-strapped coastal cities to remain virtually untouched by the 20th-century wrecking balls of "progress." By the time the rest of the country was discovering the bucolic fields of Aiken horse farms and the pristine 18th-century Palladian architecture of downtown Charleston, it was the 1980s, and historic preservation had emerged in the local consciousness. South Carolinians found themselves with an unrivaled inventory of dense forests, rolling plantations, and massive and unspoiled river deltas, rich with wildlife, untouched barrier islands, and sandy beaches as far as the eye could see. In the last three decades, this state has used these assets to build a new industry—tourism—as well as newfound respect in the annals of American history.

■ THE LANDSCAPE

South Carolina's destiny was determined not so much by its geography as by its geology. While the surface soil in the northwestern third of the state is formed by the erosion of some of Earth's oldest rocks, nowhere within its 30,111 square miles (40th in land area among the 50 states) are there geologic deposits from the Upper Silurian or Carboniferous ages—meaning there are no significant mineral deposits, no iron ore, and no coal. The rivers and waterfalls would one day be harnessed to power the state's first textile mills, but in the early decades after colonization, the economy rested on agriculture. More specifically, it rested on a single crop: first, rice and, later, cotton. And the success of this single crop depended almost entirely on the labor of slaves. Therein lies the tale of South Carolina.

The broad bands of South Carolina's geologic formations, as well as its historical development, run parallel with its Atlantic coastline, in a diagonal from southwest to northeast. These five natural regions begin at the top with the Blue Ridge, then the Piedmont, sandhills, coastal plain, and, finally, the coastal zone. The sandhills along the center contain the fall line, where the land drops and rivers form rapids and waterfalls.

Formed by 2 million years of Atlantic Ocean fluctuation, the coastal plain comprises two thirds of the state's area, running roughly from the inland capital of Columbia to the sea. It is anchored by three major river systems: the Savannah, the Santee, and the Pee Dee, which flow from headwaters up in the Blue Ridge. These rivers are unnavigable through the coastal plain, where they are blocked by the rapids and waterfalls of the fall line. For this and other reasons, the fall line has split South Carolina into three distinct economic, political, and social provinces: the Upcountry, the Midlands, and the Lowcountry.

The summers in South Carolina are famously hot and muggy, hardly alleviated at the ocean by the sea breeze. Autumn is comfortably warm and pleasant, but this is hurricane season, so the perfect weather at this time might be interrupted by a furious storm. Winter is very mild, with very little or no snow throughout the state and the blooms of camellias and narcissus to brighten the short days. Springtime is spectacular, from the early buds of azalea and dogwood to the scented jasmine, gardenia, and the crowning glory of purple wisteria vines in great oak trees.

There are no large cities on the scale of Atlanta or Charlotte. This is a state of smaller towns, farms, and a lot of water. Tourists might often come for the 185 miles of beaches, but there is also a vast network of rivers and streams, and dozens of tremendous lakes (all man-made), such as Marion, Moultrie, and Murray. Some parts have oddly shaped, elliptical wetlands known as Carolina bays, whose origin is still unknown, although some claim an ancient meteor created these landscapes. The fresh waters are filled with bass and catfish, while the ocean yields 160 species of saltwater fish and shellfish.

Still 65 percent forested, South Carolina has more than 100 types of trees (most dominant are the longleaf pine and turkey oak), 43 types of snakes, and probably more bird varieties than any other state. This was why John James Audubon spent the 1830s here, doing the bulk of his research for *The Birds of America.* Despite its small towns and soothing nature, South Carolina possesses a sophisticated undercurrent that attracts artists and philosophers to this day.

■ THE COLONISTS

The indigenous tribes inhabiting South Carolina included primarily the Cherokee, who dominated the upper third of the state until European settlers started arriving in the early 1500s. There were also native uplanders who were Iroquois, Sioux, Algonquin, Creek, and Muskogee. On the coast, there were smaller tribes of Combahee, Edisto, Kiawah, Yemassee, Etiwan, Waccamaw, Wando, and Westo. They are all gone now. The native population was, as elsewhere, quickly eliminated by disease and war when the white settlers arrived. There are only a handful of indigenous descendants from other tribes remaining, primarily on a small Catawba reservation in the mountains.

The Lowcountry was the first part to be settled, along the string of sea islands on the Atlantic coast. In the river deltas from Georgetown through Charleston to the state line at Savannah, planters, seaport financiers, and merchants would amass great wealth. These early British settlements quickly took total political control of the whole colony, and some still sense the assumption of social superiority in the

"The Indians till the soil very diligently, using a kind of hoe made from fishbone fitted to wooden handles," wrote engraver Jacques le Moyne during the Laudonnière expedition of 1564.

Lowcountry. The Upcountry was settled throughout the 1700s by small farmers and tradesmen in the valleys and rolling hills above the fall line.

The Spanish were the first European adventurers to reach South Carolina. A caravel from Santo Domingo in what now is the Dominican Republic entered St. Helena Sound between Edisto Island and Beaufort on August 18, 1521. Two more Spanish caravels from Santo Domingo explored Winyah Bay at Georgetown the following summer, both times kidnapping Native Americans to sell as slaves back in Santo Domingo. In July 1526, the Spanish don Lucas Vásquez de Ayllón of Toledo led 500 settlers back to Winyah Bay and established San Miguel. This was the first European settlement in the state, predating the English settlement at Jamestown, Virginia, by 81 years. But a severe winter, disease, and the vengeful attacks of the natives forced the Spanish to abandon the site after just one year.

On May 1, 1540, Hernando de Soto trekked up from Florida and crossed over the Savannah River into what is now Aiken, across from Augusta, Georgia. He was searching for the fabled gold of the Cofitachequi—El Dorado—but did not find it in South Carolina. It is rumored that he plundered pearls from the natives, however,

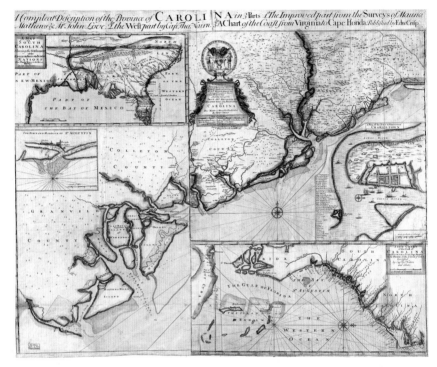

The coast and settlements of the "Province of Carolina," rendered by Edward Crisp in 1711.

and kept on going. He moved across the mountains and into the Mississippi River Valley, where he disappeared two months later and was never seen again.

The French came next. In 1562, a group of Huguenots fleeing religious persecution from their Catholic king, and led by Jean Ribault, sailed up Port Royal Sound between Beaufort and Hilton Head Island and landed near what is now the Parris Island Recruit Training Depot of the United States Marine Corps. The Huguenots erected "Charles Fort" on the island, but when a fire destroyed most of their supplies less than a year later, the colonists returned to France. Three years later, the Spanish arrived again from St. Augustine and built a fort, San Felipe, on the same site. Twenty years later, when Sir Francis Drake led English forces attacking St. Augustine, the Spanish withdrew from Fort San Felipe.

In 1663, British rice planters in Barbados sent William Hilton to the Carolina coast, in search of new lands to settle and plant. He did find an island and named it Hilton Head but, other than that, did not establish a presence for the Barbadian colonists. It was the British colonists in Bermuda who succeeded in settling, perhaps because they moved up the coastline, away from the Spanish ghost forts in Port Royal. In 1670, these Bermuda colonists settled on the west side of the Ashley River and named it Charles Town, after their king. Impoverished King Charles II deeded "Carolina," which extended from Virginia to Cape Canaveral in Spanish Florida, to eight of his backers, the Lords Proprietors. The lords recruited tough, savvy, wealthy and often unsavory sugar cane and tobacco planters from the West Indies to establish a rice industry for England's premier new colony. The colonists knew that West Africans had experience with this crop, and soon thousands of slaves were brought in to tame the new land.

By 1700, plantations spread through the Lowcountry and Sea Islands: along the Ashley, Cooper, Combahee, Pee Dee, Santee, Black, and Waccamaw rivers, and along St. Helena and Port Royal sounds near Beaufort. Settlers repeatedly fought off Spanish expeditions, as well as pirate attacks from Stede Bonnet and Edward "Blackbeard" Teach. In 1719, Carolinians threw out the assembly appointed by the Lords Proprietors to make their own laws and elect their own governor. By this time, the northern half of the new colony had taken form with a different type of settler and a different type of agriculture economy. These were primarily small farms settled by Welsh and Scots farmers, not the wide plantations and bustling port carved out by the Charles Town settlers. Since that part was now known as "North Carolina," the new governor, James Moore, presided over the royal province of what became "South Carolina."

By the 1730s, there were settlements inland: along the fall line at New Windsor (North Augusta), Fredericksburg (Camden), Saxe-Gotha (Cayce), and Orangeburg. Soon after, the Upcountry towns of York, Lancaster, and Chester were founded. These immigrants included Welsh Baptists, Swiss, Irish, Scots, and Germans, primarily from northern American colonies. They came to South Carolina via overland routes, getting away from harsh winters or vengeful native tribes. These pioneer Upcountry settlers, by inclination and background, differed from the aristocratic planter class who ran the state from Charles Town. They found themselves frozen out of the colony's new government, denied even their own courts and law officers. As a result, the Upcountry became a land of vigilante law during the 1760s, and posses called themselves Regulators.

Meanwhile, the Barbadian planters and English aristocrats grabbed up the land along the coastline and continued bringing in African slaves, primarily natives

A rendition of the Yemassee Indian massacre of 100 settlers near Port Royal in April of 1715.

from the areas that are now Senegal and Sierra Leone. There were soon 30,000 slaves on the plantations, compared to roughly 7,000 whites. Charles Town was the premier destination of the slave ships operating out of England. Between 1700 and 1775, 40 percent of all African slaves transported to North America came through Charles Town.

The Africans cleared swamps and built dikes and canals on plantations along the Lowcountry rivers near Beaufort, Charles Town, and especially Georgetown. These slaves developed a pidgin English that became a creole language called Gullah, and this language can still be heard in communities throughout the Lowcountry. In 1754, the slave colony's rice crop was almost 100,000 barrels, which weighed roughly 600 pounds each. Millions of English pounds poured into the accounts of a few hundred plantation owners, Charles Town merchants, and seaport shippers. No other group anywhere in the American colonies had such wealth.

History Timeline

1400s Between 15,000 and 20,000 indigenous people reside in the Carolinas.

1521 Spaniards from Santo Domingo visit South Carolina.

1562 French Huguenots build Charles Fort on what is today Parris Island, predating St. Augustine in Florida by three years.

1665 Eight Lords Proprietors receive a charter from King Charles II to establish the colony of Carolina.

1670 First permanent European (English) settlement is established on the west bank of the Ashley River at Albemarle Point.

1670s British planters from Barbados arrive in the Carolinas with African slaves.

1680 First English settlement moves to location of present-day Charleston.

1680s Scots and French Huguenots settle in the Carolinas.

1708 Colony's population includes 3,960 free white men, women, and children and 4,100 African slaves.

1715 Yemassee Indians attack colonial settlements.

1720 European population reaches 19,000.

1729 Colony divides into northern and southern provinces.

1730s Germans move into Midlands, Welsh along Big Pee Dee River.

1731 Georgia is carved out of the southern part of the original grant.

1739 Slaves burn plantations along Stono River and kill whites before they are stopped by the local militia.

1750s Scots-Irish move into Piedmont area through the 1760s.

1770 College of Charleston is founded; chartered in 1785.

1776 South Carolina sends four delegates to the Continental Congress in Philadelphia. They sign the Declaration of Independence.

1770s During the Revolutionary War 137 battles are fought in South Carolina up until 1783.

1780 British troops occupy Charles Town.

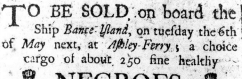

Slave sale advertisement 1744

1786   Capital moves from Charleston to Columbia.

1788   South Carolina ratifies the U. S. Constitution and becomes the eighth state in the Union.

1800s   Close to one-third of the slaves who arrive in the U. S. come through Sullivan's Island.

1801   University of South Carolina is chartered; opens as a college in 1805.

1822   Denmark Vesey, a free black carpenter, leads a slave revolt and is hanged.

1860   South Carolina secedes from the Union. Ten states follow to form the Confederate States of America in February 1861.

1861   First engagement of the American Civil War begins on April 12, when Confederate troops attack (Union) Fort Sumter in Charleston Harbor.

1863 Union assault and siege of Fort Wagner begin. After 58 days fort falls.

1865 The Union's General Sherman invades South Carolina. Confederate general Robert E. Lee surrenders at Appomattox.

1867 Reconstruction: During the next 10 years, under the Union's military and political supervision, the state reestablishes its government.

1877 Old guard (planters and merchants) establish "Bourbon Rule."

1880s Textile mills are built in the Piedmont.

1890 Benjamin R. Tillman, leader of the farmers' movement, is voted into the State House and later the U.S. Senate, ending the domination of the old guard.

1918 During World War I, more than 70,000 men from South Carolina join the armed services.

1923 Revenue from manufactured goods exceeds that of agricultural products for the first time.

1928 Julia Peterkin (of Calhoun County) is awarded the Pulitzer Prize for her novel *Scarlet Sister Mary.*

1941 Military training centers are established at Fort Jackson, Camp Croft, and Shaw Field; 173,642 people from South Carolina serve in World War II.

1960 Civil rights demonstrations begin.

1961 Desegregation is extended to city buses, railway, and bus station facilities.

1975 James Edwards becomes first Republican governor in 100 years.

1977 The Spoleto arts festival is inaugurated in Charleston.

1989 Hurricane Hugo destroys much of the coastline and inland for 200 miles.

1995 The Citadel, the Military College of South Carolina, is forced by federal courts to open its doors to women.

2001 The 1865 U.S.S. *Hunley* submarine is excavated from Charleston Harbor.

2005 State population reaches 4,218,460.

■ AMERICAN REVOLUTION

South Carolina's history of slavery, its antebellum Old South image, and its instigation of the Civil War have eclipsed in the minds of many Americans the Palmetto State's tremendous role in the Revolutionary War. Yet more patriot battles (137) took place in South Carolina than in any other state.

One month after the Battle of Bunker Hill in Massachusetts, South Carolina rebels seized the first British military installation taken by force in the war—Fort Charlotte, in McCormick County—on July 12, 1775. As historian David Duncan Wallace put it, from 1778 through 1780, South Carolina experienced "three years of war of a constancy and severity unparalleled in the North."

The landed Lowcountry planters were accustomed to getting their way, hated paying taxes to the Crown, and were leery of a growing British sensibility to eradicate slavery. They embraced the revolutionary cause with fervor. During the summer of 1775 in Charleston, Tory loyalists to the British crown were tarred, feathered, and paraded through the streets. Francis Marion, scion of French

Marion Crossing the Pee Dee *on his way to raid British forces at Georgetown, as depicted by artist William Tylee Ranney.*

FRANCIS MARION, THE SWAMP FOX

Born in 1732 of French Huguenot heritage in Winyah, near Georgetown, Francis Marion grew up in the forests and swamps of wild, young South Carolina. At the age of 29, he joined the army to fight in the Upcountry Cherokee wars, where he studied the art of guerilla warfare. He proved an attentive student.

Commissioned as an officer during the Revolutionary War, Marion served at Fort Moultrie in the defense of Charleston. When the city fell to the British in 1780, he took to the countryside to organize motley bands of South Carolina partisans against the British.

Before long, Marion's "armies" were attacking British wagon convoys and soldiers, inflicting sharp losses, and disappearing into the swamps, where pursuit was hopeless. From bases hidden on islands and trails unknown even to locals, Marion sent out spies who kept him posted on British plans and movements. Even with meager supplies and small numbers of fighting men, he successfully mired British operations, tying up soldiers and supplies in skirmishes for two years, without losing a battle.

When British general Banastre Tarleton was sent to capture Marion near Kingstree, he fought his last battle of the war before disappearing into Ox Swamp. Whipped and retreating, the English general supposedly snarled that the devil himself couldn't catch that "damned fox."

After the American Revolution, Marion served in the state senate and died in 1795. The Swamp Fox lives on in fiction, film, and history, and not least in William Cullen Bryant's poem "Song of Marion's Men." Actor Mel Gibson starred as a character based on Marion in the movie *The Patriot,* which was filmed in Chester, York, and Charleston counties.

Francis "the Swamp Fox" Marion.

THE STATE FLAG

The American Revolutionary victory at Fort Moultrie on June 28, 1776, inspired the symbols on the state flag: the native palmetto tree provided the logs from which the impenetrable fort was built. The state flag bears the silhouette of the palmetto on a blue field, under a crescent moon that was inspired by the insignia on the hats worn by Col. William Moultrie's militia. In recent years, some historians suggested that this crescent was not a moon but a gorget, the bygone metal plate worn to protect the neck of an officer. But most still agree the flag symbol came from the moon worn by Moultrie's uniformed heroes.

Huguenots, left his plantation on the Cooper River above Charleston to become a general known as "the Swamp Fox," raiding the British near Georgetown and on the Pee Dee River, then hiding his forces in Lowcountry swamps. When the young Marquis de Lafayette sailed from France to join the cause, it was South Carolina, near Georgetown, where he chose to land. Lowcountry rebels built a log fort of palmettos (now the state tree and emblem of the state flag) at Fort Moultrie on Sullivan's Island near the mouth of Charleston Harbor, then withstood shelling by nine British warships and blocked the land advance of 2,000 British troops. The victory delayed the British occupation of Charleston for four years, until 1780.

If in 1776 Lowcountry planters sent four delegates to sign the Declaration of Independence in Philadelphia, Upcountry settlers remained Tory Loyalists. These small farmers and merchants were unaffected by and indifferent to rising British taxes on imports and exports and considered their enemy to be the Lowcountry planter, not the British. In November 1775, it was these Tories who laid siege to a Patriot fort at the Piedmont town of Ninety Six, and there was not a British officer on the field of battle.

Lord Cornwallis established his British headquarters at Camden, surviving 14 battles in the vicinity, and finally captured Charleston in 1780. Later that year, when British forces massacred a surrendering force of the Continental Army near Lancaster, the Upcountry colonials got angry and finally joined forces with the

Lowcountry rebels. Cornwallis's strategy had been to join his regulars with the Upcountry Tories and march north to defeat George Washington in Virginia. Cornwallis had marched as far as North Carolina when the vengeful Upcountry rebels attacked and defeated British troops in the Battle of Kings Mountain, near the Piedmont town of Gaffney. Many historians consider that battle the turning point of the Revolution, since Cornwallis was forced to split his forces, returning half to South Carolina, leaving him too weak to defeat Washington, and leading to his surrender at Yorktown.

In 1790, Lowcountry planters appeased the Upcountry by moving the state capital to Columbia. Not far away, an inventor named Eli Whitney was tinkering with a contraption that would change forever the face of South Carolina industry.

■ ANTEBELLUM ERA AND CIVIL WAR

Cotton meant almost nothing to the rice barons of the Lowcountry until after the Revolutionary War. During the 1790s, cotton seed from Bermuda, the Bahamas, and the Caribbean was planted extensively on Sea Islands such as Edisto and St. Helena. The long, silky fibers of this Sea Island cotton were prized for laces and fine muslins. But rice remained the fortune maker until Eli Whitney invented the cotton gin in 1793, at a plantation on the Savannah River. The machine separated seeds from fibers in the cotton boll, or flower, freeing slaves from that task and enabling them to work on clearing, planting, and tilling new cotton fields. Whitney's gin made profitable the bulk production of shorter-fibered, cheaper cotton, as long as free labor worked the fields.

By 1811, South Carolina's cotton crop totaled 40 million pounds, 26 times the total just two decades earlier. By 1834, the state's crop reached 65.5 million pounds. At the outbreak of the Civil War in 1861, cotton accounted for 57 percent of the entire nation's exports. No other crop in the history of the United States has been so influential, and to see a cotton field in bloom today, usually by late August or mid-September, is to see a historic battlefield, of a sort.

Farmers in the coastal plain, fall line, and Upcountry wanted in on the cotton boom, and Charleston's cotton shippers and bankers were happy to help. They built canals to spread cotton and slavery into the interior. After New York's Erie Canal, the most important shipping canal in 1800 was the Santee, linking Charleston's Cooper River to the inland Santee River system. That 22-mile-long canal was followed by another, 67 miles long, linking the Catawba and Wateree rivers in the Upcountry near Lancaster, and other canals soon opened river routes for cotton barges all across the fall line.

In 1833, the South Carolina Canal & Railroad Company, owned by Charleston investors, began running the nation's first railroad—its first engine was named *The Best Friend of Charleston*—on a route from the port city southwest to Aiken and the Savannah River. Within a decade, the canals were virtually forgotten as railroads extended from Charleston to Columbia, Camden, and beyond into the Upcountry.

By then, Georgia and Alabama, where land was cheaper, had surpassed South Carolina in cotton production, and many Charleston cotton merchants and bankers, as well as Lowcountry cotton planters, were on the brink of ruin from overexpansion. Despite that, South Carolina continued to control virtually all Southern politics in these antebellum decades. And South Carolina's politics were controlled by the Lowcountry planters and Charleston financiers.

The most prominent politician was John C. Calhoun, an Upcountry congressman from Abbeville who had married a Lowcountry plantation heiress. As David Duncan Wallace, a South Carolinian himself, wrote, "Calhoun's career is one of the saddest tragedies of American history—a great mind and character caught up in a mistaken cause without being great enough to perceive and conquer the error."

The economy of Calhoun's home state and the fortunes of his planter supporters rested on cotton and slavery. He devoted his life to the preservation of both, resigning as President Andrew Jackson's vice president in 1832 to enter the U.S. Senate and lead the fight against federal export taxes on cotton. South Carolina threatened to secede from the Union over the tariff issue as far back as 1828, when Calhoun declared that "states' rights" should have more power than the federal government.

Calhoun died in 1850, leaving South Carolinians without a strong and temperate voice for resolution. They pressed the issue, however, trying and failing through the 1850s to recruit other Southern states into the idea of secession. By the time Abraham Lincoln was elected president, Lowcountry planters and Charleston financiers felt the only way to force other Southern states to join was with an irrevocable act.

On December 20, 1860, a special convention at St. Andrews Hall in Charleston voted to have South Carolina secede from the Union.

Portrait of John C. Calhoun by George P. A. Healy.

WHY SOUTH CAROLINA WILL SECEDE

Abraham Lincoln's election in 1860 was won without a single electoral vote from south of the Mason-Dixon line. Most Southerners felt that the election of a Republican president would end any Southern influence over the policies of the national government, and also end the Southern way of life. Resisting the warnings of moderates, South Carolina became the first state to secede from the Union, on December 20, 1860. It was soon followed by 10 other Southern states. The South Carolina "Declaration" lists the conditions that induced its secession.

On the 4th of March next this party will take possession of the government. It has announced that the South shall be excluded from the common territory, that the judicial tribunal shall be made sectional, and that a war must be waged against slavery until it shall cease throughout the United States.

The guarantees of the Constitution will then no longer exist; the equal rights of the states will be lost. The slaveholding states will no longer have the power of self-government or self-protection, and the federal government will have become their enemy.

Sectional interest and animosity will deepen the irritation; and all hope of remedy is rendered vain by the fact that the public opinion at the North has invested a great political error with the sanctions of more erroneous religious belief.

We, therefore, the people of South Carolina, by our delegates in convention assembled, appealing to the Supreme Judge of the world for the rectitude of our intentions, have solemnly declared that the Union heretofore existing between this state and the other states of North America is dissolved; and that the state of South Carolina has resumed her position among the nations of the world, as [a] separate and independent state, with full power to levy war, conclude peace, contract alliances, establish commerce, and to do all other acts and things which independent states may of right do.

Commissioners were dispatched to other southern states seeking a confederacy, and the South Carolina militia occupied without resistance the lightly guarded Union forts of Castle Pinckney, at the mouth of the Cooper River, and Fort Moultrie on Sullivan's Island, near the entrance to Charleston Harbor. Still, no other slave state joined the secession.

On April 15, 1861, South Carolina troops bombarded the Union's Fort Sumter at the entrance to Charleston Harbor. After 34 hours of shelling, the fort surren-

The bombardment of Charleston by Union forces in 1863 resulted in the destruction of the city's Catholic cathedral.

dered. President Lincoln declared war, and by May, the 11 Confederate States of America had followed South Carolina's Lowcountry planters and cotton financiers into the Civil War they wanted.

To hear the many chapters of the Sons or Daughters of the Confederacy tell the story today, or to get it from South Carolina's roadside historical markers, one

Artist John Ross Key's painting The Bombardment of Fort Sumter *depicts the attack by rebel forces on April 15, 1861.*

might think the state was a major battleground during the military campaigns of the Civil War. In fact, only one other major battle took place on South Carolina soil, and it was minor in terms of battles fought in Virginia, Tennessee, Mississippi, and Georgia. It was the Battle of Rivers Bridge in February 1865, two months before Lee surrendered at Appomattox.

Along the banks of the Salkehatchi River between Allendale and Ehrhardt, 1,000 Confederates battled 8,000 Union soldiers for two days. The river crossing was on General Sherman's route from Savannah north through South Carolina; Rivers Bridge was the only major resistance Sherman's army encountered on its destructive march through what he called "the hellhole of secession."

Although there were no further significant battles in the state, the Union Army moved into a part of the Lowcountry and remained there throughout the Civil War. Seven months after Fort Sumter, in November 1861, the Union Army occupied Beaufort, St. Helena, Hilton Head, and the surrounding coastal plantations. In 1863, the Union began giving small tracts of these plantations to freed slaves. On January 16, 1865, from his headquarters in Savannah, General Sherman's Special Field Order Number 15 granted "the islands from Charleston south, the abandoned rice fields along the rivers for 30 miles back from the sea, and the country bordering the St. Johns River, Florida," to freed slaves. Nearly 40,000 freedmen took title to 485,000 acres of tidewater plantation land, usually in 40-acre tracts, all along the Sea Islands. At the end of 1866, however, President Andrew Johnson reversed the order and returned most of the lands to their former white owners.

Soldiers and Patriots

Confederate Monument

Let the Stranger,

Who May in Future Times

Read This Inscription,

Recognize That These Were Men

Whom Power Could not Corrupt,

Whom Death Could not Terrify,

Whom Defeat Could not Dishonor,

And Let Their Virtues Plead

For Just Judgment

Of the Cause in Which They Perished.

Let the South Carolinians

Of Another Generation

Remember

That the State Taught Them

How to Live and How to Die.

—*Inscription on the Monument to the Confederate Dead, north of the State House in Columbia.*

James Petigru

Unawed by Opinion,

Unseduced by Flattery,

Undismayed by Disaster,

He confronted Life with antique Courage,

And Death with Christian Hope.

In the Great Civil War

He withstood his People for his Country,

But his People did homage to the Man

Who held his Conscience higher than their Praise.

And his Country

Heaped her Honours upon the Grave of the Patriot,

To whom, living,

His own righteous Self-Respect sufficed like for Motive and Reward.

—*Epitaph for James Lewis Petigru, South Carolina's leading Unionist at the time of secession and the state's finest lawyer in his day. His epitaph was read by President Woodrow Wilson (who spent part of his youth in South Carolina) at the Peace Conference in France following World War I.*

■ POST–CIVIL WAR ERA

About 63,000 South Carolinians served in the Confederate forces, and more than 15,000 died. Congress removed federal troops from the Confederate states in 1877, ending the occupation of the South as well as the era of Radical Reconstruction. But it was not a true reconstruction for South Carolina, which entered many decades of deterioration. When the Great Depression of the 1930s occurred, few in South Carolina could tell the difference. What had been one of the nation's wealthiest states in 1860 became, and remains today, one of its poorest.

The collapse of slavery and of the plantation system (which could not exist without slaves) had been only the beginning. South Carolinians continued to plant more cotton, until the state's 1890 cotton production was twice its 1860 crop. This served to lower the market price severely. At the same time, cotton mills were built along the Upcountry rivers. Mill villages and small towns formed, enriching their owners and enslaving to ignorance and poverty the all-white labor force. In 1900, the state Board of Health termed mill villages "pest holes for the corruption of the whole state." In the Piedmont mill town of Union, mill hands backed by the owners physically fought public health officials trying to inoculate them against smallpox, which then became epidemic in Union and spread to other Piedmont mill towns.

During the first decade of the 20th century, there were only 13 public high schools in the state (mill owners and farmers opposed compulsory school attendance, wanting children to work for them instead), and none of the state's colleges or universities got even regional accreditation until the 1920s. As an article in the *New York Times* in 1930 said, "More than any other state of the Confederacy, South Carolina has seemed to the rushing industrial regions of the United States 'a land of monuments and memories.' " When World War II brought the military draft, illiteracy and/or poor health resulted in the rejection of 56 percent of black and 34 percent of white South Carolina draftees, among the nation's worst rates.

After the Civil War freed hundreds of thousands of slaves on cotton farms and plantations across South Carolina, they and generations of descendants had no place to live or work. Thousands of them moved to industrial jobs in northern cities during World War I and continued the migration during the Depression. By 1940, whites were the majority race in South Carolina for the first time since 1700.

The often empty and fallow Sea Island plantations succumbed to an infestation of the boll weevil in 1922, and Sea Island cotton never recovered from it. What was left of the rice plantations along rivers upstream from Georgetown was devastated by a fierce hurricane in 1911, ending commercial rice production in South Carolina. The famous financier Bernard Baruch, a native of Camden, bought two rice plantations for use as hunting preserves and winter retreats. During a three-week period in 1925, more than 1 million acres of Lowcountry real estate changed hands in this manner. By 1940, wealthy northerners owned more than 159 old plantations in the Lowcountry, using them as retreats and hunting preserves.

■ POLITICS

In his classic history of the state, David Duncan Wallace lamented, "Politics since the early colonial days have been the South Carolina bull ring. The passions profitlessly expended in it, if turned into other energies, might have produced a great literature or a triumphant industrial civilization. . . ."

Politics is a blood sport in South Carolina and, like the rest of the state's history, is unique. As Wallace noted, "Issues between Whig and Tory, coast aristocrat and Up Country farmer, slave owner and abolitionist, on which the life of the state seemed to depend, developed an intolerance making difference of opinion seem treason to class or country or race; and the desperation thus bred gave factional politics the spirit of the vendetta."

The most vindictive of South Carolina's many political feuds pitted (and sometimes still pits) the Lowcountry and Charleston against the Upcountry. It is a class conflict born in colonial and antebellum days, and it has nurtured some of the state's most bizarre political figures. One such, "Pitchfork" Ben Tillman of Edgefield County, was elected governor in 1890 and to the U.S. Senate in 1894 by fanning class antagonism. Tillman rallied small Upcountry farmers by calling himself a "clodhopper" and calling Charleston "greedy," its Citadel state military college a "dude factory" and Lowcountry planters the "broken-down, Bourbon aristocracy." Another colorful character, Cole Blease of Newberry, was elected governor in 1910, leading the "cracker proletariat"—white mill hands in the Upcountry who were recruited to the mill villages from their farms and were scorned as "lintheads" and "poor white trash" by many in the Lowcountry.

An example of the static political climate in South Carolina was the half-century reign of Edgefield native J. Strom Thurmond in the United States Senate. One of the last "Dixiecrats," or members of the States' Rights Democrats Party, he ran unsuccessfully for president in 1948 on an anti–civil rights platform, to counter

Harry Truman's call for Democrats to advocate civil rights for African-Americans. Like many other Dixiecrats, Thurmond became a Republican when Sen. Barry Goldwater ran for president in 1964, but he eventually disavowed his fervid segregationist views. After Thurmond's death in 2002, it was acknowledged that he'd fathered a child with his family's black housemaid when he was still a young adult living in his parents' home.

The most enduring legacy of South Carolina's political wars, however, is the "legislative state." It makes little difference who is governor, since members of the state legislature hold the real power over everything from state finances to the election of judges and members of various powerful state boards, which control colleges, highways, and local sewer, water, and fire districts. In 1993, the legislature relaxed its grip on state government by consolidating some agencies and changing how some boards are filled, but the reform was mostly marginal. An example of its inefficiency occurred during a 1999 hurricane evacuation: the governor did not have the authority to change the direction of traffic on Interstate 26, causing a disaster all its own when several million people jammed the highways in search of safety. "Home rule," control of local government by local officials, may now be the law, but it has yet to be fully implemented.

A series of scandals rocked state government during the late 1980s and early 1990s. The worst of these, in 1989, was "Operation Lost Trust," a sting in which a former lobbyist working undercover for the FBI offered bribes for supporting legalized betting on horses. In all, 27 persons were convicted or pleaded guilty to various charges of selling their influence, including 17 members of the legislature and a circuit court judge. At the same time, other public figures such as the president of the University of South Carolina and the chief of the highway patrol resigned due to improper activities.

Walter Edgar wrote, "For a state that prided itself on honest public service, the ever-widening circle of corruption and malfeasance caused acute embarrassment. It also aroused a lethargic citizenry." Alex M. Sanders, former legislator and appellate court judge and now president of Charleston School of Law, believes the scandals were "the darkest days for the spirit of South Carolina since the Civil War. For the whole term of its existence, South Carolina has demonstrated that it can endure guilt, but it can't endure shame, and shame is where we are today."

While South Carolina is known for racial inequality in its political representation, there is one area where the state ranks far worse: It is dead last in the nation for electing women to public office. While the national average in state representation is 23 percent women, the Palmetto State lags, with only one-half of 1 percent.

For almost all of its history, race has been the state's main political issue. Upcountry and Lowcountry political leaders have long fought with each other but united when it came to excluding African-Americans from the political, social, and economic life of the state. For a century following the Civil War and Emancipation Proclamation, they succeeded.

■ CIVIL RIGHTS

African-American citizens of the state actively voted, usually for Republicans associated with the party of Abraham Lincoln, during the 1870s and 1880s. "Pitchfork" Ben Tillman put an end to that in 1895, rewriting the state constitution to exclude their votes. This bit of tyranny went unchallenged for a half century, until the mid-1940s when Supreme Court decisions began reversing it. The essence of what Tillman had done in 1895 was to make the Democratic Party primary the only election that counted in the state. Fearing federal court decisions might admit black voters to that primary, the state legislature in 1944 passed a record 147 pieces of legislation in six days and made their state Democratic Party a private club. In retrospect, it seems incredible that white legislators thought this sham would work.

The illegal scheme was foiled in 1948 by a completely unexpected person, J. Waites Waring, son of a prominent, old, white Charleston family and the federal district court judge for the Lowcountry. Waring ruled the white-only Democratic primary unconstitutional. His decision was upheld on appeal, but Waring and his wife were ostracized and shunned by Charleston society and white South Carolina for the rest of their lives.

It took another 20 years, however—after the 1965 Voting Rights Act was passed by Congress—before African-Americans in South Carolina began to vote in large numbers. The 1968 state Democratic Party convention desegregated for the first time. In 1970, the first African-Americans elected to the legislature since 1900 took office. By 2000, there were 25 black state legislators, and across the state another 322 held local offices from small-town mayors to members of the school board.

In 1896, one year after Tillman disenfranchised African-Americans in South Carolina, the Supreme Court made "separate but equal" public accommodations and schools the law of the land in its infamous *Plessy v. Ferguson* decision. "Jim Crow" laws flew through Southern state legislatures, and in South Carolina, White

A rare pre–Civil War photo depicts a black church near Charleston with slaves worshipping under the leadership of a white minister.

and Colored signs were posted over drinking fountains, in theaters, at railroad passenger stations, and at lunch counters. Not until the late 1950s was any of this apartheid challenged, and then it was black college students who led the protest, with lunch-counter sit-ins in Orangeburg and Rock Hill.

"Separate but equal" public education had turned out to be not only separate but also wholly unequal. In 1948, about 62 percent of adult African-Americans in South Carolina were totally or functionally illiterate. In 1950, African-American parents in the small farm town of Summerton filed suit in federal court, contending that "separate" never would mean "equal." Two years later, in yet another grand but empty gesture, the legislature voted to take the state out of the public school business entirely if federal courts ordered South Carolina to desegregate its schools. Meanwhile, with Thurgood Marshall as their attorney, the Summerton parents' suit, *Briggs v. Elliott,* became part of a similar suit—*Brown v. Board of Education*—and in 1954, the U.S. Supreme Court outlawed segregated public schools.

Desegregating the school system clearly would mean desegregating much of the daily life of ordinary white and black citizens of the state. During the decade following the Brown decision, many other states of the old Confederacy resisted desegregation, with Ku Klux Klan–led beatings and murders. South Carolina did not.

> "If and when every legal remedy has been exhausted, this General Assembly must make clear South Carolina's choice, a government of laws rather than a government of men. As determined as we are, we of today must realize the lesson of one hundred years ago, and move on for the good of South Carolina and our United States. This should be done with dignity. It must be done with law and order."
> —Governor Ernest "Fritz" Hollings, 1963

In what was its last hurrah and perhaps its only act of nobility, the barons of legislature, a few influential Lowcountry planters and Upcountry textile lords, and their counterparts in the state's major banks and utilities—in short, the tiny group of white men who controlled almost everything in the state—echoed Hollings' words. There would be no violence. Nobody in South Carolina, least of all "the cowards of the KKK," dared challenge the police, courts, regulatory agencies, employment opportunities, loan money, and social status those men controlled. Charleston native (and future mayor of Charlotte) Harvey Gantt began classes at Clemson College in January 1963. Later accounts of why there was no violence—as schools slowly desegregated across South Carolina during the 1960s and 1970s—credit two motives.

The feudal lords who ran things then feared "another Ole Miss" or "another Birmingham" would chase away the manufacturing industry they were just beginning to charm, induce, and persuade to build new plants in South Carolina. The second motive, in its own way just as compelling to the lords, was a matter of style.

"If you can't appeal to the morals of a South Carolinian," said Harvey Gantt, "you can appeal to his manners."

Historian Walter Edgar, in *South Carolina: A History,* observed: "South Carolina was still a small place in the 1960s, a place where, despite segregation, people knew one another across the racial divide. A tradition of civility combined with a determination to preserve law and order enabled South Carolina to undo three generations of segregation—with dignity."

The only major aberrations in the state's nonviolent, although prolonged, desegregation of its public facilities occurred on February 8, 1968, in Orangeburg.

Students from South Carolina State College demonstrated outside a segregated bowling alley near the campus. White highway patrolmen and National Guardsmen, overreacting to a thrown wooden banister that came out of the crowd of students, opened fire with shotguns, killing 3 and wounding 27 others. One demonstrator, Cleveland Sellers, was branded an "outside agitator" and spent seven months in state prison on a riot charge. Sellers went on to earn a master's degree from Harvard, a doctorate from the University of North Carolina, worked for 18 years with the city and housing authority in Greensboro, North Carolina, then returned to his home state. He teaches sociology today, is a member of the state Board of Education, and in the summer of 1993 was granted a pardon of the riot charge. Like the best of South Carolinians, with manners and nobility, Sellers accepted the state's apology.

Cleveland Sellers was one of 6.5 million African-Americans who fled South Carolina and other southern states between 1910 and 1970. The black population plummeted from nearly 60 percent of the state's total to what is now about 30 percent. It was one of the greatest emigrations in American history. Just as Sellers eventually returned to his home state, so have others since then. The Census Bureau first noticed the quiet reverse migration in the 1990s, when the proportion of African-Americans living in the South increased, from 52 percent in 1980 to 56 percent in 1988. There are now hundreds of black elected officials throughout the state, as well as black-owned businesses, and South Carolina continues to see an influx of African-American residents. Urban decay and shifting industries in major northern and midwestern cities may account for some of the change. The poet and author Maya Angelou wrote of another reason why she returned to the South a decade ago: it's home, and, "When I walk in, they may like me or dislike me, but everybody knows I'm here."

In the fall of 1999, the NAACP called for a tourism boycott of South Carolina if lawmakers didn't remove the Confederate flag that was flying atop the statehouse dome in Columbia, as well as inside the legislative chambers. Groups within the state called for its removal, including, surprisingly, the legislators who voted to put the flag up in the first place. Former governors John West and Robert McNair had led a group of the 1962 General Assembly to raise the flag in honor of the Civil War's centennial, although the timing more closely coincided with Harvey Gantt's admission to Clemson. In a well-publicized compromise, legislators agreed to remove the flag as long as it was put in a "place of honor" on the statehouse grounds, where it flies today near a statue of the late Senator Thurmond.

■ HEIRS' PROPERTY

Throughout the state are large tracts of land known as heirs' properties, estates that are quickly disappearing under the backhoes of large-home developers. These properties were granted to or purchased by former slaves after the Civil War and have been handed down through many generations, usually without the formalities of a will, deed, or title. You can see many of these properties dotted with mobile homes and carefully tended by the descendants who farm the land or lease the timber rights. Unscrupulous investors might track down long-lost relatives, who can force the sale of the land in order to collect their share of the legacy. In 1993, for example, the Beckett family of Jasper County lost 335 acres that had been in their family since 1873. A real estate agent had paid $750 for the signature of a dying, uninformed family member and bought and resold the property for a profit of $1.7 million. The Penn Center on St. Helena Island and the Heirs' Property Preservation Project, with a Ford Foundation grant, are working to preserve the estimated 3,000 parcels that remain heirs' properties and to investigate those already lost in dubious transactions.

■ THE PEOPLE

Black and white South Carolinians share much common heritage, although some of it still appears to be segregated. Church membership is an important part of life here, and it is primarily the Pentecostals who have a longtime biracial congregation. Sixty-two percent of South Carolinians identify themselves as church members, the largest denomination being Southern Baptists, with more than 743,000 members in 2003 (one-third of the state total). The rest are Protestants and Catholics, as well as many members of a very old Jewish congregation in Charleston. There were many years when the state did not observe federal holidays such as Memorial Day or Martin Luther King Jr.'s Birthday, but this has changed in recent years. There is also statewide observance of Confederate Memorial Day on May 10.

South Carolina remains one of the poorest states in the country, and there is a 50 percent high school drop-out rate. Prosperity remains somewhat distant for most South Carolinians of either race, but in pockets of economic development throughout the state, that has been changing. In 1961, the state opened its first technical education center, in Greenville, to train workers for any specific industry that would build a new plant in South Carolina. The innovative system, since

THE BOYKIN SPANIEL

In the early 1900s, a Camden planter named L. W. "Whit" Boykin experimented with dog breeds to meet the challenges of hunters along the Wateree River. Hunting ducks and wild turkeys in the swamps, local sportsmen needed a dog that could retrieve game but also fit on a boat. Typical retrievers were large and heavy, and the flat, shallow boats were crowded enough with men, guns, and other provisions.

Boykin's friend and hunting partner, a Spartanburg banker named Alexander White, had adopted a small stray spaniel mix he found wandering on a road. He'd named him Dumpy. White saw that the dog was a good retriever and gave him to Boykin for further training. The little dog turned into an ace turkey dog and waterfowl retriever. Dumpy became the foundation for a breed that would become the Boykin spaniel, whose bloodlines also drew from the Chesapeake Bay retriever, the American water spaniel, and the springer and cocker spaniels. Boykins are eager to please and have incredible stamina in hot weather, with spaniel flushing abilities for Upcountry hunting of doves, pheasant, quail, and grouse and even tracking deer. Roughly 16 inches high and weighing 30 pounds, these dogs earned a place in the duck boat, and in the duck blind as well.

Although not yet officially recognized by international kennel clubs, the Boykin is the official dog of South Carolina. They are intelligent, agile, and strong and are very friendly family pets. When you see Boykins on your travels through the state (and you will), you may be startled by their chocolate-coated poise and heartwarming, worshiping caramel-colored gaze.

—Jane O'Boyle

copied by other states and in other nations, brought scores of new industries to the state. South Carolina's Upcountry stretch of I-85 between Anderson, Greenville, Spartanburg, and Gaffney is now lined with new factories. Many of are owned by European corporations, such as Spartanburg's BMW automobile assembly plant.

The textile industry has been eclipsed by tourism as the state's largest private employer. Four out of five tourism dollars spent in South Carolina are spent in the beachside resorts such as Myrtle Beach, historic Charleston, Kiawah Island, and Hilton Head. As often is the case for popular travel destinations, visitors are returning to retire in South Carolina.

In a nation of transients, the population of the Palmetto State remains an anomaly. Most people who are born in South Carolina—a whopping 70 percent—remain in South Carolina. In only 2 of its 46 counties are there more residents who were born elsewhere.

Agriculture remains an important factor in the state's economy, particularly tobacco, peaches, and soybeans, as well as pulpwood pine farms. In 1945, the state had more than a million acres planted in cotton. By 2000, fewer than 80,000 acres grew cotton and only 2 percent of the state population lived and worked on farms. Small towns across South Carolina either lured a new industrial plant, usually an apparel manufacturer, or became ghost towns.

But, as might be expected in a place so captured by its past, the memory of farming, if not the economy of agriculture, continues to figure in the collective South Carolina consciousness. Everyone who can, from banker to state bureaucrat to factory foreman, owns a small piece of land in the country, often for no other reason than to go look at it from time to time. Roughly 20 percent of all occupied housing in the state are mobile homes—the highest percentage in the nation—and 80 percent of those trailers rest not in a trailer park but on a small piece of rural land from which the occupants commute to school, shopping, and work.

Fall is festival season in South Carolina—from the Lee County Cotton Festival in Bishopville to the Moja Arts Festival in Charleston. The local food is delicious all year round, from fried green tomatoes to Hoppin' John (black-eyed peas with ham hocks and rice), shrimp and grits in tasso (smoked pork) gravy, pulled-pork barbecue, peaches, collard greens, and okra soup. You might carry home as many fresh pecan pralines as you can carry.

At the conclusion of Margaret Mitchell's *Gone With the Wind,* Rhett Butler declares he is leaving booming Atlanta (and the aggrieved Scarlett, of course) for his hometown of Charleston, where he would find "the slow charm . . . the calm dignity life can have when it's lived by gentle folks, the genial grace of days that are gone." Those days still exist here, despite the departure of dashing blockade runners and racial inequities. South Carolina remains an enduring model of seductive graciousness that now crosses all regional, economic, and racial differences. People will wave at you when you drive down a country road, and they'll smile at you on city sidewalks. Clerks in the shops will engage you with interested questions about your home or work and offer friendly advice on where to eat lunch, find a good fishing hole, or sunbathe in seclusion.

More than stereotypical "southern style," South Carolina is a simple, seductive way of life, a sophisticated slice of America unlike any other, and you will marvel at the way you begin to wave and smile at these strangers yourself. Then you'll know you have discovered the true South Carolina.

S E A   I S L A N D S

The Palmetto State has 187 miles of Atlantic coastline, but, if you counted all the bays, inlets, and islands along that length, there are actually 2,876 miles of sandy seashore. On these islands, pirates plundered, bathers frolicked, hurricanes carved new beaches, and black Union soldiers from Massachusetts surrendered their lives in blood and sand. The Sea Islands are still quietly patrolled by pelicans and egrets, and loggerhead turtle nestlings race from the dunes toward the moonlit surf. And if you listen carefully through the hot, salty breeze, you will hear the muse that soothes so many.

> "To describe our growing up in the lowcountry . . . I would have to take you to the marsh on a spring day, flush the great blue heron from its silent occupation, scatter marsh hens as we sink to our knees in mud, open you an oyster with a pocketknife and feed it to you from the shell and say, 'There. That taste. That's the taste of my childhood.' . . . I would say 'Breathe deeply,' and you would breathe and remember that smell for the rest of your life, the bold, fecund aroma of the tidal marsh, exquisite and sensual, the smell of the South in heat, a smell like new milk, semen, and spilled wine, all perfumed with seawater. My soul grazes like a lamb on the beauty of indrawn tides."
>
> —Pat Conroy, *The Prince of Tides,* 1986

■ LANDSCAPE

This is a gentle coast, with no cliff-and-boulder seascapes, no outer capes meeting surf whipped by storms. Its appeal is subtler: a place of low islands and saltwater marshes stretching languidly out to a horizon where earth and air blend softly into an indefinite line. Narrow country roads meander through tunnels of massive, old and gnarled live oaks dripping tendrils of gray Spanish moss.

The Sea Islands range from small, transitory outcroppings of wave-washed, wind-blown sand to large forested islands. Many of the islands are still uninhabited

One certainty of Edisto Island is catching your breath, though anglers hope for far more.

and accessible only by boat. On Capers Island, great graveyards of petrified oaks march right down into the sea while on Hilton Head sprawling homes reflect the sun onto a wide, flat beach of sunbathers. Deep-water sounds such as St. Helena and Port Royal and wide estuaries such as the Edisto and Broad rivers, once lined by rice and cotton plantations, now harbor shrimp, shad, sturgeon, and scores more species.

The islands themselves were formed by rising sea levels, which flooded the coast over the course of roughly 15,000 years. Water from melting polar ice caps caused the ocean to rise more than 400 feet. Although the rate at which it changes has slowed dramatically, sea levels continue to rise about 1 foot per century, on average. Since 1920, the sea level at Charleston Harbor has risen 14 inches.

■ HISTORY

Until the 18th century, small tribes of Native Americans inhabited the Sea Islands. Their names—Edisto, Kiawah, Stono, Combahee, Ashepoo—were adopted by European settlers to identify the countless rivers and islands. Warlike, more powerful tribes, such as the Yemassee and Westo, had already raided and weakened the Sea Island tribes so that, by the time the white Europeans arrived, the tribes had disappeared rapidly into assimilation or extinction.

From the 1750s until the Civil War, the Sea Islands were the domain of planters, their African slaves, and vast, prosperous plantations producing first "Carolina Gold" rice, then the silky, prized fibers of Sea Island cotton. War, hurricanes, low cotton prices, a boll-weevil infestation, and the end of slavery vanquished this plantation life on the Sea Islands. For more than a century, the islands remained backwaters, home to small vegetable farms, family shrimp boats, oyster factories, heavily logged pine and pulpwood forests, and isolated communities of people. These were primarily the descendants of slaves, whose unique Gullah culture still survives there. Beginning with the development of Hilton Head Island in the 1960s, much of this landscape was transformed.

■ DEVELOPMENT

The islands' remoteness was a major attraction for metropolitans in search of a retreat. Even the islands' inaccessibility had a colonial charm—until the 1980s, few were connected by bridge to the mainland. Developers of resort and retirement

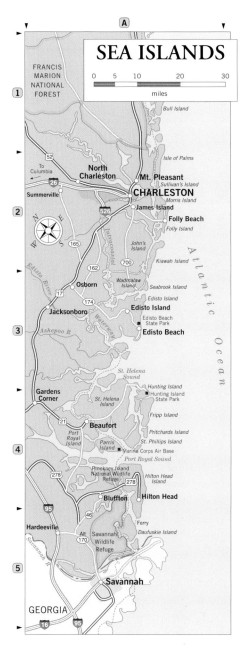

SEA ISLANDS

0   5   10   20   30

miles

FRANCIS
MARION
NATIONAL
FOREST

Bull Island

Isle of Palms

To Columbia

North
Charleston

Mt. Pleasant

Sullivan's Island

CHARLESTON

Morris Island

James Island

Folly Beach

Folly Island

John's
Island

Kiawah Island

Summerville

Osborn

Wadmalaw
Island

Seabrook Island

Edisto Island

Edisto Island

Jacksonboro

Ashepoo R

Edisto Beach
State Park

Edisto Beach

St. Helena
Sound

Hunting Island

Hunting Island
State Park

Gardens
Corner

St. Helena
Island

Fripp Island

Beaufort

Pritchards Island

Port
Royal
Island

Parris
Island

St. Phillips Island

Marine Corps Air Base

Port Royal Sound

Pinckney Island
National Wildlife
Refuge

Hilton Head
Island

Bluffton

Hilton Head

Ferry

Hardeeville

Savannah
Wildlife
Refuge

Daufuskie Island

Savannah

GEORGIA

Intracoastal Waterway

Edisto River

Edisto River

Atlantic Ocean

communities such as Hilton Head, Callawassie, Kiawah, Wild Dunes, Pawleys Island, and Myrtle Beach marketed to an upscale, out-of-state clientele. Many Sea Islands are now private, gated developments of luxurious homes with restaurants, marinas, and golf courses.

In January of 1987, a violent nor'easter stormed along the South Carolina coast, wrecking homes and washing away beaches. It accomplished what no amount of political lobbying had achieved before then: it brought legislative action to preserving the coastline. South Carolina adopted the Beachfront Management Act, which mandated that any new structure be built behind a "setback" line. It also banned construction of new seawalls and other protective beachfront "armor" that would erode the beaches. Within a few months, on September 21, 1989, Hurricane Hugo slammed into the islands. Homes disappeared into the ocean, landmark trees vanished, rivers changed course. This was the deadliest hurricane here in over a century, and some of the islands have never recovered.

Throughout the Sea Islands, environmental and conservation groups and government agencies regularly negotiate with developers to preserve the salt marshes and sand dunes, which have survived this long only

Oystermen at work among the marshes of Beaufort County.

because of the lack of economic development throughout the 20th century. South Carolina contains 25 percent of the nation's east-coast salt marshes, which, with vigilance, will remain pristine throughout the 21st.

■ COMMERCIAL OYSTERING AND SHRIMPING

There was a time when thousands of oystermen rowed weathered, wooden bateaux along the tidal creeks and rivers as thousands of other workers shucked and canned the fresh catch. In 1900, South Carolina's **commercial oyster production** was 2.2 million bushels. By 2000, that had dwindled to 70,000 bushels, with only two shucking houses and fewer than 270 licensed oyster pickers.

The last oyster-shucking house on Daufuskie Island closed in 1959, its source of supply polluted by the port, factories, and sewage of Savannah. It was an almost fatal blow to the old-time self-supporting black Gullah community on Daufuskie. Today, smoked oysters are still sold under the "Daufuski" brand and label, but

FISHING FOLKLORE

Along the coast, where fishing was once a major source of livelihood, fishermen practiced certain rituals in hopes of improving their odds. Some fishermen believed it was good luck to talk to a young girl before casting off. Dogs were not allowed to accompany the fishermen, nor was food to be eaten while the men were fishing. Other fishermen spit on their bait to ensure that fish would bite. Finally, according to one proverb,

> If the wind comes from the north
> Fish bite like a horse;
> If the wind comes from the south
> They bite like a louse;
> If the wind comes from the east
> They will bite the least;
> If the wind comes from the west
> They will bite the best.

they are imported oysters from Korea. Almost a third of the oyster beds along 60 miles of coastline from the Savannah River to Edisto Island are closed because of water pollution.

Just as oystering was once a commercial mainstay of the Sea Islands, so was **commercial shrimping.** Nearly every Sea Island village had its own small fleet of trawlers. In the early 1980s, the state still licensed about 1,100 shrimp trawlers. By the early 1990s, the fleet was estimated to number about 400.

Imported "pond shrimp," mostly from shrimp farms in Ecuador, Thailand, and China, drove down prices and dominated the U.S. market during the 1980s; they now account for almost 75 percent of all shrimp eaten in the nation. But the Sea Islands are still the main source for large shrimp, which are difficult to grow in ponds. The busiest harvest is in the fall, but to make a living, most commercial shrimpers work the entire harvesting season, usually set by state and federal agencies to last from mid-May through December or January.

In recent years, about 15 commercial shrimp-pond farms and about three dozen small crawfish farms have begun operating in South Carolina. Several of these are in

A shrimp boat heads out to sea through Port Royal Sound under the eye of the morning sun.

the Sea Islands, but so far the largest aquaculture operation offering a new source of income for the islands is a growing clam-farm industry. **Atlantic Littleneck Clam Farms** of **James Island** near Charleston has thousands of commercial clam pens in the Kiawah and Folly rivers. This is a sort of cooperative venture, where islanders (or anyone else) can invest in their own crop, which the company then harvests and sells on their behalf. You can stop in at 2107 Folly Road and observe clams growing in tanks, and then buy a few dozen to cook for supper.

You can still buy fresh-caught shrimp off the boats in several places, including **Cherry Point** on **Wadmalaw Island,** 20 miles southwest of Charleston. Locals along U.S. 17 between Beaufort and Charleston also sell shrimp from roadside coolers, with prices as low as $4 per pound.

■ CRABBING AND SHRIMPING: A PRIMER

For residents of the Sea Islands, recreational crabbing and shrimping are among the delights of the estuarine cornucopia. They are easy to learn, so newcomers can catch their own fresh crab and shrimp.

To catch your own crabs, you will need a ball of string, a small 1-ounce lead weight, a dip net, and bait—preferably chicken parts. Let the parts get hot and stinky. Find a bridge, tidal creek, or saltwater channel shallow enough to wade into. Low tide is the best time, but almost anytime is good. Tie the weight and a chicken part to one end of the twine and toss it into the water. If wading, keep the twine short enough to let the chicken part almost but not quite drag on the bottom, and walk slowly. When you feel a gentle tug on the string, slowly pull it up. The crab will hold on as long as it's submerged, so dip the net under the crab just before pulling it out of the water.

Recreational crabbing requires no license, as long as the crab is at least 5 inches across the back and has no yellow roe (eggs) on the underside. Crabs with roe are female, and keeping them is illegal. Toss your catch into an ice chest—not into a bucket of water—until you are ready to cook.

You can catch shrimp in the same salty or brackish waters, but you need slightly different equipment: a cast net and a bucket of saltwater to hold your catch. A cast net is round, with weights on the circumference that sink in the open position when the net is cast. Then a draw line is pulled, trapping whatever is inside the net. It takes an hour or so of practice to learn this simple, durable skill from ancient times. Most variety stores, convenience stores, and bait shops sell cast nets, and many marinas rent small outboards for reaching backwater creeks. Locals find the many causeway bridges just fine for cast-net shrimping.

■ THE NATURE OF THE SHORE

The mountains in northwestern South Carolina often weaken winter cold fronts dropping down from up north, and the warm waters of the Gulf Stream just 55 miles off the coast (68 degrees F and above) help create moderate winters on the Sea Islands. Warm weather and natural beauty make for wonderful beachcombing and bird-watching. The surf is placid, the sea and landscape merging together in subtle, muted blues, greens, yellows, and whites.

Depending on the time of year, you may find a wealth of marine specimens on the beach. The sand may be dotted with the shells of welks (the creatures inside are a favorite snack for shore birds), horseshoe crabs, marine snails, hermit crabs,

(following pages) Moonrise over tidewater marshes on Hilton Head Island.

bright spindle corals, starfish, ghost crabs, blue crabs, and sand dollars. In the dunes grow morning glories, pennywort, wild bamboo, and sea oats, fiercely protected by law. Walking through the dunes is generally prohibited, but there are many designated pathways that lead to the beaches. Behind the dunes grows the maritime forest, extending into the endless marshes. Here you'll see the wide-limbed live oak, with its small evergreen leaves; tall loblolly pines; palmettos, with their fan-shaped fronds bending in the breeze; and 50-foot-high red cedars.

The marsh islands are surrounded by spartina, or cord grass, which captures mainland river silt and slows erosion. The matted growth absorbs in-rushing tides, protecting the land. Four times more productive than healthy corn fields, the grass grows 10 tons to the acre. It dies, decays, and reseeds itself twice a year, pouring its nutrients into the estuarine nursery, feeding plankton, oysters, shrimp, clams, crabs, and small fish, which in turn support larger fish, birds, reptiles, and mammals.

In some offshore marshes, you'll see small islands called hummocks. These miniature refuges support live oak, red cedar, bayberry, and palmettos. Cedar waxwings, white ibis, belted kingfishers, and flycatchers flutter about the hummocks, and raccoons, deer, and bobcats are also prevalent.

The Sea Islands are an important stopover on the Atlantic flyway during the October bird migration south and the March-April migration north. Endangered wood storks have started moving their rookeries here, to live in the marshes alongside the great blue heron, snowy egrets, skimmers, pelicans, sandpipers, marsh hens, and red-winged blackbirds. Birders will see plenty of painted bunting, Carolina wrens, cardinals, titmice, Carolina chickadees, bald eagles, and great horned owls.

There are several bucolic state parks and wildlife refuges along the coast, from Cape Romain and Edisto to Pinckney Island and the Savannah Wildlife Refuge, just south of Hilton Head. In fact, a dawdling drive along U.S. 17 from Litchfield (just below Myrtle Beach) all the way to the Savannah River will take you through incredible oases of saltwater marsh and wildlife. This route passes old plantations, historic gardens, bird sanctuaries, marinas, and even old overgrown gas stations from the days when Yankees used this road to drive to Florida. Regardless of your route through the Sea Islands, a car is a necessity if you want to reach the remote parks and beaches.

Heron encounters are not uncommon on Kiawah Island.

■ SEA ISLANDS SOUTH, FROM BEAUFORT TO SAVANNAH

■ HILTON HEAD *map page 49, A-4/5*

English sea captain William Hilton claimed this island for England in 1663, although he soon left and never returned here. The island was settled by cotton planters around 1800. Among its 15 large plantations was the Stoney-Baynard Plantation at the island's southern tip, in what today is Sea Pines Plantation, the original golf course development built in the 1960s.

At the outbreak of the Civil War, Confederate forces hastily built two earthwork forts to guard the entrance to Port Royal Sound and the rice and cotton plantations within. One, Fort Walker, was on the northern tip of Hilton Head at what today is the Hilton Head Plantation development. The other, Fort Beauregard, was on St. Phillips Island on the northern side of the sound, still today an uninhabited island.

On November 7, 1861, six months after South Carolina fired the first shots of the Civil War at Charleston's Fort Sumter, a massive Union flotilla sailed into the mouth of Port Royal Sound. Eighteen Union warships led by Adm. Samuel Francis du Pont's flagship, the steam frigate *Wabash*, launched salvos from their 11-inch

FIRST SOUTH CAROLINA VOLUNTEERS, 1863

The services began at half past eleven o'clock, with prayer by our chaplain. . . . Then the President's Proclamation was read by Dr. W. H. Brisbane, a thing infinitely appropriate, a South Carolinian addressing South Carolinians; for he was reared among these very islands, and here long since emancipated his own slaves. Then followed an incident so simple, so touching, so utterly unexpected and startling that I can scarcely believe it on recalling, though it gave a key-note to the whole day. The very moment the speaker had ceased, and just as I took and waved the flag, which for the first time meant anything to these poor people, there suddenly arose, close beside the platform, a strong male voice (but rather cracked and elderly), into which two women's voices instantly blended, singing, as if by an impulse that could no more be repressed than the morning note of the song-sparrow.—

"My Country, 'tis of thee,
Sweet land of liberty,
Of thee I sing!"

People looked at each other, then at us on the platform. . . . Firmly and irrepressibly the quavering voices sang on, verse after verse; others of the colored people joined in. I never saw anything so electric; it made all other words cheap; it seemed the choked voice of a race at last unloosed.

—Col. Thomas Higginson, recalling religious services held January 1, 1863, for his
regiment, the First South Carolina Volunteers, which consisted primarily
of runaway slaves from South Carolina who fought with the Union.

cannon. Fort Beauregard and the palmetto forest behind it were leveled in minutes. Fort Walker held out for four hours, and then the rebels retreated. From 55 support craft in the Union fleet, a force of 13,000 troops then made an amphibious landing on Hilton Head. A landing of that size was not attempted again until World War II.

Hilton Head became the headquarters and supply base for the Union's naval blockade of the Confederacy's Atlantic coast, as crucial an element in the war as any land campaign. Fort Walker, rebuilt and renamed Fort Mitchell, led to the creation of nearby Mitchelville, a garrison town where some of the thousands of slaves, suddenly freed as the white planters fled the Sea Islands, found paying jobs after the war.

In the eyes of some citizens, oceanfront development is a bane to Hilton Head's pristine areas.

Within weeks, the town of Beaufort was occupied by the Union, and within months, the abandoned Sea Island plantations were being carved into small plots and sold (for a nominal price) to their former slaves. During Reconstruction, many of the deeds held by the former slaves were invalidated when the previous owners returned and wanted the land. However, many more deeds remained in the hands of the newer black owners. Known as the Port Royal Experiment, this established the Gullah communities still found today on Daufuskie, Hilton Head, St. Helena, Edisto, Wadmalaw, and Johns islands.

Today, Hilton Head is a mecca for golf, tennis, and restaurant and nightclub prowling, with scores of boutiques, discount outlet malls, and wide beaches. Its upscale, slightly swift, often crowded milieu attracts hundreds of thousands of visitors a year. There used to be an off-season at Hilton Head between November and March, but no more; Hilton Head is always busy, as many visitors have made this their retirement home.

The island's first development, **Sea Pines Plantation,** won national and international acclaim on environmental, architectural, and social grounds. During the late 1960s and 1970s, more faux "plantation" developments patterned after Sea Pines

Sea Pines Riding Stables on Hilton Head Island.

spread over the island: Port Royal, Shipyard, Wexford. Today, it's a continuous sprawl of large gated residential developments. These neighborhoods blocked through-traffic, and the slow crawl on old **U.S. 278, the William Hilton Parkway,** prompted the construction of the **Cross Island Parkway,** an elevated, four-lane expressway over its salt marshes and creeks. U.S. 278 became a four-lane expressway connecting the island to Interstate 95 at Hardeeville, some 15 miles inland.

Despite the development that accompanied these "plantations," Hilton Head has one of South Carolina's best Atlantic beaches, and nature lovers can spend hours exploring the Hilton Head shores. Area beaches are beautiful and diverse; some are broad and flat, with long tidal pools, perfect for hours of beachcombing. There are also wild beaches, muddy clamming beaches, bird-nesting spots, dolphin-watching inlets, and lounge chair rentals for sunbathers.

Dolphin Head, the island's northern shore, is within Hilton Head Plantation. The bluffs overlook Port Royal Sound and herds of bottle-nosed dolphins, but the bluffs have eroded dramatically (the land has lost 250 feet since 1860). Heading northeast, hikers will find the red cliffs of Hilton Head, in the stretch between

Dolphin Head and Fish Haul Creek. These are craggy headland bluffs facing Port Royal Sound, on comparatively high ground, though it is eroding 3 feet a year beneath storm surf, tidal currents, and rising sea levels.

Hilton Head Beach is the island's eastern "heel," the curving bit of beach and mud bordering Port Royal Sound and the Atlantic. This is where Capt. William Hilton guided his ships ashore in 1663. The beach is within Port Royal Plantation, and the best beach walking is adjacent to the "Steam Cannon," where Fort Walker Drive ends. There are views here of Port Royal Sound's headwaters and neighboring islands.

North Forest Beach (*south* of Hilton Head Beach) is submerged under 10 feet of water at high tide and suffering from extreme erosion (10 feet a year). To protect their homes, residents here constructed seawalls, great rocks that serve as hosts to such odd creatures as ghost crabs and long-tailed, brown sea cockroaches.

At the far end of Hilton Head Island is **South Beach.** Here, a southbound sea current carries in clean, fine sand eroded from North Forest Beach and flows out in Calibogue Sound's riptide. The two currents neutralize each other, and sand is dumped at the mouth of the sound. This is Hilton Head's widest beach, and it is actually getting bigger. It is a popular feeding ground for game fish, pelicans, osprey, and dolphin.

Much of Hilton Head is privately owned and gated, so it is easiest to rent a vacation house for a week to fully enjoy the island. When you inquire at rental agencies, ask for specifics about beach access from particular condos or vacation homes.

■ Inland from Hilton Head

The historic village of **Bluffton** (population 750) nestles on a high bluff along the **May River** just down SC 46 toward Savannah. Settled in 1825 as a summer haven for rice and cotton planters, Bluffton is a small town with longtime locals and newer retirees.

Shady streets, plankboard homes, and serenity typify the old Gullah communities here, which are being encroached on by development in spite of conservation efforts. Ask directions to the small public dock by the Episcopal Church of the Cross. From the dock, there is a spectacular view of the May River, saltwater marshes, and old homes along the bluff. The weathered little cypress-plank church was built in 1854 for a congregation of planters. Its cool interior and grounds shaded by cedars and live oaks offer a peaceful respite.

Rose Hill mansion in Bluffton.

South of Bluffton and Hilton Head Island lies **Daufuskie Island,** which now beckons wealthy retirees and vacationers to new golf course developments. Daufuskie is reached only by a small **passenger ferry** and private boat (check locally at Harbor Town marina for ferry schedules). Its developers promise buyers the island will never be another Hilton Head. A genuinely unique and quaint place to visit, it was the setting for Pat Conroy's first book, the memoir *The Water Is Wide.*

■ PARRIS ISLAND   *map page 49, A-4*

Anyone who knows *Semper Fidelis* ("Always Faithful"), the motto of the U.S. Marine Corps, knows Parris Island, north of Hilton Head Island across Port Royal Sound on SC 802. The 40-mile drive from Hilton Head to the Parris Island and Beaufort area, via U.S. 278 and SC 170, passes under canopies of live oaks and across broad expanses of salt marsh. It is one of the most scenic drives in the Sea Islands.

Former members of the Corps who have retired here learned of this area at the island's recruit training depot or at the Marine Corps Air Base 5 miles north of Beaufort. Unlike some military bases, Parris Island encourages visits by the public.

It's possible to drive past recruits in training, tour old navy yards, and learn Marine Corps history at the **Parris Island Museum.** The island is open every day, and events such as parades and graduation ceremonies are open to the public. The guards at the base gate will provide directions to the Douglas Visitors Center, where maps and brochures are available. Call 843-525-3650.

On what is now the seventh fairway of the marines' golf course (right behind the clubhouse) was, from 1566 to 1587, the site of Santa Elena, Spain's northern outpost in America. Santa Elena succumbed to disease, privation, and attacks by Native American tribes, whom the Spanish tried to enslave. For two decades, about 500 colonists clung to the New World settlement, which is now being explored by archaeologists. Artifacts and remnants of three forts, including the recently excavated Charles Fort, include the oldest European-style pottery kiln found in North America.

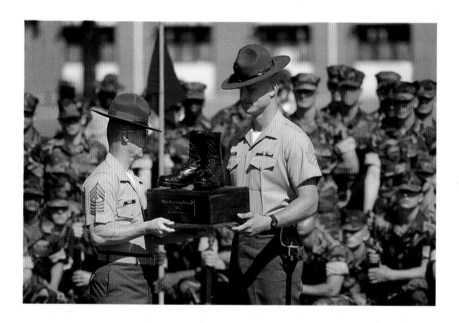

Basic training of U.S. Marine Corps cadets takes place at their Parris Island facility.

AFRICAN-AMERICAN TIMELINE

1670 Of the colony's 148 original settlers, 5 are black. Importation of slaves from Africa begins; especially valued are farmers from the rice-producing region of Ghana, as well as Ibo, Shanan, and Angolans.

1730s Two-thirds of the local population is in bondage; the other (white) third fears revolt.

1739 Slaves burn plantations along the Stono River.

1800s Forty percent of slaves come to the U.S. after quarantine on Sullivan's Island.

1818 Emanuel African Methodist Episcopal Church opens in downtown Charleston.

1820 Manumission—the act of freeing a slave—is outlawed in South Carolina.

1822 Denmark Vesey, a free black carpenter, plots a slave revolt and is executed.

1860 South Carolina secedes from Union

1861 Civil War begins.

1862 Escaped slaves form first black regiment in the U.S. Army, the First South Carolina Volunteers, and begin to fight for the Union.

Robert Smalls and other black crewmen pilot a Confederate gunship out of Charleston Harbor and deliver it to the Union.

Penn School is established on Union-occupied St. Helena Island.

1863 All-black Massachusetts 54th leads the assault on Fort Wagner in Charleston Harbor. Sgt. William Carney becomes the first African-American to be awarded the Congressional Medal of Honor.

1865 Civil War ends. Thirteenth Amendment abolishes slavery.

1868 Fourteenth Amendment makes ex-slaves citizens; Robert Smalls and Thomas Miller begin serving in Congress.

1870 Ku Klux Klan becomes active.

1895 State constitution deprives most blacks of voting rights.

1954 U.S. Supreme Court finds segregation in public schools unconstitutional.

1960s Civil rights movement begins. Harvey Gantt becomes first black student to attend an all-white college in South Carolina; public facilities desegregated; right to vote ensured.

1968 Three black students are killed and 40 injured as students integrate an Orangeburg bowling alley.

1970 Three blacks elected to state house of representatives.

1974 First black woman elected to the state house of representatives.

1994 Ernest Finney elected Chief Justice of the South Carolina Supreme Court.

GULLAH CULTURE

The word Gullah refers to the African-American descendants of plantation slaves who lived in virtual isolation for generations in the Sea Islands of South Carolina and Georgia, speaking a hybrid dialect of English and African words, passing on herbal medicines and religious ceremonies, and existing by harvesting oysters, fish, vegetables, and pulpwood. Although many Gullah remain on the islands, their population and lifestyle are threatened by encroaching developers. But as you cross over onto St. Helena and nearby islands around Beaufort, you will hear the lilting language all its own.

Here are a few Gullah proverbs and phrases:

Ef yo' play wid puppy, ee lick yo' face.	Familiarity breeds contempt.
Cut finguh f'aid ax.	A burnt child dreads the fire.
Ef yo' ent hab hoss to ride, ride cow.	Half a loaf is better than no bread.
Po' buckra an' dog walk one pat'.	The poor man and dog walk the same path.
clean gone	having left earlier
crack'e'teet'	speak
curly flower	cauliflower

A view out to sea over the marshes of St. Helena Island

■ BEAUFORT *map page 49, A-4*

On Port Royal Island, Beaufort (think of the word beautiful and pronounce it "Byew-furt") is South Carolina's second-oldest town, after Charleston. Established in 1711, it is the county seat of Beaufort County. One of Beaufort's scores of antebellum mansions and homes, **Tidalholm,** was that quintessential, baby-boomer-restored Yuppie dream house in the 1983 film *The Big Chill.*

Beaufort (population 13,600) is one of those rare towns where residents and visitors alike find that one of the most rewarding aspects of life is strolling the quiet, shady streets of the large national historic district downtown, **Old Point.** From U.S. 21, take Bay Street into the historic district. There you'll find more than 170 public buildings and private houses of historic distinction. You may walk, or take a guided, horse-drawn carriage tour that departs from the visitors office near the Beaufort River public marina. Town maps for self-guided walks and event listings are also available here. Waterfront Park and Bay Street are lined with galleries, bookstores, and restaurants.

The Union victory over the Confederacy in the Battle of Port Royal Sound was so swift and complete that Beaufort was abandoned without serious resistance. Since it was held by the Union for the rest of the Civil War, the town's historic buildings were not destroyed when Sherman's Union army advanced through South Carolina. For example, the **George Parsons Elliot House Museum,** at 1001 Bay Street (now a private home) served as a Union hospital during the Civil War, and the **John Mark Verdier House,** at 801 Bay Street (open to the public; 843-379-6335), housed Federal officers from 1861 to 1865.

You will also find local mansions that were memorable movie sets, early-18th-century homes, antebellum mansions, the national cemetery (established during the Civil War by President Lincoln), and the 1724 **St. Helena Episcopal Church** (843-522-1712). While many private houses in Old Point are not usually open to the public, some may open their doors during the annual **Historic Tour of Homes and Plantations,** in mid-October, and the **Spring Tour of Homes and Gardens,** in April or May.

■ **ST. HELENA ISLAND AND BEYOND** *map page 49, A-3/4*

> The winding road is deeply rutted in sand and crosses numerous tidal rivulets. In summer the wild phlox spreads a varicolored carpet over uncultivated fields, and the aroma of sweet myrtle is brought in by the ocean breezes.
>
> —*South Carolina, the WPA Guide to the Palmetto State,* 1941

The largest of Beaufort County's 65 islands, St. Helena is pronounced "S'int Hellena." Native Indians here were eradicated between 1715 and 1718, after which European planters became wealthy, first growing indigo, then rice, then the more successful long-fibered Sea Island cotton. Legend has it that these planters were dismayed, in 1815, to learn that Napoleon was to be exiled to St. Helena Island. They wrote protests to the English government, which informed them that there was more than one St. Helena.

The crop of cotton here was so fine that French mills often bought the crop before it was planted, making St. Helena Island planters quite wealthy and allowing them to purchase large numbers of slaves. When their owners fled Union ships in 1861, the slaves remained, living on their former owners' properties. These

Basket weaving is a popular folk art that has endured on St. Helena Island.

Digging in the sand is a Sea Islands pastime.

details and other mementos of African-American history can be found in St. Helena Island's **Penn Center Historic District.**

Every January in the early 1960s, the late Dr. Martin Luther King Jr. and his Southern Christian Leadership Conference met privately in the cottages and dormitories of the Penn Center to plan their next civil rights campaigns. It was here that King scheduled marches on Selma and Birmingham, Chicago and Cicero, Memphis and Jackson, Mississippi, as well as the Poor People's March on Washington. The Retreat House was built expressly for Dr. King, who would not live to see its completion in spring 1968.

Penn Center's 49 acres and 16 buildings along Land's End Road are a National Historic District themselves, not because of Dr. King and the SCLC but because of something that occurred a century earlier. In 1862, soon after the Union occupied Beaufort, two Quaker women from Philadelphia opened the first southern school for freed slaves, here at Penn Center. It became the cultural and community center of the freedmen on St. Helena Island. The school closed in 1953, but Penn Center remains a living museum, preserving the language, culture, and history of the Sea Island's Gullah population. The center's York W. Bailey Museum is open Tuesday through Friday; call 843-838-2432 for more information.

There are no beaches on St. Helena Island, but several can be found at the eastern end of U.S. 21. That route reaches the ocean just across the marshes of Johnson Creek at **Hunting Island,** which is now almost entirely a state park.

Within the park are more than 5,000 acres of wide "boneyard" beaches (named for the bonelike driftwood sculptures left by cypress, palmettos, and pines) as well as a maritime forest, sand dunes, a 19th-century lighthouse that provides awesome views from 140 feet, and a boardwalk through the salt marshes. Hikers may see many small game animals, birds of prey, and giant sea turtles, but hunting is no longer allowed here.

Hunting Island is far from crowds, noise, and nighttime light pollution. The park has rental cabins and hundreds of campsites. For more information, call 843-838-2011.

Fripp Island, just south of Hunting Island, was purchased from the Yamassee by Capt. Johannes Fripp after his victory over the Spanish, and the golf course here served as the Vietnamese movie set for the 1994 film *Forrest Gump*. It is now an entirely private resort with homes and villas for rent, as well as the Fripp Island Inn (843-838-3535 or 800-845-4100).

■ THE TWO EDISTOES   *map page 49, A-3 and map page 169, C-4*

Up U.S. 17 on the road to Charleston, Highway 174 takes you to the two Edistoes, which retain much of their old character, in part because residents actively curtail massive development. The small island town of **Edisto Beach** still has very few accommodations or commercial businesses other than a small fleet of shrimp trawlers. The much bigger community of **Edisto Island**, inland from the beach island across the tidal creek, still has family descendants living on colonial-era plantations, attending the same historic Edisto Island churches their ancestors did.

In Edisto Beach, you can rent one of the modest, one-story, fully furnished houses by the week. Although there are some newer, prefabricated homes, most are the kind of shacks that were built a hundred years ago when owners accepted the likelihood that nature would come along one day and blow them all away.

There are some newer golf rentals on Edisto Beach Island, such as Fairfield Ocean Ridge rental villas and Bay Creek Villas, at the south end of the island. **Edisto Beach State Park** offers more than a hundred oceanside campsites at the north end of the island and five fully-furnished, heated, air-conditioned cabins overlooking the marsh. It's a popular site, and reservations are recommended (843-538-8206).

(following pages) Edisto Island remains one of the least developed of the state's Sea Islands.

Casual seafood restaurants at Edisto Beach serve what the local trawlers and fishermen just caught. For fine dining, the **Old Post Office** on Edisto Island is as renowned as any in Charleston. Retail fresh seafood markets and roadside fresh vegetable stands provide epicurean delights for preparation in your own rented kitchen (843-869-2339).

■ SEA ISLANDS FROM CHARLESTON ENVIRONS TO MYRTLE BEACH

■ KIAWAH ISLAND   *map page 49, A-2/3*

Immediately northeast of Edisto is Seabrook Island, a resort that is primarily a residential suburb of Charleston. The Bohicket Marina has boat rentals, charter sea fishing, and a handful of very good restaurants. The next island is Kiawah, a five-star resort with a luxury hotel, the Sanctuary, as well as breathtaking private homes for rent.

The colonization of Kiawah began in the 1690s when the English Lords Proprietors bought it from its namesake Indian tribe, mostly in exchange for cloth, hatchets, and beads. The lords granted the 2,700-acre island to Capt. George Raynor, believed to be one of the many pirates who sometimes sailed for the English against the Spanish. In the 1730s, John Stanyarne, a wealthy merchant and planter, bought Kiawah to raise cattle and grow indigo. For the next 120 years, Kiawah was owned by Stanyarne's descendants, the Vanderhorsts, who also used the island to raise cattle and grow crops.

In 1953, the Vanderhorst estate sold Kiawah to a wealthy timberman from Aiken, C. C. Royal, who used the island for logging and as a family vacation retreat. Royal also built the

Tidelands at Kiawah Island.

Tee off and spot wildlife at the Kiawah Island Resort's Ocean Course.

first bridge linking Kiawah to neighboring Johns Island, which already had bridges linking it to the mainland and Charleston. In 1974, in a deal that shocked the Sea Islands, the Royal family sold Kiawah to an investment group led by the oil-rich sheikdom of Kuwait, which developed the island as a golf and tennis resort. The resort has changed hands several times since then and has expanded its development to attract visitors from around the world to play on its championship golf courses.

The Ocean Course, protected under the federal Coastal Barrier Resources Act, has hosted the Ryder Cup and the World Cup on several occasions. Two other island courses also have challenging oceanfront holes. The freshwater lagoons are home to hundreds of alligators, who frequently emerge to sun themselves on the grassy banks. Pelicans, herons, osprey, bobcats, deer, and other wildlife are usually visible from the 30 miles of bike paths. The beach on Kiawah Island is more than 12 miles long, and at low tide, you can ride bicycles on the sand to hunt for shells and sand dollars.

There are several inland islands in the area here, such as Johns Island, home to fresh vegetable stands, sweetgrass basket weavers, and the Angel Oak. This massive live oak, in a city park off Maybank Highway, is believed to be about 1,400 years old, the largest living tree east of the Mississippi. Nearby is rural Wadmalaw Island, where you can visit the nation's only surviving tea plantation. You can also buy shrimp in season fresh off the boat at Cherry Point Park, and pick your own strawberries at Leland Farms.

■ **FOLLY BEACH** *map page 49, A-2*
A small bridge crosses over the Folly River from James Island to the self-proclaimed "Edge of America," Folly Beach, a narrow island populated by aging surfers and huge sculptural wisteria vines. This is where George Gershwin stayed while composing the music for *Porgy and Bess,* although the modest shacks are quickly being renovated into chic beach houses.

During the 1930s and 1940s, Folly's Pier Pavilion and Atlantic Boardwalk drew big crowds and big bands such as Tommy Dorsey, Artie Shaw, Harry James, Guy Lombardo, and Vaughn Monroe. One section has been cleared of homes by the storms, a beach with tempestuous surf known as "The Washout," where surfers gather to ride out the swells year-round. You can park your car along the street and take a delightful walk in the sand.

You can see the 1876 Morris Island lighthouse from the northern end of Folly. Preservationists are trying to save the structure, which is now 50 feet in the surf. Morris Island, now uninhabited and guarding Charleston Harbor, was the site for the 1862 Battle of Secessionville. It was here that the all-black Union regiment, the Massachusetts 54th, ran a suicide charge, an event depicted in the 1989 movie *Glory.*

■ **SULLIVAN'S ISLAND AND MT. PLEASANT**
map page 49, A-1/2 and map page 109, C-3/4 and C-5
North of Charleston over the striking Cooper River Bridge, Sullivan's Island retains a low-key Victorian feel, with beautiful large homes and a refreshing lack of hotels. Once a quarantine stop for hundreds of thousands of slaves imported from Africa, Sullivan's later became a respite for locals who wanted to escape the stifling summers of downtown Charleston. The surf is not as high as at Folly Beach, but the strong winds here attract plenty of windsurfers and kite surfers. At the southern tip, Fort Moultrie State Park overlooks Fort Sumter and the shipping channel, providing a close look at the tremendous container ships on their way into port. There are several batteries on Sullivan's, some of which date back

to the Revolutionary War, and some have even been converted into unusual subterranean homes.

Edgar Allan Poe spent 13 months during 1827–28 on Sullivan's Island, where he absorbed images he later used in his blood-curdling short story of buried pirate treasure, "The Gold-Bug." Poe, then 18, was in an army artillery unit assigned to Fort Moultrie, guarding the entrance to the harbor. He described Sullivan's Island in the story: "This island is a very singular one. It consists of little else than the sea sand, and is about three miles long . . . . It is separated from the mainland by a scarcely perceptible creek, oozing its way through a wilderness of reeds and slime, a favorite resort of the marsh-hen."

The island has no hotels but many lovely Victorian homes and lively restaurants. You can also continue up the shore to other laid-back islands such as Isle of Palms, where Wild Dunes Beach and Racquet Club has vacation rentals, golf, and a marina.

Sullivan's and Isle of Palms are in the northeast direction from Charleston via U.S. 17 over the Cooper River Bridge. The route passes through historic **Mt. Pleasant,** where colonial Charlestonians first began summering around 1700. The world's largest naval and maritime museum is located here on **Patriot's Point;** berthed offshore is the aircraft carrier *Yorktown.* Call 843-884-2727 for more information. Turn right off U.S. 17 just beyond the bridge onto SC 703, passing by Mt. Pleasant's Shem Creek, where a small shrimp boat fleet and a number of charter deep-sea fishing boats are based and where some of the area's most popular seafood restaurants are located.

With a rental boat from the Wild Dunes marina, it is a short trip via the Intracoastal Waterway or along the beach past Dewees Island (under development for private homes) to **Capers Island,** a state Heritage Preserve. Capers' long beach usually is deserted, but overnight camping is available by permit.

There are no facilities on Capers, fishing is allowed only from the beach, and campers should bring their own water, food, and charcoal or firewood. Pets are not allowed. Reservations should be made a week in advance: S.C. Department of Natural Resources on James Island (843-762-5043).

If you want to experience wildlife and nature as they may have existed hundreds of years ago, all of the coastline's islands are worth exploring. And one way to see them is through the eyes of the planters and their slaves, by visiting the many public plantation museums that dot the Lowcountry.

COASTAL PLANTATIONS

The colonial and antebellum rice, indigo, and cotton plantations of South Carolina grew fat on the fruit of a tragic condition: entire industries built with slavery. It is an emotional part of American history, accompanied by romantic accoutrements such as grand architecture, unforgettable gardens, infamous mythological characters (from Scarlett O'Hara to the great Santini), renegade soldiers, and heartbreaking music.

■ SLAVES, RICE, AND INDIGO

In September of 1670, five months after the first English settlers landed at Albemarle Point, a ship from the British colony of Bermuda sailed into Charleston Harbor. On board were the first African slaves to be recorded by name in North America.

The Carolina colony was the only English colony on the continent where African slaves were introduced virtually at the outset. Although they were called simply "Africans," they included a disparate variety of people from the Congo, Ibos, Coromantees from the Gold Coast, Gambian Muslims, and others. Placed together on plantations, these individuals eventually formed an entirely new culture—a mixture of language, custom, and ethnicities paralleling that of the Europeans in its complexity. By 1708, the colony's population included 3,960 free white men, women, and children; 4,100 African slaves; and 1,400 Native American slaves.

The Africans were enslaved, and the plantations created, to grow rice from a seed imported from Madagascar in 1672 by one of the colony's most respected and learned settlers, Dr. Henry Woodward. His agricultural experiment promised to give the colony its first export product.

For the next three decades, Dr. Woodward's rice crept up the tidal rivers of the Lowcountry. Slaves from the rice-growing areas of West Africa were not only experienced with the crop, but they were also resistant to the malaria endemic to both regions. River swamps were cleared and drained. Marshes were enclosed and divided by earthen dikes into square fields watered by a series of trunks and sluices. The seeds were planted in spring and the fields subsequently flooded. Throughout

Drayton Hall is the only Ashley River plantation mansion to survive the Civil War.

the summer, the rice grass was stimulated and insects controlled by periodic drain-ing, flooding, and hoeing. In early autumn, when the stalks turned golden brown, they were harvested by sickles, tied into bundles, and transported on flatboats to plantation rice mills for threshing.

By the 1730s, rice had made the Carolina planters the richest men in America, and then, indigo made them richer. The indigo plant can be processed to yield a dye that colors fabric indigo blue—between blue and violet in the color spectrum. England's rapidly expanding textile factories were launching the Industrial Revolution and clamoring for more indigo dye. In 1749, Parliament began award-ing a bounty, a kind of bonus, to indigo suppliers.

Indigo is a difficult crop to cultivate and process. During the 1740s, a young Carolina plantation mistress named Eliza Lucas Pinckney developed an efficient method of processing the plant to yield the valuable dye. She let it ferment in a vat of water for 12 hours. The liquid was then drawn off into a lower vat and stirred vigorously with paddles for several hours. When it turned the desired color, lime was added to stop the fermentation and fix the color. The heavier dye settled to the bottom, and the water was drawn off, leaving a paste. That was strained to remove excess water, cut into cubes, then set out in the sun to dry.

River systems, along with slaves, were the life blood of the rice and indigo plan-tations. Neighborhoods formed along the tidal streams, most notably along the Ashley, Cooper, Wando, and Stono rivers near Charleston; the Pee Dee, Waccamaw, Black, Sampit, and Santee rivers near Georgetown; and the Edisto, Ashepoo, and Combahee rivers near Beaufort. Twice a day, ocean tides forced the rivers to back up, while plantation tidal gates let in fresh water for irrigating the fields. Down the same rivers came the crop, on shallow-draft flatboats, en route to the docks and ships of Charleston and Georgetown. As the crop went downstream to port, supplies came up the river, hauling furnishings and fabrics for the new mansions, as well as new slaves.

Imports of slaves rose faster than exports of rice, and the planters usually paid for their slaves with rice. Import duties on slaves, paid to the colonial treasury, financed nearly half the annual budget of the colonial government in Carolina dur-ing the 1730s. Not until after the American Revolution did South Carolina stop importing slaves. Between 1803 and 1808, 40,000 more slaves were the last to be imported, and then the United States Congress outlawed their importation. By then, however, hundreds of thousands were already at work on the plantations, and slavery continued for nearly six more decades.

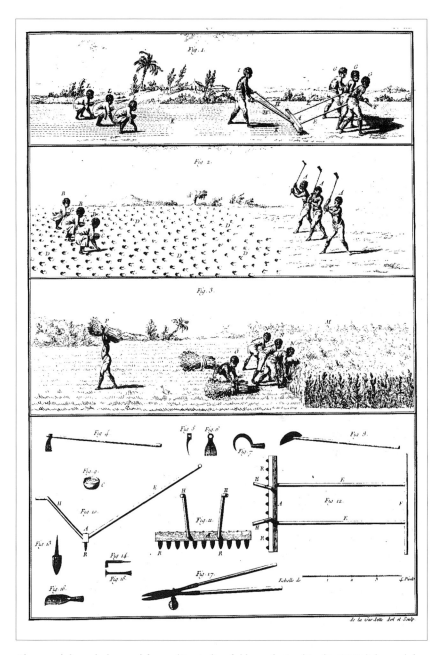

Slaves and the tools they used for working indigo fields are depicted in this 1770 lithograph by Beauvais de Raseau.

■ ANTEBELLUM MANSIONS

It is remarkable that any of the plantation houses are left standing. Accidental fire was the most frequent cause of destruction on South Carolina's Lowcountry and Sea Island plantations, and war was a close second. In 1715, the Yemassee Indians destroyed nearly all of the plantations south of Charleston after the owners abandoned them and fled to the safety of the port. During the Revolutionary War, and again during the Civil War, more plantations were burned. Hurricanes, earthquakes, termites, heat and humidity, Reconstruction-era neglect, and the Great Depression took their toll on the magnificent mansions.

The manors that survived the ravages of time did so, in part, because cypress was the favored building material. Resistant to rot and termites, cypress shrinks very little over time. Heart pine was used for flooring, poplar and mahogany for trim. In the colonial period, masonry was the preferred exterior, and bricks were usually made at the site. In later years before the Civil War, wood became the popular siding.

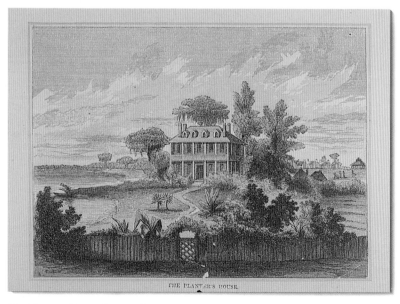

THE PLANTER'S HOUSE.

The Planters House *by an unknown artist.*

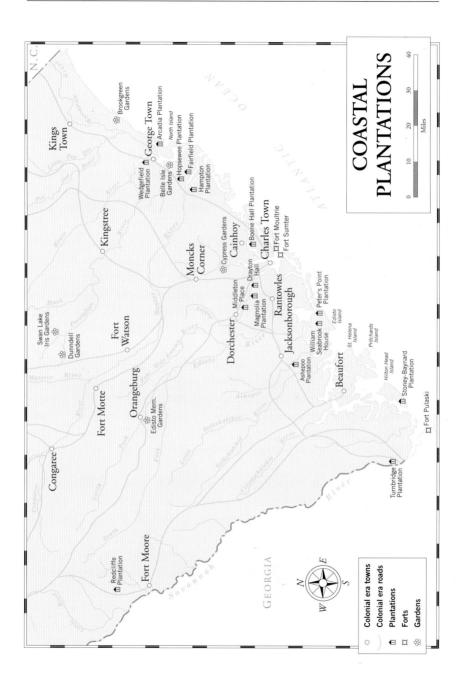

COASTAL
PLANTATIONS

Miles

0   10   20   30   40

N.C.

OCEAN

ATLANTIC

Brookgreen
Gardens

Kings
Town

George Town
Arcadia Plantation
North Island
Fairfield Plantation
Belle Isle
Gardens
Hopsewee Plantation
Wedgefield
Plantation
Hampton
Plantation

Kingstree

Moncks
Corner

Cypress Gardens
Cainhoy
Boone Hall Plantation
Charles Town
Fort Moultrie
Fort Sumter

Middleton
Place
Drayton
Hall
Magnolia
Plantation
Rantowles
Peter's Point
Plantation

Dorchester

Jacksonborough

William
Seabrook
House

Edisto
Island

Pritchards
Island

St. Helena
Island

Ashepoo
Plantation

Beaufort

Hilton Head
Island

Stoney-Baynard
Plantation

Fort Pulaski

Swan Lake
Iris Gardens
Dunndell
Gardens

Fort
Watson

Orangeburg

Edisto Mem.
Gardens

Fort Morte

Congaree

Redcliffe
Plantation
Fort Moore

Turnbridge
Plantation

GEORGIA

N
W   E
S

Colonial era towns
Colonial era roads
Plantations
Forts
Gardens

The wealthy planters were not trained architects, for the most part, but they often designed their own houses, borrowing from the schools of Georgian, Federal, Gothic Revival, and early colonial architecture.

■ ASHLEY RIVER BARONS   *map page 83*

The Ashley River, which empties into Charleston Harbor, is only about 30 miles long, but it is packed with history. The fabulously wealthy rice and indigo planters here were the men who overthrew the English Lords Proprietors; signed the Declaration of Independence; served as governors, state justices, and members of the Continental Congress; and signed the Ordinance of Secession to launch the Civil War.

Drayton Hall, Magnolia Plantation and Gardens, and a third extraordinary plantation and garden, Middleton Place, come one after another on a 10-mile stretch of **SC Scenic Highway 61,** which parallels the Ashley River up from Charleston. Together, the three provide a composite picture of the grandeur the Ashley River barons lavished upon themselves. All three houses are on the National Register of Historic Places, Drayton and Middleton also being National Historic Landmarks. All three are open to the public.

John Drayton built Drayton Hall between 1738 and 1742, and his descendants kept the mansion in the family through the next seven generations. Drayton designed an exquisite Palladian home where slaves fanned him with peacock plumes. He died one of the wealthiest men in colonial America, leaving behind rice and indigo plantations with 500 slaves, and an epitaph: "Such was his character, he lived in riches, but without public esteem. He died in a tavern, but without public commiseration."

Today, **Drayton Hall** (3380 Ashley River Road off Route 61, 9 miles from downtown Charleston; 843-766-0188) is a museum of the National Trust for Historic Preservation, owned jointly by the trust and the state of South Carolina. It is the only Ashley River plantation mansion to survive the Civil War, spared by Union troops because it was being used as a smallpox hospital for the just-freed slaves of the Drayton plantations. It was they who burned the newel posts for firewood, and perhaps the missing false doors as well.

Drayton Hall, a massive Palladian portico, is perhaps the finest early Georgian house in the nation. Inside are rich, hand-crafted details, delicate mahogany carvings, painted cypress paneling, and a hand-molded drawing-room ceiling executed

The beautiful gardens of Magnolia Plantation.

in wet plaster that is the only one that survives in this country. In keeping with historic preservation, there is no running water, electric lighting, or central heating, even though this remained the home of Miss Charlotte Drayton for much of the 20th century.

Magnolia Plantation and Gardens (10 miles northwest of downtown Charleston on Route 61; 843-571-1266) was the first home of the Draytons, established by Thomas Drayton, one of the wealthy planter-colonists from Barbados, whose son built Drayton Hall. The original house is long gone, but unlike at Drayton Hall, the gardens are intact and magnificent. Fifty acres of lawn and gardens yield 250 varieties of azaleas and 900 types of camellias. They were built in the 1840s by Dr. John Drayton and have been open to the public since 1870. Dr. Drayton was an anomaly among the Ashley River barons. He became an Anglican priest and, despite state laws against it, taught his 300 slaves to read and write. He also invited artist John J. Audubon to visit and obtain waterbird specimens. The **Audubon Swamp Garden** rises from 60 acres of black water in a cypress and tupelo swamp adjoining the plantation. Boardwalks, dikes, bridges, rental canoes, and walking and biking trails make both gardens accessible.

Middleton Place (14 miles northwest of Charleston, 4300 Ashley River Road; 843-556-6020), the nation's oldest landscaped gardens, was owned by the same family for three centuries—in this case, the Middletons. Of course, the Ashley River barons intermarried so much, it is hard to say which family name applies. Henry Middleton established this duchy in 1740. He built his holdings into 20 plantations, 50,000 acres, and 800 slaves and was president of the First Continental Congress. Each of his children respectively married a Drayton, a Pinckney, a Rutledge, a Manigault, an Izard, a Smith, and a Parker. His son, Arthur Middleton, signed the Declaration of Independence, and Arthur's children married into almost all the same families, as did their children after them.

The original plantation mansion was burned to the ground by Union troops in the final days of the Civil War. The family then moved into what was built in 1755 as a gentlemen's guest wing but, today, seems as elegant as any mansion should be, with Empire furnishings, Aubusson carpet, and a portrait of Czar Nicholas I. (Henry the Second served 10 years as the nation's minister to Russia.)

While the house is open for guided tours, the main draw at Middleton Place is the grounds. The formal gardens and butterfly ponds were modeled after 17th-century European gardens. They blaze with color almost year-round, camellias in winter, azaleas in spring, kalmias, magnolias, crepe myrtles, and roses in summer. These are not merely well-tended grounds; they are closely barbered. There are pea hens roaming the grounds, as well as cows and sheep grazing on the huge front lawn, and you can visit the outbuildings to watch yarn spinning and black-smithing. There's a fine restaurant overlooking one of the rice ponds, as well as a superb gift shop selling local crafts. There is also a ¼-acre demonstration rice field, planted by Carolina Gold, the company that has been cultivating rice in the Lowcountry since the mid-1680s. Middleton offers self-guided tours as well as guided tours, and African-American focus tours.

While the entrance fee to each plantation is relatively high, you may purchase a one-week pass that permits entry to Middleton and Drayton, as well as three museum houses in downtown Charleston.

As you continue up Route 61, Old Dorchester State Park is the site of what once was the frontier outpost, and then the colony's third-largest town, **Dorchester.** Founded in 1697 by Congregationalists from Dorchester in the

The Audubon Swamp Garden rises from a cypress and tupelo swamp adjoining Magnolia Plantation.

Massachusetts colony, it was the limit of navigation on the Ashley and the beginning of a major Indian trading trail.

Dorchester's colonial merchants traded finished goods from Charleston for plantation products such as rice and indigo and naval supplies. Its craftsmen included carpenters, tailors, and blacksmiths. A small fort guarded the town, which was seized by the British during the Revolution. By the end of that war, Dorchester was abandoned. Today, only the tabby walls of the fort, the ghostly remains of a church bell tower, and the tombstones of an old cemetery remain, sheltered by huge live oaks and stately pines. Archaeological excavations are ongoing, and outdoor kiosks detail the town's history.

To get to **Old Dorchester State Park,** go north on SC 61 about 5 miles beyond Middleton Place to SC 165, turn right and drive north about 1 mile to SC 642, then go right again and drive about a mile. Old Dorchester is open 9 AM to 6 PM free of charge, closed Tuesday and Wednesday.

■ GOOSE CREEK BARBADIANS   *map page 83*

While the Ashley River barons' plantations are the best known in South Carolina, the Goose Creek Barbadians were the men who first launched the plantation system in the colony. They imported the first African slaves, enslaved Yemassee despite protests from England, and controlled government in the Carolina province throughout its early decades.

Goose Creek branches off the Cooper River on the other side of the Charleston peninsula from the Ashley River in what today is a center of industrial development and suburban sprawl. In the 1670s, during the first decade of the colony's existence, each year brought more immigrants from the West Indies, especially from the British colony of Barbados.

Edward Middleton, whose son built Middleton Place on the Ashley, was among these early Barbadians who settled on Goose Creek and the Cooper River. So was William Rhett, or "Colonel Rhett" as he put it, who led the expedition of planters and merchants that put an end to pirate raids on shipping through the port of Charleston. The Barbadians brought slaves to the colony, and also a culture combining Old World elegance and frontier boisterousness. By the time of the Revolution, their influence was no longer distinct within the planter-merchant oligarchy of the Lowcountry and Sea Islands. Today, their plantations are home to subdivisions, shopping centers, and industry.

Colonial and antebellum rice plantations spread farther up the Cooper River from Goose Creek, and one of those was **Dean Hall.** The plantation was settled by a family of Scottish baronets, the Nesbetts of Dean, then sold to William Carson in 1821. For his son, the plantation was not a happy place. Writing after the Civil War, he said, "My father, William A. Carson, was a rice planter who wore out his life watching a salty river, and died at the age of 56, when I was 10 years old."

In 1909, Dean Hall plantation was sold to Benjamin Kittredge, who had no interest in planting the land but instead conceived of a garden of azaleas, camellias, and other flowers rising out of the cypress and tupelo swamps of the plantation. Dean Hall is now called **Cypress Gardens** (843-553-0515), donated to the city of Charleston in 1963 and open to the public.

■ GEORGETOWN RICE PLANTATIONS *map page 83*

By 1840, plantations along five rivers in the Georgetown region, 60 miles north of Charleston, grew almost half the rice produced in the nation. During the 1840s and 1850s, more rice was shipped from Georgetown than from any other port in the world, and nearly all of the crop was grown by 91 planters who, until the Civil War, lived as richly and lavishly as the Ashley River barons of the colonial period.

Four rivers empty into Winyah Bay at Georgetown: the Sampit, Black, Great Pee Dee, and Waccamaw; a fifth, the Santee, empties into the Atlantic Ocean 15 miles south of the port. The first plantations in the region were near the mouth of the Santee, where Huguenots seeking religious freedom began settling in 1689, after being forced from France by the Edict of Nantes.

Within a decade, about 70 French Huguenot families were diking the marshes of the lower Santee for rice and indigo, in a stretch of the river that became known as French Santee. The legendary guerrilla raider of the Revolutionary War, Gen. Francis "the Swamp Fox" Marion, was born into this French Huguenot community in 1732.

A few miles farther up the Santee, equally illustrious figures in South Carolina and American history were born into "English Santee" plantation families. Thomas Lynch, a delegate to the Continental Congress, founded **Fairfield Plantation.** His son, Thomas Jr., a signer of the Declaration of Independence, lived across the river at **Hopsewee Plantation** (843-546-7891).

Perhaps the most influential of all the Santee River settlers, however, was a young English millwright, Jonathan Lucas, who emigrated to the colony shortly before the Revolution. The ship Lucas was aboard ran aground on sand bars at the

A large portion of rice grown in South Carolina was produced on tidal deltas. Here a sluice is opened to flood a rice field at high tide.

mouth of the Santee River, and so the Santee and its rice plantations defined the first experiences the inventive immigrant had in his new homeland.

The laborious mortar-and-pestle method used to clean the hull from the rice struck Lucas as inefficient, and he invented a pounding mill in 1787. This machine was powered by the rising and falling tides of the river and revolutionized the processing of rice. Lucas became wealthy, with a town house in Charleston, a summer retreat in the fall-line town of Aiken, and a 4,000-acre rice plantation with 500 slaves on Murphy Island, not far from where his ship ran aground.

■ HAMPTON PLANTATION

Perhaps the most celebrated—certainly the most accessible—of all the Santee River rice plantations is just north of U.S. 17, and about 15 miles south of Georgetown at **Hampton Plantation State Park.** Begun in 1700 by the Huguenot Elias Horry (pronounced "*Oar*-ee") and expanded shortly before the Revolution (with a massive, columned Adams portico and a ballroom with a sky-blue ceiling), the mansion and plantation were home to Horrys, Pinckneys, and Rutledges and are now open to the public.

Harriott Horry, daughter of Eliza Lucas Pinckney (who'd perfected indigo processing), brought Hampton to its architectural glory and greatest prosperity. She owned it and managed it as a widow from the 1780s until her death in 1830. President George Washington came there in 1791 and was greeted by Harriott and Eliza, who wore sashes painted with his likeness (the Washington Oak is planted in front of the house). Harriott's daughter had married a Rutledge, and it was a descendant born two generations later, Archibald Rutledge, who became Hampton's most famous resident.

Archibald Rutledge was born at Hampton in 1883, grew up hunting, fishing, and playing on the plantation, then left as a young man to pursue a teaching career at private schools in Pennsylvania. For 15 years, after the death of his parents in 1921 and 1923, the mansion stood empty and slipped into disrepair. But it was not left entirely alone.

Young Archie Rutledge grew up with a childhood best friend, Prince Alston, who also lived at Hampton. The Alstons were descendants of the slaves who had worked Hampton's rice fields and, after the Civil War and freedom, had simply stayed where they were.

Upon his retirement from teaching in 1937, Archibald Rutledge came home. "When I came to where the gate used to be, I could hardly see the house for the tall weeds and taller bushes. It was as if the blessing of fecundity had been laid on everything natural, and on everything human, the curse of the decay," he later wrote.

Rutledge and his old friends the Alstons set to work restoring the mansion and grounds as a labor of love. In the mansion's front room, Rutledge sat before the fire late in the days, a board laid across the arms of his big chair, and wrote. He became South Carolina's first poet laureate, and wrote two books about the area: *Home by the River* and *The World Around Hampton*.

THE POET LAUREATE COMES HOME

Bowered in its reticent grove of massive old live-oaks, there stands the ancient Southern colonial home, beautiful, wistful, almost like some dreamy fair memory of days long gone . . . . Architecturally, the place stands revealed; but subjectively it is veiled and mysterious. Only by actually living near such a place, by reading its history—if any is recorded—and, best of all, by gossiping with the oldest and most alert of the neighbors can one secure stories of an intimate nature regarding such a remote and magnificent edifice, tales of the more vivid of its inhabitants in far-off times, glimpses of those who now call it home. As I was born and reared in a plantation region, and as I always have taken a certain strange delight in the semi-legendary tales of these ancient picturesque estates and a deep interest in their more modern lore, perhaps it may be possible for me to set ajar certain doors of the enchanted Past, thereby calling to memory life as it was on the old Carolina plantations. . . .

The setting for this strange yet delightful culture was romantic and picturesque to an extraordinary degree. There were the immense tracts of lonely woods, timbered with virgin pine and oak; dark, misty, impenetrable swamps, the haunts of many wild and some savage creatures; noble rivers, difficult to navigate and harder to bridge; sunny shrubberies of a tropical luxuriance of growth; solitary reaches of melancholy coastline, beautiful with the forbidding charm of a spiritual autumn. Nowhere else in the world has nature been so kind to her children as in those regions where the plantations were formed out of the Edenlike wilderness of the Low-Country. And that charm is an eternal one; though the civilization that it cradled and nourished has passed away, the charm survives. The home remains lovely after the guests are gone.

—Archibald Rutledge, *The Carolina Low-Country,* 1931

A second and more scientific restoration of this National Historic Landmark was completed during the 1980s by the state Department of Parks, Recreation, and Tourism. In rebuilding the interior of the mansion, cross-sections of walls were left open to show visitors colonial and antebellum construction techniques. The plantation is 8 miles north of McClellanville off U.S. 17. The Hampton house is open to visitors Thursday through Monday from 1 to 4 PM, and the plantation grounds are open from 9 AM to 6 PM on the same days. For more information, call 843-546-9361.

■ WACCAMAW NECK *map page 83*

North of Georgetown, the rice plantations spread along the Black, Waccamaw, and Great Pee Dee rivers. The most accessible to visitors, and easily the most interesting simply because of what became of them, are along U.S. 17 in the short peninsula between the Waccamaw River and the Atlantic Ocean. The southern end of the peninsula is called **Waccamaw Neck,** and next to it, where Winyah Bay enters the ocean, is **North Island.** When the Marquis de Lafayette sailed to America to join the revolution against the English, he landed at North Island, to be welcomed by Maj. Benjamin Huger, one of the Waccamaw Neck rice planters.

The colonial and antebellum planters made fortunes growing rice on the Neck, and they also spent summer months at the beach here, away from the swamps and marshes where "the fever"—malaria—struck from May through September. North Island was one such planters' resort, until September of 1822, when a hurricane swept over the island and drowned 40 members of plantation families and their servant-slaves.

Prospect Hill, Clifton, Arcadia, and Litchfield rice plantations stretched from ocean to river across the peninsula, but the biggest of them all was the barony given to Lord Carteret, one of the original Lords Proprietors, by King George II in 1718. Carteret, never much interested in the colony, sold it and eventually the barony was divided into plantation parcels of 1,000 to 3,000 acres. Between 1790 and 1900, as many as 10 rice plantations thrived on the barony, which covered all of Waccamaw Neck. Then, in the winter of 1905, a young native of Camden came back to South Carolina on a hunting vacation to a place of his childhood memories, Waccamaw Neck. His name was Bernard Baruch.

As the first half of the 20th century progressed, Baruch became the nation's premier private financier, an advisor to presidents, and a friend of Prime Minister Winston Churchill and President Franklin Roosevelt. But that winter of 1905, already a wealthy stockbroker in New York, Baruch had more personal plans: buying Waccamaw Neck. Within two years, he had it all: 17,500 acres of pristine beach, marsh, rice fields, and maritime forest, more land than Lord Carteret had been given by the king.

Baruch named his vast estate **Hobcaw Barony,** from a Waccamaw Indian word meaning "between the waters." He used a small cabin for hunting trips and winter retreats, then in 1931 built a mansion on the bluffs overlooking Winyah Bay, where he hosted Churchill, FDR, and other world leaders.

Baruch's daughter, Belle, also loved life at Hobcaw and, in 1936, built her own mansion on a plantation-size parcel of the barony she named Bellefield. She acquired all of Hobcaw after her father's death, and before she died in 1964, she established the Belle W. Baruch Foundation, a trust that owns the old barony and maintains it with Clemson University and the University of South Carolina.

Clemson scientists study the maritime forest on the barony's high ground and Carolina scientists the saltwater marsh and estuarine area. **North Inlet,** about 9,000 acres of beach, tidal wetlands, oyster reefs, old rice fields, and creeks, is one of just 21 pockets of pristine nature set aside as national benchmarks to measure environmental changes in a program managed by the National Science Foundation and National Oceanic and Atmospheric Administration. The coastal area along portions of Waccamaw Neck contains some of the last pristine stretches of beach to be found in the state.

The North Inlet-Winyah Bay National Estuarine Research Reserve, the **Bellefield Nature Center,** and **Hobcaw Barony** all are open to the public for a variety of van and walking tours, seminars, lectures, and short-course field studies. The programs are so popular that reservations are recommended several months in advance. For program information and reservations, phone 843-546-4623.

■ BROOKGREEN GARDENS

Joshua Ward, inventor of the water-powered rice thresher, once owned this magnificent plantation just north of Pawleys Island. During the 1920s, Julia Peterkin used Brookgreen as the setting for her novel *Scarlet Sister Mary,* which won the Pulitzer Prize for fiction in 1928. In the 1930s, the wealthy New York art patrons Archer and Anna Hyatt Huntington purchased these 6,600 acres and then began to transform the formal gardens into an outdoor museum of 19th- and 20th-century sculpture. It is an unparalleled setting all year round, with 800 works of art commingling with 2,000 species of plants, art deco ponds, and endless oak-filled marshes along the Waccamaw River. The collection includes sculptures by Anna Huntington herself, as well as Donald DeLue, Marshall Fredericks, James Earle Fraser, Henry Clews, Carl Jennewein, and Jo Davidson, among others. For more information about Brookgreen Gardens, call 843-237-4218.

The coastal area along portions of Waccamaw Neck contains some of the last pristine stretches of beach to be found in the state.

■ GEORGETOWN   *map page 83*

There are dozens of old plantations along the five rice rivers of Georgetown, and for the private, less accessible ones, the best (often the only) way to see them is via boat or van tours from Georgetown.

Every April, the **Prince George Winyah Parish Episcopal Church** holds a two-day tour that includes private mansions and gardens. Throughout the year, tour boats from marinas in Georgetown and the Waccamaw Neck peninsula cruise the rice rivers for views from the water. For more information about the plantation tours, call 843-546-4358.

The old rice port of Georgetown itself, founded in 1729 on the banks of the Sampit River and Winyah Bay, has several dozen residential, religious, and public structures from the 18th and antebellum 19th centuries in its downtown **National Register historic district.** There are guided walking and trolley tours of the district.

Among the notable buildings are the Episcopal church and the **Rice Museum** (843-546-7423), with its maps, dioramas, and artifacts illustrating the heyday of the plantations. A renovated Front Street and Harborwalk along the docks, with galleries, boutiques, and restaurants along a 3½- block stretch of Front Street, invite idle strolling, and the shady, quiet streets of the residential portion of the historic district are within a few blocks.

■ SEA ISLAND COTTON

After the American Revolution, the cultivation of rice became almost exclusively the domain of the Georgetown region, because a new crop took over the plantations south of Charleston on the Sea Islands. By 1800, Sea Island cotton had transformed the coastal economy, creating more antebellum millionaires.

The first seeds for the prized cotton—whose silky fibers grow up to 2 inches in length, twice that of cotton grown inland—were imported from Bermuda, the Bahamas, and other British colonies in the Caribbean. It was a perfect cash crop for the Sea Islands, needing only relatively small fields to produce enormous profit and only the nutrients of marsh mud for fertilizer.

Two of the Sea Islands south of Charleston, Edisto and St. Helena, just east of Beaufort, became rich and famous in their plantation heyday. Today, both islands

Brookgreen Gardens includes 800 pieces of sculpture collected by Archer and Anna Huntington.

The Grove Plantation house in the Sea Islands is privately owned but open to the public.

provide not only a window upon what happened then but also examples of how it all turned out, nearly two centuries later, for the descendants of the two races that created the Sea Island cotton plantations.

On Edisto, among the many plantation mansions now on the National Register of Historic Places is the William Seabrook House (private), built in 1810 by the first Sea Island cotton planter to make a fortune on the crop, and the first to use marsh mud as fertilizer. Seabrook's son, William, won a medal for his cotton at the 1851 World's Fair in London (where McCormick won a medal for his reaper, Colt for his revolving pistol, and Goodyear for his India rubber).

The cotton, the climate, and slavery on Edisto Island produced an isolated 1808 society of 236 free whites and 2,600 African slaves. This was the norm on the Sea Islands. On the eve of the Civil War, in 1860, the dependency upon slavery and fervor to secede from the Union were so intense on Edisto Island that its planters began calling it "the royal principality of Edisto." One of them, Col. Joseph E. Jenkins, told a secessionist meeting, "Gentlemen, if South Carolina does not secede from the Union, Edisto Island will." The colonel had no idea that, in its mind, South Carolina already had.

Cotton pickers return from the fields on a Mt. Pleasant plantation carrying the day's harvest on their heads, ca. 1875.

By 1860, there were nearly 10,000 slaves on Edisto's plantations. Today's African-American community on the island numbers about 1,600, and the white population about 900. Most of them are descendants of the masters and slaves who owned and worked the same colonial and antebellum plantation lands they all live on today, family descendants still attending the same historic churches their ancestors founded, some living in the mansions their ancestors built.

The Emancipation Proclamation brought an end to any pretensions of being a "royal principality" at Edisto. Sea Island cotton continued to be cultivated on Edisto and other nearby islands until a 1921 infestation of the boll weevil finally wiped out the last of the crop. The old Sea Island cotton fields now produce large crops of vegetables and melons, fresh produce sold daily at roadside stands usually set in the shade of the twisted, gnarled limbs of a live-oak canopy.

The physical remnants of the Sea Island cotton plantations are neither as numerous nor as accessible to visitors today as the plantations of the Georgetown rice rivers or the Ashley River barons. Various church and civic groups organize guided or self-guided tours of the privately owned Sea Islands cotton and Lowcountry rice plantations on occasional weekends throughout the year, especially during the fall and spring. A check with the local chambers of commerce in Edisto and Beaufort (843-869-3867 and 843-986-5400, respectively) will yield the most recent information on these changing dates and tours.

■ SLAVE UPRISINGS

White South Carolinians lived in constant fear of a slave uprising, of violent reprisals for the abuses endured by the Africans. Whippings for the most trifling provocation were routine, often ending in death. Even white children had personal slaves on the wealthy plantations, and those slaves often were tyrannized and abused for sport. The penalty for escape was 40 lashes for the first offense. Branding, mutilation, or public execution could be applied to repeat offenders.

On the morning of September 9, 1739, at the Stono River bridge, 20 miles south of Charleston, the bloodiest slave revolt in the history of colonial America erupted. About 50 slaves attacked a store and nearby plantation homes, murdering more than a dozen whites and burning their houses. The band of slaves then set out on foot through the Lowcountry in hopes of reaching Spanish Florida, where runaways were given freedom by Spanish forces hoping to weaken the Carolina plantation economy.

A force of armed and mounted planters caught the slaves near Jacksonboro at the Edisto River on what today is U.S. 17. Fourteen slaves were shot on the spot, while others fled into the woods. Within weeks, the militia had arrested and killed more than 40 more runaway slaves accused of taking part in the rebellion.

Some former slaves continued to serve their masters after the Civil War as illustrated in this photo from a Carolinian family album of the 1870s

One year later, up the Cooper River at Goose Creek, a similar slave revolt was betrayed by other slaves before it began. Scores of slaves were tried in the plot. Some were hanged, some had ears sliced off, others were branded or whipped.

■ PLANTATIONS TODAY

The end of slavery and the ravages of the Civil War itself devastated South Carolina's rice and Sea Island cotton plantations. A bumper crop was harvested in 1920, but by 1921 the boll weevil infestation finally finished off the maritime cotton kingdom. A series of hurricanes around 1900, especially a 1911 storm, finally brought an end to commercial rice production near Georgetown, where gaping holes were ripped in the dikes, and the rice fields were soaked in saltwater.

Bernard Baruch's purchase of Hobcaw (the vast land parcel on Waccamaw Neck) set off a real estate boom on the old rice plantations. A new aristocracy—mainly wealthy northerners—bought the old fields and mansions for use as hunting preserves and winter retreats. By the 1940s, more than half the 38 major rice

plantations of Georgetown County and another 159 Lowcountry rice or cotton plantations were in the hands of out-of-staters and used exclusively as hunting retreats. Birds and deer now flock to the old fields to feed and nest.

Carolina Gold, the strain of rice that made millionaires along the plantation rice rivers from Waccamaw Neck to the Savannah River, is being revived on islands throughout the Lowcountry. It is grown at Plumfield Plantation on the Pee Dee River, on Prospect Hill near Edisto Island, and in a demonstration field at Middleton Place plantation.

In recent years, thousands of acres of old plantations have been developed for residential use and retirement communities. Some of the old plantations are used for deer- and bird-hunting clubs and movie sets, and others are owned by major timber and pulpwood corporations who harvest the pines. Through the spring and summer months, from Georgetown to the Savannah River and inland for 30 miles, you can smell the thick, sweet scent of pine sap and freshly cut trees. Forestry is the largest segment of South Carolina's agriculture, and most of the pines are used not for lumber but for pulp and paper products.

Not all of the old plantations have become the domain of the chainsaw and double-aught buckshot. One of the unique and most innovative conservation programs in the nation was begun by wealthy, out-of-state owners of historic rice and cotton plantations along three Lowcounty rivers between Charleston and Beaufort.

In 1966, Gaylord Donnelley, retired chairman of a Chicago printing company, bought the 10,000-acre Ashepoo Plantation (private) at the mouth of the Ashepoo River along St. Helena Sound near Beaufort. He and his family used the private land for their own recreation, allowing only friends and business associates to hunt there. Donnelley and other wealthy owners of the long-dormant plantations, some from out of state but some of them descendants of the original plantation families, opposed development and sought a way to protect their lands for future generations.

In 1988, Donnelley and other private owners (including mogul Ted Turner) formed the ACE Basin Task Force, a coalition including the Nature Conservancy, Ducks' Unlimited, the South Carolina Department of Natural Resources, and the U.S. Fish and Wildlife Service. The private plantation owners are making conservation easements a permanent part of their deed restrictions, as well as donating land for use as research reserves and future scientific and educational centers.

Summer Day Under Spanish Moss *by William de Leftwich Dodge captures the feeling of a past era of gracious living in the rural South.*

Boone Hill, six miles northeast of Charleston. The plantation harvests pecans and raises cattle.

The basin is bordered on the north by the Edisto River; on the south by the Combahee River; on the west (inland) by an irregular pattern of watersheds, uplands, and highways; and on the east by St. Helena Sound, where all three rivers converge. Its 350,000 acres, which include 91,000 acres of marsh and 55,000 acres of forested wetlands, make it one of the largest, most pristine estuarine ecosystems in North America. It's home to 17 endangered or threatened species, including the wood stork and loggerhead sea turtle and protects the largest nesting population of bald eagles in the state. About 25 private plantations along the Ashepoo, Combahee, and Edisto rivers account for the bulk of the land in the area and form the core of the conservation project. A similar program of protective easements recently began on private plantations along the old rice rivers near Georgetown.

C H A R L E S T O N

Natives of Charleston prefer to believe that the Ashley River and the Cooper River come together in their harbor to form the Atlantic Ocean. And it's hard not to be seduced into this way of thinking, as Charleston often seems like the lively meeting point between watery wilderness and elegantly outfitted human indulgence. Perhaps this is why so many travel magazines rank Charleston at the top of our nation's destinations, right next to New York City and San Francisco.

The "Port City" is the jewel of South Carolina. When Edgar Allan Poe (a one-time resident of nearby Sullivan's Island), in his poem "Annabel Lee," wrote of a "kingdom by the sea," Charleston was the place he described. From a distance, the peninsular city between the Ashley and Cooper rivers resembles an antebellum watercolor, but for the soaring new suspension bridge that was completed in 2005. Away from the bridge, the city's low profile is pierced by the spires and steeples of 181 churches, a phenomenon of urban architecture that has also earned its nickname the "Holy City."

Tradd Street cuts across the tip of historic Charleston.

After 350 years of epidemics, wars, pirates, fires, earthquakes, hurricanes, and hubris, Charleston remains one of the nation's best-preserved cities. South of Broad Street (a.k.a. "S.O.B."), along South Battery and East Battery, elegant and airy old homes influenced by the style of 18th-century West Indies planters face the harbor. Many who lived here stood at their windows and watched the Civil War begin.

The Charleston vernacular architecture includes stucco town houses that date to 1670 as well as antebellum wood-sided beauties with double porches (which the locals call piazzas). There are cobblestone lanes, wrought-iron gates leading to hidden gardens, and ancient gravestones in pockets of land behind small retail shops. The unparalleled surviving collection of architecture is a result of Charleston's singular history of antebellum wealth and postbellum poverty. The city simply was too poor to tear down its old homes and public buildings and replace them with later styles.

There are many levels to Charleston. There is the glittering natural harbor, one of the finest on the East Coast and protected from the sea by sun-baked sandy barrier islands. There is the splendid, epic old seaport, now restored and accessible as never before, with guided tours and waterfront parks and rows of stately palmetto trees. Then there is the Charleston known only by those who are born here, whose ancestors created this splendor whether they were aristocrats or not. And there is the tale of how this "kingdom by the sea" came to be, and how it endures, from the Battery mansions to the parade ground of the Citadel military college, from the old markets to the container shipping docks.

For most of its long history, Charleston was South Carolina's only city. In terms of character and history, in many ways it is still the only city.

■ COLONIAL PORT

Nine years after the first English settlers landed a few miles up the Ashley River at Albemarle Point in 1670, the Lords Proprietors, ruling the Carolina colony from London, decided that location wasn't adequately defendable. They preferred the tip of the peninsula, then called Oyster Point, now known as the Battery and White Point Gardens. In 1680, the little Ashley River settlement packed up and sailed back to the harbor.

The new location, Charles Town, was an immediate success. Deerskins and furs were the settlement's early exports, soon followed by naval supplies such as tar,

The Adventurer *idles at Charles Town Landing.*

City of Charleston, South Carolina, Looking Across Cooper River, *1838, by William James Bennett. Seaborne trade caused the city to grow into the fourth largest in America during the 18th century.*

turpentine, and timber, all harvested from the vast coastal pine forests. These were shipped to England for the Royal Navy and merchant fleets. The harbor became thick with sailing ships. The town's dirt streets teemed with sailors, Royal Marines, prostitutes, river planters and farmers, merchants, fur traders, African slaves, indentured white servants, and an occasional Indian chief in ceremonial dress.

The first planters, Barbadians who settled up the Cooper River at Goose Creek, then up the Ashley River, soon were joined by new planters and religious refugees from Europe. Protestant French Huguenots, Quakers, Presbyterians, and Baptists from England, Scotland, and Ireland established plantations along the coastal rivers north and south of Charles Town, and the port became much like a Greek city-state, the plantations its surrounding province.

It also became a pirate's prize.

Charles Town lay between two major pirate haunts—the West Indies and the hiding places of the inlets along North Carolina's coast. At first, Charles Town merchants welcomed freebooters, privateers, and pirates for their free spending. Then, in June of 1718, the notorious Edward "Blackbeard" Teach, with four ships and 400

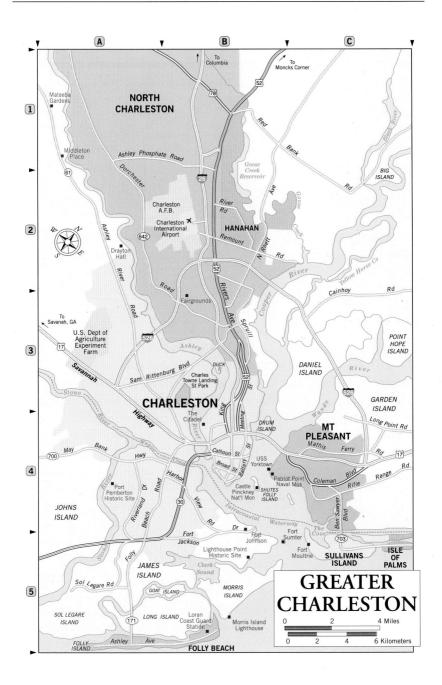

GREATER CHARLESTON

men, plundered the merchant vessels anchored in Charles Town Harbor. Teach seized passengers, held them for a ransom of medical supplies, and departed when paid.

Two months later, in late August, Stede Bonnet, "the gentleman pirate" from Barbados, seized and plundered merchant ships off the entrance to the harbor. This time, enraged merchants led by Col. William Rhett, one of the Goose Creek Barbadian planters, struck back. With two sloops and 130 men, Rhett's force captured Bonnet up the Cape Fear River near what is now Wilmington, North Carolina. Though he begged for his life, Bonnet and dozens of other pirates were hanged in Charles Town during the winter of 1718. The harbor was no longer threatened by pirate attacks, and merchant ships could safely come and go.

By the end of the 1730s, with a population of more than 6,000, Charles Town was the fourth-largest town in North America, after Boston, New York, and Philadelphia.

■ REVOLUTIONARY WAR

The first British attempt to capture Charles Town began in May 1776. A sea and land force attacked Sullivan's Island while the patriot rebels scurried to complete Fort Moultrie on the north side of the harbor entrance. While British troops advanced ashore, British ships opened fire, but the new fort had been built with a material virtually impervious to cannon shot—palmetto logs. The spongy, freshly cut logs absorbed most of the shots without damage, and the patriots returned fire from behind Fort Moultrie's walls. This proved too fierce for both the British naval and land forces, and they withdrew, sailing north to battle Gen. George Washington's army in the North. The palmetto tree became the state symbol, incorporated on the midnight blue background of the state flag.

The British were unable to defeat Washington in the northern colonies, so in the spring of 1779, they launched a southern strategy to rally the considerable number of British loyalists in the South. In May, they plundered by land through the Ashley River rice plantations and reached the outskirts of Charles Town. By early 1780, the entire rebel army of South Carolina, about 3,000 men, was walled inside the town without an escape route.

Led by Lord Charles Cornwallis, a massive British force bore down on Charles Town from land and sea. After more than 30 days of resistance, Fort Moultrie on Sullivan's Island finally fell, on May 7, 1780. Five days later, the British captured Charles Town, the colonies' last open seaport.

A view of the British siege of Charles Town in the spring of 1780. The American force of 3,000 men under Gen. Benjamin Lincoln surrendered in May 1780.

Loyalists to the English crown streamed into Charles Town. Cornwallis and his armies marched inland, to Camden, then on to the surprising British losses at Kings Mountain and Cowpens. A ruthless guerrilla war raged inland from Charles Town in the swamps of the Lowcountry rivers as far as the hills of the Piedmont. During the spring of 1782, British outposts fell one by one to the southern patriot forces, led by Gen. Nathanael Greene. Finally, Greene's army came within 15 miles of Charles Town and threatened to trap the British inside the town.

After Cornwallis's defeat at Yorktown, Virginia, the year before, Charles Town was the only major British outpost left. In the summer of 1782, the British commander at Charles Town fled, and negotiations began for the surrender of the port. On October 27, 1782, a convoy of 40 ships departed Charles Town carrying away most of the British army, as well as more than 3,700 civilians loyal to the crown and their 5,000 slaves. Many of these white and black civilians ended up settling on the islands of the northern Bahamas, where their descendants still live. The remaining British troops formally surrendered and evacuated Charles Town on December 14, 1782, and Greene's army took possession of the seaport after 2½ years of British occupation and rule.

In August 1783, the new South Carolina legislature, convening in the port city, changed the name from Charles Town to Charleston.

■ SLAVE TRADE

Many African-American historians today characterize slavery as the African holocaust. Hundreds of thousands of persons were taken from Africa to what is now the southern United States, from the late 17th century until the early 19th century. By the time of the Civil War, the slave population in the United States was 4 million. And these were only the ones who had survived the Atlantic crossing from Africa. Thousands died during the voyage, and those who survived entered a life of unremitting toil. Of those who came to North America, roughly 40 percent first entered through Charleston. They were quarantined on Sullivan's Island, and most were then sold in the slave markets of Charleston.

Enormous personal fortunes were made by the slave traders of the port city. During the 1730s, for example, nearly 20,000 slaves, most of them from Angola, were imported through the city, almost a third of them by Joseph Wragg & Co., the biggest slave trader in town.

Merchant vessels calling at Charleston included a fleet of 140 British-owned trading ships. More than 800 vessels a year were using the port shortly before the Revolutionary War, and Charleston's annual import-export tonnage exceeded that of New York, even though the southern city had only half the population.

Ships entering the port from England brought consumer items and wines, while ships entering from the West Indies brought sugar and rum. Ships leaving Charleston carried tar, pitch, turpentine, leather, deerskins, corn, peas, beef, pork, and rice.

By far, rice was the most profitable export, and, by far, the labor that grew the rice—slaves—was the most profitable import.

During the early 1770s, the slave trade through Charleston boomed. More than 65 vessels with more than 10,000 Africans came through the port in one year alone. It was the core of the shipping trade and the economic foundation upon which Charleston grew. The traffic in humans officially ended in January 1808, when Congress outlawed the importation of slaves, but another 250,000 African

A slave auction in the streets of Charleston is depicted in this issue of The Illustrated London News *in 1856.*

slaves were smuggled into the nation, many via Charleston, from 1808 until the Civil War. And, of course, the ones who were already here remained slaves for 60 more years.

Visitors to Charleston, and many residents, mistakenly believe that City Market, a two-block-long structure on Market between Meeting and East Bay streets, was the city's slave mart (slaves were never sold there). In fact, there was no single slave mart but instead a number of vacant buildings or lots, sometimes simply in the street, where slavers conducted business. Advertisements announcing auctions were placed in the Charleston newspapers, and most of the auctions were held in various locales along Chalmers and State streets near the Exchange (East Bay at Broad), where South Carolina's delegates to the First Continental Congress were elected in 1774.

Despite the fact that the ancestors of so many of today's American citizens reached this nation through Sullivan's Island and the slave marts of Charleston, there is no museum, not even a historical marker, memorializing—or admitting—the enormous tragedy. However, the history of slavery and artifacts of black life in

Charleston can be found in the exhibits and archives of the Avery Research Center for African-American History and Culture, operated by the College of Charleston (843-727-2009) at 125 Bull Street.

A rare and extraordinary collection of "hire badges" at the Charleston Museum reveals a strange aspect of "the peculiar institution" of slavery. These thin pieces of copper listing the slave's occupation, badge number, and year of issue were worn (beginning in 1751) by artisan slaves hired out by their owners to work for others.

Very few members of Charleston's powerful aristocracy opposed—or dared to voice opposition to—the slavery of antebellum and colonial times or the racial segregation of the 20th century. Some Charlestonians did oppose slavery, however, and their breach of custom struck the elite as both philosophically and socially aberrant.

Sara Grimke, eldest daughter of an eminent Charleston jurist, left town in 1821 to join the abolitionist movement in Philadelphia. Her sister, Angelina, soon joined her. The two women, also advocates of women's suffrage, opposed slavery on humanitarian grounds.

Other Charleston women of the slave-owning class quietly opposed it for the opportunity it offered their husbands for extramarital sex. An excerpt from the writings of Mary Boykin Chesnut of plantation and Charleston elite circles:

> Like the patriarchs of old, our men live all in one house with their wives and their concubines; and the mulattos one sees in every family partly resemble the white children. Any lady is ready to tell you who the father is of all the mulatto children in everybody's household but her own.

Unlike other southern states, South Carolina did not prohibit interracial marriage until after the Civil War. In Charleston, mulatto women and well-regarded white men occasionally married during antebellum years. The city had a free black population of more than 3,000 (rivaled in numbers only by New Orleans), and within that group was an elite of about 500 free mulattos.

By 1820, about 58 percent of the city's population was black. White residents were anxious about the large numbers of slaves living in town and the many other slaves who came to Charleston on Sundays on their days off (and sometimes to run away and disappear among the large number of blacks in the community).

Romanticists and apologists for the Old South who portray the slaves as happy and singing should ponder the story of Denmark Vesey.

Denmark, owned by Capt. Joseph Vesey, could read, write, and speak several languages. Vesey used him on a ship shuttling between Charleston, St. Thomas, and Santo Domingo in the West Indies. Denmark bought a ticket in the popular Charleston East Bay Lottery, won $1,500, and promptly bought his freedom for $600.

Taking the name Vesey, he became a skilled and prosperous carpenter. His property in Charleston included a home at 20 Bull Street. Vesey helped found the African Methodist Episcopal (AME) Church, where he became well known among town and plantation slaves and was respected for his powerful personality, quick mind, and sophistication.

In June of 1822, rumors swept through the white community of a slave rebellion planned for the night of June 16. That night, 2,500 armed whites patrolled the city, and in the days following, 10 blacks were arrested as leaders of the alleged plot, including Vesey. On July 2, Vesey and five other blacks were hanged.

Terrified slaves began turning in others, and before long, 35 blacks were hanged. The AME church, at Reed and Hanover streets, was suspected to be a gathering place for rebel slaves and was demolished. While the plot was never actually proven to exist, Vesey is considered a hero by many, and a new AME church was constructed at 110 Calhoun in 1865.

In December 1822, the legislature passed a law requiring all free black males older than 15 to have a white guardian or risk being seized and sold into slavery. In Charleston, the repression went further. A "workhouse" on the southwest corner of Magazine and Mazyck streets was created for the purpose of giving slaves perceived as "uppity" "a little sugar" on a tortuous treadmill. The arms of men or women were fastened to an overhead rail and a treadmill put in motion beneath their feet. Those unable to keep pace suffered a constant beating of legs and knees against the treadmill steps while "drivers" also flogged them with a cat-o'-nine-tails whip.

The abolition of slavery would take decades longer, but it was foreshadowed in 1833 when the English Parliament outlawed slavery in the British West Indies and, in Philadelphia that same year, the American Anti-Slavery Society was founded.

A superb van tour focusing on the African-American history of Charleston is offered by Gullah Tours, which departs twice a day from Gallery Chuma on John Street (843-722-7568).

■ CIVIL WAR

Secessionist fever inflamed Charleston and the rest of the state for more than two years before the first shots of the Civil War were fired. One of the few Unionists left in Lowcountry aristocratic circles, James Petigru, advised a secessionist meeting in Charleston that "South Carolina is too small to be a republic and too large to be an insane asylum."

Frederick Law Olmsted, visiting Charleston in 1859, wrote, "the cannon in position on the parade ground, The Citadel . . . with its martial ceremonies, the frequent parades of militia . . . the numerous armed police, might lead one to imagine that the town was in a state of siege or revolution."

The most strategic fort in Charleston, Fort Sumter, was a small island in the center of the entrance to Charleston Harbor from the Atlantic Ocean. At 4 AM, April 12, 1861, cadets from the Citadel military academy fired a cannon at the Union soldiers at the fort. By 5 AM, 43 batteries and mortars were bombarding Fort Sumter from Fort Moultrie on Sullivan's Island as well as from Fort Johnson on James Island, on the southern side of the harbor entrance. Fort Sumter's Maj. Robert Anderson, a Southerner who was also a Union army commander, refused to surrender.

Charlestonians rushed to the Battery, to wharves and rooftops, for a view of the pyrotechnics. By nightfall, 2,500 rounds of shot and shell had been fired onto the fort. Major Anderson's cannon, meant only to engage ships in the harbor entrance, lacked the range to inflict damage on the rebel cannon. On the afternoon of April 13, after 34 hours of almost continuous bombardment, and with his isolated outpost ablaze, Anderson surrendered.

By mid-July, 11 warships of the Union's Atlantic Blockading Squadron were cruising off the South Carolina coastline in an effort to disrupt all trade with the South's richest city. On November 7, 1861, a Federal fleet swept into Port Royal Sound, launched an amphibious assault, and captured Hilton Head, Port Royal, Beaufort, and the nearby Sea Islands. The occupation shocked Charleston, and it tightened the shipping blockade.

At first, blockade-running ships regularly slipped through the Union fleet and into Charleston Harbor. They turned around and carried goods to Bermuda, Nassau, and all the way to Liverpool. They exported cotton bales and brought back military and medical supplies, dry goods, groceries, and occasional luxury items. Estimates are that about 80 percent of all blockade runners based in

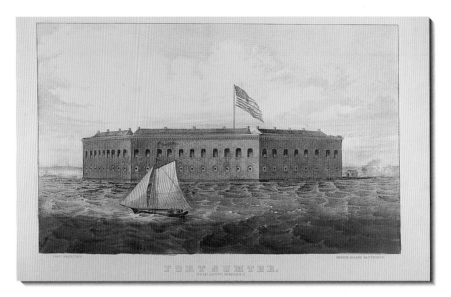

Fort Sumter flying the Union Jack in a pre-war illustration.

Charleston eluded capture. Their captains, crew, and investors reaped huge profits, but the overall tonnage was a small portion of the port trade before the war.

By early 1863, more than 10,000 rebel troops were encamped in and around Charleston, which by then had changed dramatically. Streets were almost deserted, and stores closed as the Union's naval blockade drove up prices, making ordinary goods such as shoes unobtainable in stores.

The Union made three attempts to capture Charleston.

The first came on June 15, 1862, on James Island. More than 6,000 troops landed on the island and began an assault across a narrow peninsula against a fortified Confederate breastwork where cannon awaited them. After three charges and 2½ hours of fierce hand-to-hand fighting, the Union withdrew.

The second attempt came April 7, 1863, when nine Union ironclads steamed into the harbor mouth and shelled Fort Sumter. After heavy damage inflicted by Confederate cannon from the fort and shore batteries, they withdrew.

The third assault came in July 1863, by a combined land and sea force. It, too, failed but is notable as the first time black soldiers—commanded by white officers—fought in the Civil War. The 54th Massachusetts Volunteer Infantry Regiment assaulted Battery Wagner on Morris Island. The black Union soldiers were almost entirely eviscerated, but the Confederates eventually abandoned the outpost. The story of this battle was recounted in the 1989 movie *Glory.* Morris Island is no longer occupied, but you can see its "new" 1876 lighthouse from Folly Beach.

After those three failures, the Union decided to simply lay siege to Charleston and its port. Bombardment began August 27, 1863, and continued until the city was abandoned by Confederate troops several months later. During one nine-day period in January 1864, about 1,500 Union shells were fired onto Charleston, but because the city south of Broad Street was nearly deserted, there were few casualties.

A curiosity of the war in Charleston occurred later in 1864, when the Confederate submarine *Hunley* sank the Union sloop *Housatonic* in the harbor. It was the first submarine in history to sink an enemy vessel, and in so doing, the *Hunley* itself went down with all hands. In 1995, the 40-foot *Hunley* was found by author-adventurer Clive Cussler, and in the summer of 2001 it was hoisted up onto a barge and carried to a holding tank in North Charleston. You can visit the submarine on the grounds of the old navy base on the Cooper River. The remains of the sailors were buried at historic Magnolia Cemetery in a colorful tribute in April 2004.

Union general William Tecumseh Sherman, with 60,000 battle-toughened soldiers, marched through Georgia and took Savannah on December 22, 1864. Expecting Charleston would be next, about 16,000 rebel troops were deployed around the city. In January 1865, Sherman crossed the Savannah River into South Carolina. He kept his enemy guessing as to his intentions but told his aides to march north to Columbia. Charleston, Sherman said, was "a mere desolated wreck hardly worth the time it would take to starve it out."

Outflanked by Sherman's march north, the Confederate army abandoned Charleston on February 17 and 18, 1865. The rebels marched up the peninsula, then north toward the state border. On the morning of February 18, 1865, Union troops landed at the foot of Broad Street near East Bay Street, established headquarters in the Citadel, declared martial law, and ordered the Stars and Stripes hoisted over all public buildings and fortifications. Thousands of newly freed slaves deserted plantations all around Charleston and poured into the city to celebrate, to search for family members, and to enlist in the Union army.

For two centuries, Charleston had been the most prominent, and certainly the most politically important, city in the South. Her aristocracy controlled South Carolina's politics, and South Carolina led southern politics. After the war, however, the "kingdom by the sea" lost forever both its fabled wealth and its influence.

Rhett Butler

Everyone knew now that the fate of the Confederacy rested as much upon the skill of the blockade boats in eluding the Yankee fleet as it did upon the soldiers at the front.

Rumor had it that Captain Butler was one of the best pilots in the South and that he was reckless and utterly without nerves. Reared in Charleston, he knew every inlet, creek, shoal and rock of the Carolina coast near that port, and he was equally at home in the waters around Wilmington. He had never lost a boat or even been forced to dump a cargo. At the onset of the war, he had emerged from obscurity with enough money to buy a small swift boat and now, when blockaded goods realized two thousand percent on each cargo, he owned four boats. He had good pilots and paid them well, and they slid out of Charleston and Wilmington on dark nights, bearing cotton for Nassau, England and Canada. The cotton mills of England were standing idle and the workers were starving, and any blockader who could outwit the Yankee fleet could command his own price in Liverpool. Rhett's boats were singularly lucky both in taking out cotton for the Confederacy and bringing in the war materials for which the South was desperate. Yes, the ladies felt they could forgive and forget a great many things for such a brave man.

—Margaret Mitchell, *Gone With the Wind*, 1936

■ Charleston Aristocracy

Three of the most revered (at least by their social peers) old Charleston family names are Porcher, Huger, and Petigru. The first two are pronounced "Por-shay" and "*Yew*-gee," making things rhyme in the antebellum doggerel that explains just how important family ancestry is to Charleston's aristocracy:

> "I thank Thee, Lord, on bended knee,
> I'm half Porcher and half Huger,
> For other blessings thank Thee too,
> My grandpa was a Petigru."

For two centuries, from its founding until the 1900s, the same families controlled virtually everything in Charleston, from membership in the St. Cecelia Society to the selection of the next mayor. While its influence beyond a small social circle no longer approaches political or financial supremacy, the old aristocracy remains a

INDELICACIES OF WAR

August 29, 1861

. . . We are Americans as well as the Yankees—& Russell cannot do us justice—he even repeats those hateful & *hideous* falsehoods as to our treatment of wounded & prisoners, when their own officers write such different stories—& one of the head surgeons writes to thank our surgeons. It is really amusing to see the accounts of the way Mrs. Gwin & Phillips & Greenhow are treated—houses guarded. Our women are now in a nice condition—traveling, your false hair is developed & taken off to see if papers are rolled in it—& you are turned up instantly to see if you have pistols concealed—not to speak of their having women to examine if you are a *man*—in disguise. I think *these* times make all women feel their humiliation in the affairs of the world. With *men* it is on to the field—"glory, honour, praise, &c, power." Women can only stay at home—& every paper reminds us that women are to be *violated*—ravished & all manner of humiliation. How are the daughters of Eve punished.

—The diary of Mary Boykin Chesnut, daughter and wife of U.S. senators, 1861

power to be reckoned with in Charleston. The same elite, for example, were responsible for the preservation movement that saved the city's architectural beauty, including the buildings their ancestors constructed.

By the 1730s in colonial Charles Town, the aristocracy had established itself. Prominent mercantile families were marrying into prominent coastal plantation families, and a plutocracy emerged. Merchant and planter families intermarried so thoroughly that they became "one great tangled cousinry."

Almost from the city's beginnings, the aristocracy set out to entertain itself in style. In 1703, Charles Town had what generally is considered to be the first professional theatrical performance in North America. Formation of the South Carolina Jockey Club in 1735 and the club's annual "race week" in February gave definition to a social season that began in November and ended in May. The aristocracy created the colonies' first natural history museum, first public library, first theater, first musical society, and first scientific society. For all that, however, the cultivation of good times, as opposed to the culture of enlightened learning, was the elite's raison d'être.

By the 1770s, more than 23 singing and dancing masters offered lessons in Charles Town. Unlike Boston, Philadelphia, or New York, however, Charles Town had no institution of higher learning. The College of Charleston was founded in 1770 and claims to be the oldest municipal college in the nation. However, in its early decades, the college was actually a high school and often closed. On the eve of the American Revolution, fewer than 20 Charles Town *and* coastal plantation Carolinians held college or university degrees.

Historian Walter J. Fraser Jr., in his history of the city, *Charleston! Charleston!,* explains: "It was a society that placed a premium on good looks, good companionship, bright conversation and a rounded personality. It embraced the sparkling dilettante, avoided the solitary thinker."

It also was a society whose fortunes were based not merely upon slavery but also upon the slave trade.

The three wealthiest men in what came to be called Charleston were Henry Laurens, Gabriel Manigault, and Benjamin Smith, and the fortunes of all three came from the slave trade. Laurens, said to be the richest man in colonial America, was the principal partner in the firm of slave importers owned by Laurens, George Austin, and George Appleby, three family names still prominent in Charleston society.

The Civil War devastated the Charleston aristocracy, both financially and emotionally. Many were forced to take in boarders merely to live. Still, the same families who ruled antebellum Charleston continued to rule the city after the war—Gibbes, Rutledge, Huger, Middleton, Pinckney, Ravenel, and Rhett among them. Unlike the emerging "New South" cities such as Atlanta, Nashville, and Charlotte, where in the absence of an old aristocracy there was room for a vibrant civic leadership to emerge, in Charleston nothing changed.

"Conviviality over diligence, dilettantism over specialization, and leisure over work," as Fraser put it, continued to be the Charleston style.

The usual business day barely had time for business, what with the long mid-morning coffee break; the extended dinner (known elsewhere as lunch) from two to four o'clock in the afternoon, with several courses, wine and liquor; then a return to the office for no more than an hour or two.

Charleston's old plutocracy purposely prevented railroads from entering the city limits, and restricted the building of steam-powered mills and factories to outside the town, in part to keep out free white laborers seen by the elite as "antagonistic to our institutions."

Henry Laurens was a prominent Charleston aristocrat and Huguenot of the 18th century. Originally a merchant and planter, Laurens served in the state assembly, and was president of the Continental Congress from 1777 to 1779. He was captured by the British during the Revolutionary War while on a diplomatic mission and imprisoned in the Tower of London, then traded for Lord Cornwallis. Upon his release, Laurens was billed for his meals.

One of the most scandalous episodes "South of Broad," which heralded the aristocracy's forced entry into the modern era, began in 1947. One of their own, J. Waites Waring, federal district court judge and member of a prominent, old Charleston family, outlawed the exclusion of blacks from the state Democratic Party primary elections.

Soon after Judge Waring's decision, both his family and the aristocracy began to ostracize him. To this day, some claim the shunning was due to Waring's divorce from a member of another elite family and his rapid marriage to a northern divorcée.

Waring ended segregated seating in his courtroom and ordered all court personnel, including attorneys, to address blacks as "Mister, Missus, and Miss."

His second wife, Elizabeth, invited black civil rights activists to the Waring home on fashionable Meeting Street, south of Broad. On February 11, 1950, Mrs. Waring appeared on NBC television's "Meet the Press" and spoke in favor of a complete end to racial segregation in the South, as well as of racial intermarriage. About the same time, Judge Waring said in a speech to a New York City church group, "We don't have a Negro problem in the South; we have a white problem."

Early in March 1950, a cross was burned in front of the Waring home. The judge resigned his membership in the St. Cecilia Society, his captaincy in the elite Charleston Light Dragoons, and his affiliation with the local Episcopal church. On January 29, 1952, Waring announced his retirement from the federal bench, and he and Elizabeth immediately moved to New York.

Waring's written opinions in a public-school desegregation case from Clarendon County in 1950 eventually became much of the legal reasoning for the Supreme Court's 1954 decision that racially separate educational facilities are inherently unequal, and thus, unconstitutional. After the high court's decision, more than 500 members of the local, state, and national NAACP gave a testimonial dinner for the Warings at a black church in Charleston.

It was the couple's only return visit to Charleston. They returned to New York immediately after the banquet and never came back. However, on January 17, 1968, J. Waites Waring was buried in Charleston's Magnolia Cemetery.

A further crumbling of the elite's traditions—albeit one unlikely to result in social ostracism—came on July 22, 1994, when the 152-year-old, men-only admissions policy at the Citadel military college was ruled unconstitutional by U.S. District Court judge C. Weston Houck. The college, with Virginia Military Institute the last two state-supported military colleges in the nation, had been a creation of Charleston's aristocracy. From its founding in 1842, the Citadel has reflected the Charleston aristocracy's love for military trappings and ceremony. The state school now has scores of female cadets, and on Friday afternoons from September through May, the cadet corps marches on its parade grounds and the public is invited to observe.

■ MODERN SEAPORT

Until the 1820s, the single most important and dominant seaport in the nation was Charleston. Then, the advent of steam-powered vessels meant merchant ships from England and Europe no longer had to follow the trade-winds route via Bermuda, the Bahamas, or the West Indies. With steam, the merchant ships took the direct route to Baltimore, Philadelphia, and New York.

About the same time, fertile, new lands for growing cotton were opened to migrating farmers in Alabama, Mississippi, Louisiana, Arkansas, and Texas. Mobile and New Orleans emerged as major cotton ports, surpassing Charleston.

After nearly a century of decline, the navy created its base up the Cooper River in 1912, and it grew to be one of the largest in the nation through World Wars I and II and the Korean War. It also became a Polaris and ballistic missile submarine base. The military complex includes a large army "point of embarkation" for troops, supplies, and equipment. During the 1970s, as many as 90 ships with nearly 20,000 officers and men called Charleston their home port, and 11,000 civilians were directly employed at the naval base.

It was at this time that the port of Charleston began to return to national status. Today, it is one of the nation's busiest seaports for container cargo, fourth in the nation and second only to New York on the East Coast. The State Port Authority's huge cargo terminal on the Wando River, a tributary of the Cooper River just northeast of the city, is among the largest in the nation.

Although merchant shipping is thriving, the future of the naval station remains unclear. In 1993, Charleston's economy and tradition were rocked when the navy announced it would close the huge Charleston Naval Station and Charleston Naval Shipyard in early 1996, which resulted in a loss of about 30,000 jobs. City planners in North Charleston are still finding new uses for the old navy base, such as light industry and residential neighborhoods. Some navy units remain, such as the naval hospital and a communications unit. The army has a fleet of 15 freighters based at the old navy base, the ships loaded with ammunition and supplies at all times and ready to sail immediately to wherever army troops are deployed.

Cotton piled on a Charleston wharf in 1870 awaiting shipment.

■ ARCHITECTURE

The historic streets of Charleston, where nearly every structure—church, home, courthouse, or office—has a plaque facing the sidewalk, seem at first to be not a living part of the city but a guidebook neighborhood. They are both.

Marriages, funerals, and worship services routinely go on in St. Philip's Episcopal church. Families, some old Charleston aristocracy, many others well-to-do newcomers, bathe, dine, raise children, and entertain inside the old homes on Tradd and Legare streets. Mundane records still are filed at the new county courthouse at Broad and Meeting streets, and shipping agents consign cargo to ports around the world from offices on East Bay Street.

CHARLESTON ARCHITECTURE

Popular styles of architecture in the historic district include:

COLONIAL
(1690–1740)
Defining features:
Low foundations
Clapboard sidings
High, pitched roofs

*John Lining house at
106 Broad at King*

GEORGIAN
(1700–1790)
Defining features:
Hipped roofs
Box chimneys
Flattened columns
Raised basements

*Miles Brewton house
at 27 King Street*

FEDERAL
(1790–1820)
(also known as Adam)
Defining features:
Geometric rooms
Iron balconies
Exterior trip, spiral stairs

*Nathaniel Russell House
at 61 Meeting Street*

GREEK REVIVAL
(1820–1875)
Defining features:
Large heavy columns
and capitals
Gabled or hipped roof
Wide band of trim

*Beth Elohim Reform
Temple at 90 Hasell*

French Huguenot Church at 136 Church Street

GOTHIC REVIVAL
(1850–1885)
Defining features:
Pointed arches
Buttressed stone tracery

ITALIANATE
(1830–1900)
Defining features:
Balustrades
Low pitched roofs
Verandas

Colonel John Ashe House at 26 South Battery

VICTORIAN
(1860–1915)
Defining features:
Multi-gabled roofs
Gingerbread trim
Turrets

Sottile house at Green Street on the College of Charleston campus.

CHARLESTON SINGLE HOUSE
(late 1700s)
Defining features:
Single room width.
Set at right angles
to the street.

Colonel Robert Brewton House at 71 Church

There are more than 1,000 residential, commercial, civic, and religious structures within Charleston's sprawling historic district, including 73 from the colonial period, 136 from the late 18th century, and more than 600 built prior to the 1840s. Inside almost all of them the details of daily living continue while hundreds of thousands of visitors stroll by outside.

In addition to Charleston's historical appeal and uniquely bucolic urban charm, the old streets are a living museum for admirers and students of architecture and design. Many of Charleston's colonial houses used yellow pine and cypress from trees felled in the coastal forests during wintertime, when the sap was down. They were cut into 40- to 70-foot lengths at river sawmills and then floated to Charleston. Cured in saltwater and then air-dried, the wood became nearly iron-hard, almost impervious to termites or fungus, enduring today after centuries of exposure.

Ornamental wrought iron is another creative aspect of architecture that can be seen throughout the historic district, nearly all of it created by black artisans, first as slaves, later as freedmen, and today as nationally recognized treasures such as Phillip Simmons. Born in 1912, Simmons began as a blacksmith at the age of 13. Over the years, his work evolved from farm implements to car bodies to ornamental iron. More than 200 of his gates, fences, balconies, and grills adorn homes in the historic district.

Simmons' gates are ornate designs sometimes 10 to 15 feet high, decorated with fauna, fish, snakes, and palmetto trees. In the early 1990s, the Smithsonian Institution named Simmons a National Heritage Fellow and commissioned him to produce a gate for display. He also has been recognized by the Folk Arts Program of the National Endowment for the Arts as a master traditional artist. His work has been reproduced as jewelry, bookmarks, and picture frames, making him as "South Carolina" as sweetgrass baskets and Beaufort stew.

Simmons is the descendant of Charleston's tradition of black artisans whose skills made their owners rich. At one time, nearly 200 black cabinetmakers practiced their craft in Charleston, serving the city and plantation elite. Some of the artisans became wealthy themselves, such as Thomas Elfe, a slave whose cabinetry from the 1760s and 1770s now is eagerly sought by collectors.

That anyone can still live in or see the architectural and design beauty of historic Charleston today is the result of a meeting held on April 21, 1920, in a home at 20 South Battery. The city was about to widen its streets to accommodate automobiles, and that meant the destruction of historic structures throughout the lower peninsula, a prospect that moved 32 of Charleston's aristocratic families to attend that April meeting.

This group called themselves the Charleston Society for the Preservation of Old Dwellings, later renamed the Preservation Society of Charleston.

Still running most of Charleston in those days, the aristocracy pressured the city council in 1929 to pass the nation's first zoning ordinance to protect historic structures. In 1931, the city council set aside 23 square blocks of the lower peninsula—today's principal historic district—as an architectural preserve, limiting owners in what they could do with their property and establishing a Board of Architectural Review.

Charleston's historic preservation laws became models for historic districts across the nation. In 1946, the Historic Charleston Foundation was created and assumed the lead in the city's preservation movement.

That movement, however, is not limited to the wealthy, nor aimed at the gentrification of low-income areas. Historic Charleston is rehabilitating vintage buildings in economically depressed neighborhoods throughout the peninsula and helping low-income Charlestonians finance ownership. The foundation also administers a crafts program that trains young adults in carpentry and masonry restoration. Charleston natives helped found the four-year College of the Building Arts, opened in 2005, for those who want to learn masonry, timber-framing, stone carving, and blacksmithing.

Charleston's municipal government, with the help of the city's architects, continues to build several hundred small-scale public housing facilities. The program refused to use the usual standard design of brick duplexes or high-rise apartments. Instead, it builds single-family units on vacant lots.

■ TOUR OF HISTORIC CHARLESTON   *map page 130*

The 1923 musical *Runnin' Wild* introduced one dance number that swept the nation in the 1920s flapper heyday. It was "the Charleston," a knee-knocking, palm-slapping, leg-kicking forerunner of the jitterbug.

There is absolutely nothing that quick—human or motorized—in today's historic Charleston.

The historic districts of the city's lower peninsula, and for that matter most of the residential and commercial neighborhoods without the "historic" designation,

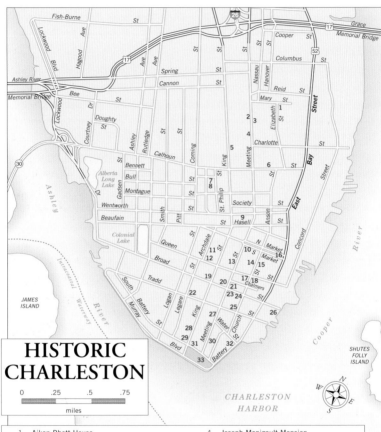

HISTORIC CHARLESTON

0   .25   .5   .75

miles

1	Aiken-Rhett House	4	Joseph Manigault Mansion
6	AME Church	10	Market Hall (Confederate Museum)
10	Kahal Kadosh Beth Elohim Reform Temple	28	Miles Brewton House
30	Calhoun Mansion	27	Nathaniel Russell House
3	Charleston Museum	5	Old Citadel Building
2	Charleston Visitor Center	16	Old City Market
21	City Hall	26	Old Exchange Building & Provost Dungeon
7	College of Charleston	14	Old Powder Magazine
20	County Courthouse	29	Patrick O'Donnell House
17	Dock Street Theater	25	Colonel Robert Brewton House
32	Edmondston-Alston House	8	Sottile House
13	Gibbes Museum of Art	11	St. John's Lutheran Church
24	Heyward-Washington House	23	St. Michael's Episcopal Church
18	French Protestant (Huguenot) Church	15	St. Philip's (Episcopal) Church
31	John Ashe House	22	Stuart House
19	John Lining House	12	Unitarian Church
		33	White Point Gardens

are a theater of detail. The best of Charleston can be noticed best at foot speed and eye level.

Visitors to Charleston eager to orient themselves and understand the old city should stop first at the **Charleston Visitor Center** in the heart of the commercial district, north of the historic district, at 375 Meeting Street. Parking is a problem anywhere, any time, any day, in the historic district; however, it is simple to park at the visitor center lots and then take a trolley south to the historic district.

Inside the center is an overview of the city and surrounding area in the form of a large diorama and multimedia videos, as well as a comprehensive collection of brochures, maps, flyers, and other notices. Free shuttle buses leave the visitors center at 15- to 20-minute intervals to and from the Old City Market on Market at East Bay Street, on the northern edge of the historic district. The center is open 8:30 AM–5 PM daily; 843-724-7174.

Guided tours in air-conditioned buses or horse-drawn carriages are available at the visitors center and other locations in the historic district. (There are so many horse-drawn carriage tours in historic Charleston that the horses wear diapers. If there is an "accident" the carriage driver drops a marker at the spot and special trucks clean the street, then spray it with a perfumed disinfectant.)

Not far from the visitors center in the historic district are several fascinating old buildings worth exploring.

The **Aiken-Rhett House** is at 48 Elizabeth Street; 843-723-1159. When Gov. William Aiken inherited the house from his father in 1833, he added Greek Revival features to the original Federal-style design. Aiken spent three years in Europe collecting furniture and chandeliers for his home. In 1863 Jefferson Davis spent a week as Aiken's house guest, and Confederate general P. G. T. Beauregard used the house as his headquarters during the Civil War. Aiken lost his fortune during the war, and Federal troops ransacked his house.

The **Charleston Museum** at 360 Meeting Street (843-722-2996), founded in 1773, is the oldest museum in the United States, although its current incarnation falls short of the architectural standards set elsewhere in the city. This brown block building includes artifacts, treasures, and exhibits on the history of the Lowcountry, as well as an inventive "Discover Me" room for children.

Across the street is the **Joseph Manigault Mansion** (843-723-2926). This splendid Federal-style home was built in 1803 by a wealthy planter, Joseph Manigault, and designed by Joseph's brother Gabriel Manigault, a lawyer fascinated with architecture. Educated in Europe, Gabriel brought elements of the

Franco-English villa style into his design, seen best in the elegant breezeway and graceful staircase. The original gatehouse stands in the garden and represents a small Roman temple.

Farther down Meeting Street is the **Old Citadel Building** (843-723-6900), built in 1822 at Marion Square to house state arms and troops. It was here that the famous South Carolina Military College—the Citadel—first began. (The new site is at Hampton Park, on Moultrie Street off Ashley Avenue.) A portion of the tabby wall that once marked the town's northern fortifications can still be seen. Today, the Old Citadel is an Embassy Suites hotel; in its lobby are several Citadel artifacts.

At 110 Calhoun Street is the **Emanuel African Methodist Episcopal Church** (843-722-2561), home of the South's oldest AME congregation, which had its beginnings in 1818 at another location. In 1822, authorities demolished the original church, claiming it was the sanctuary where Denmark Vesey planned his slave insurrection of that year. The congregation's new location opened in 1865.

At this point visitors might want to make a tour of the shops on **King Street,** long a center of commerce for the city. The **Patrick O'Donnell House** at 21 King Street (private) was built in the 1850s in the Italianate style. O'Donnell was an Irish immigrant and master builder who undertook the building of this house for his fiancée. Unfortunately, the building took so long that she married someone else.

At 27 King Street, visitors can see the handsome brick **Miles Brewton House** (also private). With its two-tiered piazza, the house is an elegant example of the Charleston double house in the Palladian style. It was completed in 1769 for Brewton, a colonial merchant and leading slave trader who was lost at sea with his family in 1775. The house served as headquarters for Sir Henry Clinton and Lord Charles Cornwallis during the American Revolution as well as Union generals George Meade and Edward Hatch during the Civil War.

Just off King Street, at 90 Hasell Street, is **Kahal Kadosh Beth Elohim Reform Temple** (843-723-1090). The original synagogue, the birthplace of American Reform Judaism, was destroyed by fire and replaced by this structure in 1840. It is considered one of the finest examples of Greek Revival architecture in the country.

East of King, at 8 Archdale Street, is the **Unitarian Church** (843-723-4617). The oldest Unitarian church in the South, it was built between 1772 and 1787. In 1852, Francis D. Lee began extensive remodeling in the Gothic Revival style popular at the time. He added the Gothic arched window, buttresses, and a fan-tracery vaulted ceiling based upon that of Gloucester Cathedral.

The historic district of downtown Charleston includes a row of brightly painted homes, known as Rainbow Row, along East Bay Street.

The Greek Revival **St. John's Lutheran Church,** on the corner of Clifford and Archdale streets (843-723-2426), was built in 1817. Note the fine craftsmanship in the wrought-iron gates and fence, as well as the 1823 Thomas Hall organ case.

Back at the intersection of Meeting and Market streets is **Market Hall** (843-723-1541), a National Historic Landmark built in 1841 and modeled after the Temple of Nike in Athens. The **Confederate Museum** is located here; founded in 1898 by the Daughters of the Confederacy, the museum still displays flags and other Confederate memorabilia.

At 135 Meeting Street is **Gibbes Museum of Art** (843-722-2706), an outstanding collection of American art and portraits relating to southern history. Specialties of the museum include the collection of more than 300 miniature portraits and the miniature rooms, detailed with fabrics and furnishings. The rotunda's Tiffany-style stained-glass window is also worth noting.

Nearby, at 79 Cumberland (one of Charleston's few remaining cobblestone thoroughfares), is the **Old Powder Magazine** (private). Built in 1713, it is the oldest public building in the city and was used during the Revolution to store munitions. It is now a museum operated by the Colonial Dames of America, with costumes, furniture, armor, and other artifacts from 18th-century Charleston.

On Church Street rises the sand-colored spire of **St. Philip's (Episcopal) Church** (843-722-7734), built in 1838. The church lies right in the middle of the street (hence the name Church Street), and the graveyard behind it is the resting place of Revolutionary statesmen such as Edward Rutledge (who signed the Declaration of Independence) and John C. Calhoun.

The starkly white Gothic **French Protestant (Huguenot) Church** (843-722-4385), on the same street, once had services only in French. While this building dates from the mid-1800s, the congregation worshipped on this site beginning in 1687. In 2003, this street was filled with dirt so moviemakers could film a scene with actor Jude Law for the movie *Cold Mountain.*

The **Old Exchange Building & Provost Dungeon** (843-727-2165) at the foot of Broad Street on East Bay stands on the site of the original British fort. This 1751 former customhouse (which stored the tea during Charleston's Revolution-era tax revolt) has been renovated into a colorful history museum.

Most carriage tours begin and end at the 1841 **Old City Market,** now a fresh-air souvenir shopping venue. Visitors can explore the market, then walk south along East Bay Street, past the row of pastel-colored houses (called **Rainbow Row**) near Tradd Street, or along any of the cool, palmetto-shaded streets. There are private gardens and churches hidden about, waiting to be discovered by the curious.

The intersection of Broad and Meeting streets is known as the **Four Corners of Law,** for its elegant, longtime occupants. Each of them represents a different branch of law: the federal courthouse, the county courthouse (which includes the magnificently restored stucco statehouse), city hall, and the wedding-cake 1751 steeple of **St. Michael's Episcopal Church** (843-723-0603). It is said that one might presumably get baptized, married, divorced and buried, all at this intersection. St. Michael's graveyard bears the remains of two signers of the Declaration of Independence: John Rutledge and Charles Cotesworth Pinckney.

Returning to Church Street and continuing south, visitors will enter the neighborhood known as **Cabbage Row.** At 87 Church Street is the **Heyward-Washington House** (843-722-2996), built in 1772 by rice king Daniel Heyward, and the setting (as Catfish Row) for Du Bose Heyward's *Porgy* and, later, *Porgy and Bess.* President George Washington stayed here during his 1791 visit.

St. Michael's Episcopal Church is one of more than 180 churches in Charleston, locally called the Holy City.

CULTURAL TIMELINE

1670 First permanent settlement, Charles Town, established.

1718 After a summer of pirate attacks by the notorious Blackbeard and Stede Bonnet, Gov. Robert Johnson and Col. William Rhett rid the Carolina coast of pirates. Bonnet and others are hanged.

1736 Dock Street Theater opens in Charles Town. Site of what is considered the first play produced in the United States: *The Orphan.*

1744 Teenage plantation mistress Eliza Lucas (later Pinckney) brings a good crop of indigo seed to maturity. Develops an indigo-processing technique.

1762 St. Cecilia Society founded as a musical organization in Charles Town. Functions today as an exclusive social club.

1773 Charleston Museum—the oldest in the United States—is founded.

1780 Henry Laurens, in England as a diplomat representing the rebellious colonies during the Revolutionary War, is charged with high treason and imprisoned in the Tower of London. He is later billed for meals.

1783 Name of Charles Town changed to Charleston.

1812 Theodosia Burr Alston, daughter of Aaron Burr, sails to New York and is never heard from again. Later a pirate confesses she had been forced to walk the plank.

At 51 Meeting Street is the **Nathaniel Russell House** (843-724-8481), headquarters of the Historic Charleston Foundation. Built in 1808, it is one of the nation's finest examples of Federal-style architecture and has a three-story staircase that spirals upwards without touching the walls, seemingly without support. Nathaniel Russell was a native of Rhode Island who arrived in Charleston in 1765 and established a mercantile empire on rice, indigo, cotton, and slaves.

Farther south is the area where somewhat more lavish mansions reflect the wealth of a later era. At 16 Meeting Street is the 35-room **Calhoun Mansion** (private), opulent even by Charleston's standards. For this house built in 1876 by George W. Williams, no expense was spared. His son-in-law, Patrick Calhoun (a grandson of John C. Calhoun), inherited it, but the house passed out of the family in the 1930s and the building was on the verge of being condemned when restoration began in 1970. It is an interesting example of Victorian taste, notable for its

1827 Edgar Allan Poe's artillery unit is assigned to Fort Moultrie on Sullivan's Island. Poe gets ideas for his 1843 short story "The Gold-Bug."

1880 Col. E. B. C. Cash and Col. William S. Shannon fight (with pistols) the last legal duel in the state over an inheritance. Shannon is mortally wounded.

1915 Charleston becomes the place to drink when statewide prohibition is enacted.

1920s Author DuBose Heyward writes *Porgy*, the basis for George Gershwin's operatic work *Porgy and Bess*.

1923 The musical *Runnin' Wild* introduces "the Charleston," which becomes a national craze.

1928 Julia Peterkin wins the Pulitzer Prize for her novel *Scarlet Sister Mary*.

1930 Anna Hyatt Huntington begins her sculpture collection at Brookgreen Gardens.

1950s Teenagers on the Strand start dancing "the Shag."

1990s Numerous films are filmed in South Carolina, including *The Prince of Tides*, *Sleeping with the Enemy*, *Rich in Love*, *Chasers*, *Forrest Gump*, and *Scarlett*.

Hootie and the Blowfish, a pop-rock band from Columbia, sells a million copies of its first CD, *Crack'd Rear View*.

ornate plasterwork, fine wood moldings, and 75-foot domed ceiling. While private, the house is occasionally open for tours; call 843-577-1100 for information.

At 21 East Battery is the **Edmondston-Alston House** (843-722-7171), built by the Scottish merchant Charles Edmondston in 1828. The financial panic of 1837 forced Edmondston to sell the mansion, and the new owner, Charles Aston, immediately set about remodeling it. The result is the handsome Greek Revival mansion with its three-story piazza and commanding view of the harbor. The house has remained in the family since its purchase, but the bottom two floors are open to the public. This house and the Nathaniel Russell House sell weeklong value passes that also provide entry to Middleton Place, Drayton Hall, and the Gibbes Museum.

A tranquil spot for relaxing is the **White Point Gardens,** in Battery Park, facing the harbor and shaded by palmettos and oak trees. Once the site where pirates hung from gallows, it is now the most romantic spot in Charleston for several

George and Ira Gershwin's presentation photo to DuBose Heyward upon completion of Porgy and Bess. *Gershwin wrote a portion of the hit musical while staying at Folly Beach.*

hundred couples a year. The park offers a spectacular view of Charleston Harbor, with Fort Sumter in the distance, and some of the historic district's finest old homes behind the park on Battery Street. Today, visitors from as far off as Oregon and New Jersey, recalling the locale from earlier visits, reserve the gazebo in White Point Gardens a year in advance for their weddings. Strolling visitors to the historic district are likely to become spectators at the nuptials. To reserve the gazebo, contact the City of Charleston Recreation Department at 843-724-7327.

For several weeks every March and April, the Historic Charleston Foundation (843-723-1623) holds a fund-raising festival of house tours. Every October, the Preservation Society of Charleston (843-722-4630) conducts a monthlong tour of houses and gardens, which may also include plantation oyster roasts, symphony galas, and candlelight tours.

Boat tours to Fort Sumter and through the fort leave frequently each day from a pier next door to the contemporary State Aquarium up on Concord Street. Fort Moultrie is also open to the public, but you need to drive to Sullivan's Island to reach it.

BLIND TIGERS

South Carolinians of the non-temperance temperament first made Charleston a place to visit during the 1890s. They came looking for a drink, because no government on earth has ever succeeded in telling Charlestonians how, when, or where they should consume alcoholic beverages. When Gov. "Pitchfork" Ben Tillman tried to dry up the town in 1893, Charleston's saloon keepers, city council, municipal court judges, and citizenry, including the aristocracy, more or less said, "You betcha, Ben," and turned a blind eye to the whole business.

The "blind tigers" thrived. These were the same old taverns, only now the saloon keepers paid protection money to city police and state liquor agents. Any raids made were pro forma, usually coordinated with the saloon.

Most of Charleston, then and now, believes the role of government police forces is to prevent crime, not sin. When federal prohibition came along in 1919, Charleston and its "blind tigers" ignored that too.

So, by the time Charleston's city fathers decided during the 1920s to officially promote tourism in "America's most historic city," there already was a core of regulars visiting the port city to drink, and perhaps to commit other acts, away from home-town eyes.

■ DAY TRIPS FROM CHARLESTON

The preceding chapters on the Sea Islands and coastal plantations include several great destinations near Charleston. It's an easy car trip to Folly Beach, Sullivan's Island, the Francis Marion National Forest, and Brookgreen Gardens. And it's only a 20-minute drive inland up SC 61 to explore the Ashley River plantations.

■ CAPE ROMAIN NATIONAL WILDLIFE REFUGE   *map page 151, A-5*
One of the most pristine stretches of Atlantic coastline is 30 miles northeast of Charleston in the Cape Romain National Wildlife Refuge. Access is tightly controlled to its 60,000 acres of open water and saltwater marsh and 4,000 acres of high land, but day visitors will find the trip worthwhile. Cape Island on the northeast boundary of the refuge is one of the nation's largest nesting grounds for sea turtles, and Marsh Island in Bulls Bay is a rookery for brown pelicans. Fishing, birding, and hiking trails are available on Bull Island. The Seewee tribe harvested oysters and clams here in pre-colonial times, and visitors today can do the same.

DIGGING FOR TREASURE ON SULLIVAN'S ISLAND

I dug eagerly, and now and then caught myself actually looking, with something that very much resembled expectation, for the fancied treasure, the vision of which had demented my unfortunate companion. At a period when such vagaries of thought most fully possessed me, and when we had been at work perhaps an hour and a half, we were again interrupted by the violent howlings of the dog. His uneasiness, in the first instance, had been, evidently, but the result of playfulness or caprice, but he now assumed a bitter and serious tone. Upon Jupiter's again attempting to muzzle him, he made a furious resistance, and, leaping into the hole, tore up the mould frantically with his claws. In a few seconds he had uncovered a mass of human bones, forming two complete skeletons, and intermingled with several buttons of metal, and what appeared to be the dust of decayed woollen. One or two strokes of a spade upturned the blade of a large Spanish knife, and, as we dug farther, three or four loose pieces of gold and silver coin came to light . . . . We now worked in good earnest, and never did I pass ten minutes of more intense excitement. During this interval we had fairly unearthed an oblong chest of wood . . . . It was firmly secured by bands of wrought iron, riveted and forming a kind of open trellis-work over the whole . . . . Luckily, the sole fastenings of the lid consisted of two sliding bolts. These we drew back—trembling and panting with anxiety. In an instant, a treasure of incalculable value lay gleaming before us. As the rays of the lanterns fell within the pit, there flashed upwards a glow and a glare, from a confused heap of gold and of jewels, that absolutely dazzled our eyes.

■ ■ ■

"What are we to make of the skeletons found in the hole?"

This is a question I am no more able to answer than yourself. There seems, however, only one plausible way of accounting for them—and yet it is dreadful to believe in such atrocity as my suggestion would imply. It is clear that Kidd—if Kidd indeed secreted this treasure, which I doubt not—it is clear that he must have had assistance in the labor. But this labor concluded, he may have thought it expedient to remove all participants in his secret. Perhaps a couple of blows with a mattock were sufficient, while his coadjutors were busy in the pit; perhaps it required a dozen—who shall tell?"

—Edgar Allan Poe, "The Gold-Bug," 1843

SWEETGRASS BASKETS

In South Carolina, sweetgrass basketry was first practiced in slave quarters by West African women accustomed to weaving grass baskets at home. In the Carolinas they used sweetgrass—not to be confused with the cord grass, spartina—a long-stemmed plant that once grew plentifully in the Sea Island and mainland marshes from South Carolina into north Florida.

Basketmakers coiled sweetgrass with strips of leaves from the palmetto tree and with pine straw from longleaf pines. (Coiling is a process of sewing or stitching, once done with a bone, now with a metal spoon handle.)

Today sweetgrass baskets are becoming scarce and valuable. Fewer people make them—basketmakers once numbered about 1,200, but now it's closer to 200—and the supply of sweetgrass has diminished due to development. An attempt to renew the supply is under way on James Island in the suburbs of Charleston, financed by the Agricultural Society of South Carolina (founded 1785) as well as the Sea Grant Consortium and the Historic Charleston Foundation.

"Basket ladies" today are almost exclusively African-American women, Gullah descendants who display their skills and sell their wares in roadside stands along U.S. 17 east of Mt. Pleasant. In Charleston, they are found at the Old City Market (Market and East Bay streets) and "the Four Corners of Law" at Broad and Meeting streets. One of the most well known is Mary Jane Manigault, a 1984 National Heritage Fellow.

Access to the refuge is by boat only. Look for refuge headquarters signs on U.S. 17 at Awendaw. Private boats can be launched at high tide only from Moore's Landing at refuge headquarters on the Intracoastal Waterway. A public ferry from Moore's Landing takes day visitors (no vehicles) to Bull Island at 9 AM Tuesday, Friday, and Saturday, returning at 4 PM. No overnight camping is permitted within the refuge. For details, call the refuge headquarters at 843-928-3368.

■ **FRANCIS MARION NATIONAL FOREST** *map page 151, A-5*
About 40 miles north of Charleston via U.S. 52, this site comprises 250,000 acres of swamps, vast oaks, pines, and little lakes thought to have been formed by meteors.

Home to Indians for 10,000 years, this is where Gen. Francis Marion, "the Swamp Fox," stealthily battled British colonel Banastre Tarleton during the Revolutionary War.

After the Civil War, the land was bought up by lumber companies, who established logging camps and laid down railroads for transporting timber to Charleston and other cities. The lumber companies in turn sold the land to the government in the 1930s, and the area was declared a National Forest in 1936. Today, the forest encompasses numerous campsites as well as a few small towns.

Buck Hall, located just off of U.S. 17, is the largest and most developed campground in the forest. It includes full facilities and is the only campsite for which there is a fee. The Guilliard Lake campground is in the Guilliard Lake Scenic Area on the Santee River. There are also "hunt camps," unimproved camping areas that do not require a fee. Among these are Elmwood, Canal, Halfway Creek, and Honey Hill. In addition, camping in the general forest is allowed with a permit, obtainable at the two district offices (see below).

Huger Recreation Area is open for day use only and is a good place for picnicking. It has a boat launch on the nearby creek and is one of the most popular spots in the forest.

The Wambaw District office of the Francis Marion National Forest is in McClellanville, at 843-887-3257. The Witherbee District office is in Moncks Corner, at 843-336-3248. Permits, needed only if visitors plan to camp in the forest outside of camping areas, can be obtained at these two locations.

Brown pelicans are one of many species of birdlife that can be seen along the shoreline of Cape Romain National Wildlife Refuge.

MYRTLE BEACH
AND THE GRAND STRAND

Officially, the Grand Strand (meaning shore) begins at Winyah Bay and Georgetown in old rice plantation country and runs northeast for 60 miles to Little River Neck, on the North Carolina state line. Unofficially, but perhaps more commonly understood, the Grand Strand is Myrtle Beach, heart and soul of one of the nation's top three Southeast vacation destinations. It is also one of the South's more eclectic places.

Dozens of old beach towns and new retirement communities are packed to capacity during the height of the summer season at the Grand Strand. The old summer retreat of Pawleys Island anchors down the south end of the Strand. Little River, on the north end, is a veritable string of all-you-can-eat seafood restaurants. What's in between Pawleys and Little River is more or less sprawling Myrtle Beach, with its boardwalks, arcades, amusement parks, roller coasters, cotton candy, candy apples, and more waterslides and miniature golf courses than trees.

There are plenty of real golf courses as well; in fact, many consider this to be a golfer's heaven. And just up the road at Ocean Drive Beach—"OD" to the cognoscenti—new generations of teenagers still learn the steps to South Carolina's official state dance, the shag. The open-air dance halls are gone, but there is still a summer ritual of shuffling to old soul music (here it is called beach music). During spring break vacations, more teenagers arrive from up north, playing volleyball on the sand, cavorting at motel pools, and cruising down Ocean Boulevard. There's a wonderful old music shop, Judy's House of Oldies, at 300 Main Street (843-249-8649), still a great source for beach music.

The Grand Strand is filled with outlet malls, fast-food restaurants, and the occasional country-music emporium offering shows, dinners, and star performers. There aren't a lot of trees left, but there are RV parks right on the dune line, fishing piers that extend more than 1,000 feet into the ocean, and fleets of charter and party fishing boats.

There is a beach too, sometimes out of sight, just on the other side of the row of high-rise time-share and retirement condos that thickens every year. And no matter the season, whether it's jam-packed in summer or only mildly packed in fall and winter, everyone is having a good time.

Umbrellas freckle the sands at Myrtle Beach.

■ Early Visitors

While rice, indigo, and cotton plantations were creating lavish wealth in Georgetown, Charleston, the Sea Islands, and along Lowcountry rivers, the eastern corner of colonial and antebellum South Carolina was a place most settlers avoided. It wasn't known as the Grand Strand back then but rather the Great Swamp.

Watery thickets of tupelo gum and bald cypress made the region nearly impenetrable. Rice plantations spread up the Waccamaw River only as far north of Georgetown as today's Brookgreen Gardens, and planter families summered on the beach only as far north as Pawleys.

Unlike along the rest of the state's coastline, there are no rivers emptying into the Atlantic Ocean along the Grand Strand. Without river-borne sediments, no coastal islands were formed (Pawleys Island is essentially just a big sand dune), and the runoff simply sat in the swamps, making travel virtually impossible. But in the 1940s, the Army Corps of Engineers built the **Atlantic Intracoastal Waterway (ICW)**, inland a few miles from the beach from Little River Inlet south to the Waccamaw River, and then south all the way to Florida. This stretch is known as

BEASTS OF PREY ON THE SANTEE

We were awaken'd with the dismall'st and most hideous Noise that ever pierc'd my Ears . . . our Indian Pilot (who knew these Parts very well) acquainted us that it was customary to hear such Musick along that Swamp-Side, there being endless numbers of Panthers, Tygers, Wolves, and other Beasts of Prey, which make this Swamp their Abode . . . making this frightful Ditty 'till Day appears.

—Explorer John Lawson on the Santee, 1701

the **Pine Island Cut**, and it makes it seem as though the Grand Strand is a 60-mile-long island. Unlike the rest of the waterway through South Carolina, this stretch of the ICW is treeless and barren.

Colonial settlers, most of them one-mule, Scots-Irish farmers, first trickled into this area from North Carolina. They built small cabins and houses, farmed a few acres, established a settlement at Little River, and were ignored or forgotten by the rest of the region. A French Huguenot planter, Peter Horry, and a Charleston entrepreneur, Robert Conway, settled in the area during the Revolutionary War. Both men became major landowners, largely of swamps. Horry County (pronounced "*Oar*-ee"), which includes Myrtle Beach, and the county seat, Conway, were named after the two gentlemen.

Horry County remained in the hands of small farmers and the Great Swamp until the 1890s, when F. G. Burroughs of Conway began timbering the swamp. He bought land as he cleared his path, built a lumber mill at Pine Island, and laid railroad tracks to the sea—the Conway Seashore Railroad—to ship his wood and turpentine to Conway and from there down the Waccamaw to Georgetown.

The seashore terminus of the railroad was called New Town for a few years until Burroughs renamed it Myrtle Beach in 1900, for the evergreen shrub with small, dark leaves and scented, white flowers. These were once abundant along the shore and still are found in the Charleston area, but here they are primarily found in Myrtle Beach State Park. Farm families and small-town storekeepers began riding Burroughs's lumber train to Myrtle Beach, and in the summer of 1901 he opened the resort's first hotel, the Sea Side Inn, as well as a commissary and pavilion. A sandy dirt road from Conway to the lumber village of Socastee was extended to the beach in 1914, and a few more farmers and shopkeepers

OCEAN FOREST HOTEL, MYRTLE BEACH, S. C., "AMERICA'S FINEST STRAND"

670 MILES SOUTH OF NEW YORK, 735 MILES NORTH OF MIAMI

The Ocean Forest Hotel, built in 1926, was Myrtle Beach's first grand hotel.

began vacationing at Myrtle Beach. Most of them pitched tents on the beach and in the dunes, where there are still more than 7,000 campsites in public or private parks along the Strand.

In 1926, a cotton-mill magnate from the Upcountry, John T. Woodside of Greenville, led a group of investors in building a huge, grand Myrtle Beach hotel—the Ocean Forest, which is now, alas, gone. Woodside and his associates bought most of the town, laid out streets, and began selling lots. It was a banner year for the Strand. Beach communities were founded, incorporated, and began developing with small inns, casual seafood cafés, and beach houses at Garden City just south of Myrtle Beach and at Ocean Drive and Cherry Grove to the north.

The Great Depression of the 1930s halted the boom launched by Woodside, until the post–World War II boom of the 1950s. The Strand, however, never severed its Greenville connections. Until the 1970s, its visitors were primarily vacationing textile executives and cotton-mill hands from Greenville and other upstate communities. Even today, the daily Greenville newspaper, published 242 miles from Myrtle Beach, includes the "Grand Strand Forecast" in its weather report.

The row of high- and low-rises on the Grand Strand thickens every year.

The Strand also became known as "the beach" since it is the closest seashore for all of North Carolina west of Raleigh.

In the late 1960s and early 1970s, Myrtle Beach and the Grand Strand were put on the national map by a tourism visionary. In 1967, the late George "Buster" Bryan, a Myrtle Beach businessman, envisioned his hometown becoming a mecca for golf. He built two courses and then created "golf-weekend vacation packages" and "golfotels," special lodgings just for golfers. Bryan predicted golfers would come between Labor Day and late spring, when Myrtle Beach and the Strand were like a ghost town.

The venture was slow to take off, until a few winters later, when a snowstorm closed the famous golf courses at Pinehurst and Southern Pines. The North Carolina resorts sent their vacationing golfers 100 miles south to Myrtle Beach. For a few days, golfers filled hotels, restaurants, and courses. Thus a vacation mecca was born.

During these same winters, New England residents and Canadians traditionally jammed Interstate 95 for the drive south to the Florida sun. When oil embargoes in the 1970s sent gasoline prices soaring, winter travelers checked their roadmaps for destinations closer to home and discovered that they could avoid hundreds of miles on Interstate 95 if they turned off at the Grand Strand of South Carolina.

■ BIG BOOM AT MYRTLE BEACH

The beachfront here is now a wall of high-rise condominiums, not unlike Ocean City and Fort Lauderdale. The Federal Aviation Administration had to warn banner planes (flying low and slowly up and down the beach and trailing banners: Bikini Contest Trader Bubba 9 Tonight) to watch out for parasail riders and the flight paths of scheduled jetliners using the Myrtle Beach Airport.

Many visitors came and never left. What was once a small town of roughly 37,000 in the 1960s has grown to include more than 200,000 full-time residents, with an extra 20,000 tourists during any given day during the off-season. During the summer, the Grand Strand receives as many as 13.5 million visitors.

In the course of this big boom, the development of swamps and massive new expressways, Horry County became a place of two sharply differing personalities. Drive over the waterway and 15 miles inland, and the rhythms of life are not those of the winter and summer tourist seasons but of spring planting and late-summer harvesting. Horry County is still the most productive in the state for farming—

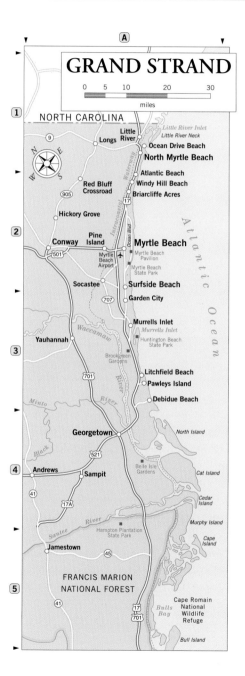

GRAND STRAND

there are more soybeans, oats, and tobacco grown here than any other county, worth more than $50 million per year. But tourism is now bringing in more than $5 billion per year. The men in bib overalls driving tractors around hamlets such as Cool Spring, Galivants Ferry, and Hickory Grove are hugely successful in their industry, but they are no longer as politically powerful as the restaurant owners and hoteliers of Myrtle Beach.

The Horry County Council and the Myrtle Beach City Council have been feuding for years over what to do with **Myrtle Beach Air Force Base,** which closed in 1992. The base once had a fighter wing of 70 jets, and its last squadron of A-10 "Warthog" anti-tank planes flew 1,492 combat missions during the Gulf War. They are mothballed in an Arizona desert now, but the air base still serves as the Grand Strand's commercial airport.

■ **MUSIC THEATERS**

The Strand already is considered the number three locale in the nation for country music, behind Nashville and Branson, Missouri. Today, a number of country music theaters are open in Myrtle Beach and on the Strand, plus **Dolly**

Spanish Galleon is billed as one of the area's top shaggin' venues.

Parton's Dixie Stampede with "a horse racing, whip cracking, wagon busting good time," a creation of Dolly Parton's Dollywood Productions. Performed in huge, new auditoriums and theaters, country music is bringing a new life to old Myrtle Beach.

In retrospect, country music seems to be a natural for Myrtle Beach. The golf complexes around North Myrtle Beach, and the social airs, real or imagined, of Pawleys and DeBordieu attract mostly upscale visitors. Myrtle Beach, however, always has been a blue-collar family resort of two-week vacationers driving campers, cooking their own meals, and listening to "The Grand Ole Opry" on the radio.

Until 1986 there was little vacationers could do together, as a family, once the sun set. That was the year Calvin Gilmore, an entrepreneur from the Ozarks of Missouri and frequent vacationer at Myrtle Beach, opened his 2,200-seat **Carolina Opry.**

GRAND STRAND MUSIC VENUES

Afterdeck. U.S. 17, Restaurant Row; 843-449-1550. An open-air club with live music, dancing, and comedy.

Alabama Theater. 4750 U.S. 17 South, North Myrtle Beach; 843-272-1111. Celebrity concerts each week and a musical variety show six nights a week. Special appearances throughout the year by the owners, the musical group Alabama.

Carolina Opry. 8901A 82nd Ave., Myrtle Beach; 843-913-1400. This popular music hall hosts a talented cast of country-western singers and dancers.

Crook and Chase Theatre. Fantasy Harbor-Waccamaw, Intracoastal Waterway; 843-236-8500.

Dolly Parton's Dixie Stampede. North junction of U.S. 17 and U.S. 17 Business; 800-433-4401. Dolly Parton's dinner theater presents music, comedy, rodeo, Wild West performances, and a four-course country-style meal.

Ducks. 229 Main St., North Myrtle Beach; 843-249-3858.

Fat Harolds. 212 Main St., North Myrtle Beach; 843-249-5779.

Forum Theater and Savoy Theater. Both at Fantasy Harbor-Waccamaw, Intracoastal Waterway; Forum 843-236-9700, Savoy 843-236-2200. Both theaters offer several musical acts throughout the year.

The House of Blues. Barefoot Landing on U.S. 17 North; 843-272-3000. Offers an eclectic venue attracting blues, jazz, gospel, and rock stars. Sunday gospel brunches are especially popular.

Legends in Concert. U.S. 17 Business and Third Ave. South, Surfside Beach; 843-238-7827. Elvis, Hank Williams Jr., Marilyn Monroe, and the Blues Brothers, among others, are impersonated.

Medieval Times Dinner and Tournament Show. Fantasy Harbor-Waccamaw, Intracoastal Waterway; 888-935-6878. Audience dines while knights battle in 11th-century setting.

The Palace Theater. Broadway at the Beach, 21st Ave. North and U.S. 17 Bypass; 843-448-0588. Kenny Rogers, the Oak Ridge Boys, and the Radio City Rockettes have performed in this new theater.

Spanish Galleon. 100 Main St., North Myrtle Beach; 843-249-1047. Shaggin' offered, some nights.

Studebaker's. 2000 N. Kings Hwy., Myrtle Beach; 843-626-3855. DJ spins old-time rock-and-roll beach music nightly.

A country rock band at work in the Alabama Theater.

Some of the biggest names in country music joined in what Gilmore began. The mega-group Alabama, which once played for tips in Myrtle Beach nightclubs, opened the **Alabama Theater** at Barefoot Landing in North Myrtle Beach. And almost every week another rumor hits Myrtle Beach about another country music star said to be following the crowd of theater founders, Lee Greenwood, Garth Brooks, Mel Tillis, Crystal Gale, Travis Tritt, Barbara Mandrell, and Mickey Gilley among them.

■ SHOPPING AND DINING

For all the excitement over golf and country music on the Grand Strand, eating and shopping still draw crowds by the thousands. A section of U.S. 17 just north of the Myrtle Beach city limits has been known locally for decades as **Restaurant Row.** The 2-mile strip no longer has the best or the most restaurants on the Strand, but it has some good ones—Cagney's (843-449-7872), Gullyfield (843-449-3111), and Chesapeake House (843-449-7933) among them. For old-time seafood, drive to Murrells Inlet and take your pick from several locally owned eateries.

SHAGGIN'

On New Year's Day, 1740, at a colonial tavern near Cedar Creek, not far from what today is Ocean Drive Beach, George Whitefield, a fiery Methodist disciple, came to baptize a child. When he encountered a group of dancers, he told them they were committing a sin. The tavern patrons stopped dancing. The preacher then baptized the child and went to bed, and the dancing resumed.

Dancing, especially dancing the shag, has never abated along the Grand Strand, and it may never stop. The "shag" is a shuffling, four-step hybrid of the jitterbug and the lindy hop, performed to Carolina "beach music," which is not Beach Boys music but a rhythm-and-blues sound made famous by songs such as "Give Me Just a Little More Time" and "Sixty-Minute Man."

Teenagers from South and North Carolina began practicing the shag during spring and summer vacations from school in hangouts along the Strand during the 1950s. There's a shag hangout in every beach community here, from **Ocean Boulevard**, a kind of teenager's Bourbon Street, to the birthplace of the shag, **Ocean Drive Beach**. At OD, in the legendary shag hangout, the Pad, countless middle-class, white southerners discovered black rhythm-and-blues bands. The Pad closed in 1987 after being damaged in a fire. Its remains were finally demolished in 1994, witnessed by nearly 200 of its old regulars, by then middle-aged.

"Shaggin' " remains so popular that it has its own preservation society, the **Society of Stranders,** who gather in OD and Strand hangouts every April and September, in numbers nearing 10,000 strong, to lay down some steps to the Temptations' original version of "My Girl" or Bill Withers's "Lean on Me."

The area specialty is seafood, and favorite Lowcountry dishes are she-crab soup, deep-fried or sautéed seafood, and spicy crab cakes. Many restaurants offer all-you-can-eat deals, and some combine dining with entertainment.

The **Waccamaw Factory Shoppes** (800-444-8258) on the waterway and U.S. 501 just outside Myrtle Beach dwarfs everything else on the Strand. The complex consists of three large malls covering 500 acres and drawing more than 7.5 million shoppers, browsers, and curiosity seekers a year.

On U.S. 17 at the turnoff to Pawleys Island, there are 20 shops and two restaurants in a complex (843-237-8448) centered on the original **Pawleys Island Hammock Shop**, where locals still make the rope hammocks.

Barefoot Landing (843-272-8349) at North Myrtle Beach is an unusual outdoor mall on the waterway that has upscale boutiques. **Broadway at the Beach,** at 21st Avenue North and U.S. 17 Bypass, is a 350-acre complex that includes shops, restaurants, mini-golf, children's rides, an aquarium, movie theaters (including IMAX), and a NASCAR speedway.

■ PRINCE GEORGE TRACT

The last major chunk of undeveloped land on the entire South Carolina coast that was not part of a state, federal, or privately owned park, refuge, or preserve was sold for development in 1994. It is known as the Prince George tract, with nearly 2,000 acres that stretch from the beach to the Waccamaw River just south of Pawleys Island. Archaeologists found evidence of temporary camps used by passing Native American tribes in pre-colonial times. Hickory, red maple, cypress, gum, and pine trees cover much of the tract, and traces of the **Old Kings Highway,** which George Washington rode on his triumphal tour through South Carolina after the Revolutionary War, still can be found on the hilly terrain.

The Waterford and Hagley rice plantations were here, and remnants of steam-powered rice mills remain, as do a canal and dike system between the rice mill and the river. There are also remains of a boat landing used by passengers between Georgetown and Pawleys.

In 1909, as wealthy northerners began buying the failed rice plantations for use as hunting preserves and winter retreats, Isaac E. Emerson of Baltimore bought one of the properties and named it **Arcadia Plantation.** It was inherited in 1931 by his grandson, George W. Vanderbilt, son of the industrialist Cornelius Vanderbilt. In 1971, Lucille Vanderbilt Pate sold some of the beachfront to developers, who changed the name of Debidue Beach to **DeBordieu Colony** (still pronounced "*Deb*-a-doo"), a posh resort. In 1985, some of the DeBordieu developers bought the rest of the Prince George tract from Mrs. Pate for $17.5 million. By 1988, however, both the Prince George project, which never got off the ground, and the DeBordieu Colony, like Kiawah Island, struggled through financial challenges.

DeBordieu was successfully revived. The Melrose Corporation, one of the developers of Daufuskie Island and Hilton Head, hooked up with the Georgetown County Council. The county and the developers proposed golf courses, hotels, restaurants, and marinas for most of the 2,000 acres, with 250 acres set aside for a state park. But the University of South Carolina and its developer partners offered a different land-use plan. About 1,300 acres would be set aside as a coastal research center, a habitat for the endangered red-cockaded woodpecker, and protected wetlands, with the rest of the tract cut into residential lots to finance the deal.

The university's developer partners are two of the same investors who now run DeBordieu Colony, and luxury homes have been built on the beach.

■ PAWLEYS ISLAND   *map page 151, A-3*

Families have returned year after year, generation to generation, to the same ramshackle cottages and gently dilapidated two- and three-story old beach homes on Pawleys Island. Ownership, as well as summer reservations, has passed through the hands of relatives or friends—the same family gets the same month year after year.

They have come to the tiny, 3.5-mile-long island for what it continues to be: laid-back, simple beyond modern conveniences, offering relaxation on an unspoiled family beach, without arcades, theme parks, restaurant rows, condo rows, traffic, nightclubs, noise, or even—yes, truly—a golf course.

The permanent islanders, about 200 of them, have happily coexisted with the 400,000 or so mid-spring to early-fall visitors, most of them regular renters. The day's options include sitting on the uncrowded beach; crabbing in the tidal creeks of the saltwater marsh separating Pawleys from the mainland; enjoying a big midday Carolina dinner of perhaps fresh broiled flounder, corn fritters, yams, biscuits, lima beans, and ice tea; and taking a nap on a cool, yawning porch in one of the wide, and now-famous, Pawleys Island rope hammocks.

The Pawleys year-rounders and property owners voted to incorporate the island in 1985 to prevent Grand Strand commercialism in any form, from luxury condos to boutique mini-malls. The only commercial property on the island today remains an aging, small condo and two small, almost historic beach inns, the **Pelican** and the **Sea View.** A duplex is the only new multi-family housing that town zoning ordinances permit. Even soft drink machines are banned.

The plan—the only plan ever accepted by the islanders—seemed to be working. And then, in 1989, Hurricane Hugo's outer reaches hit Pawleys. Hugo sliced a new inlet through Pawleys and leveled 90 houses, most of them ramshackle cottages in the south end known as Bird's Nest.

This had happened to Pawleys before, in 1822, when the rice plantation families and their slaves summered on the island. The difference this time was that, in

Saltwater Fishing

"Snagging lip (stuffed, baked flounder) does not come from the cabbage patch."

Every day of the year, saltwater anglers are out surf casting from the beach, fishing from piers, prowling the coastal inlets and waterways, and riding deep-sea charter boats far off shore to the Gulf Stream, which flows roughly 60 miles off the coast of South Carolina.

All over the shore, you can find fleets of the big, shining, chrome charter boats, as well as "party boats" carrying dozens of visitors. The major sportfishing marinas for these fleets are at Little River and Murrells Inlet on the Grand Strand; Georgetown; Mt. Pleasant's Shem Creek across the Cooper River from Charleston; and Edisto Beach, Beaufort, and Hilton Head Island in the Sea Islands.

The prime fishing season is from March to November, when the catch includes king and Spanish mackerel, flounder, spot-tail bass, cobia, bluefish, sheepshead, Atlantic croaker—and from June to October, Florida pompano in coastal waters (off piers or in the surf). Spotted sea trout, pinfish, kingfish, and whiting are taken year-round in the same waters. The usual baits are live shrimp, minnows, small live fish, dead shrimp, sand fleas, and cut bait.

Various sportfishing clubs and the state Marine Resource Division have created dozens of artificial reefs, sinking cast-off tugboats, landing craft, Liberty ships, barges, and old bridges 10 to 20 miles offshore to attract fish. Maps with loran coordinates to the artificial reefs, as well as the *Seasonal Guide to Saltwater Fishing in South Carolina*, both published by the South Carolina Department of Natural Resources, are available from MRD, in Charleston (843-953-9300).

Big-game fishing for sailfish, tuna, and shark on charter boats in waters near the Gulf Stream has yielded several world-record catches in recent years. Check local marinas and bait-and-tackle shops for dates and entry information regarding big-game fishing tournaments.

1989, Pawleys had what was considered almost priceless beachfront property, and the new houses that replaced the old ones after the hurricane are mammoth and expensive. What was once the Bird's Nest is now an avenue of enormous homes.

Barry McCall, magistrate of the island and year-rounder, suspects the protective motives that led to the island's incorporating itself into a town might have altered the spirit of what was supposed to be protected.

The magistrate told an interviewer: "It's regressed from what it was 20, 30 years ago. There was a bowling alley, trampolines, miniature golf, raft rentals, the Pavilion. Now, it's so residential people have become possessive of their property. It never used to bother us when young people parked in our yard to get to the beach."

■ MURRELLS INLET   *map page 151, A-3*

Murrells Inlet, halfway between Pawleys and Myrtle Beach, was named for a simple 1740 planter who settled the island and not for a pirate, as some would like you to believe. This community is a holdout of individualists, including two-fisted, blond-bombshell-loving, commie-hating, private-eyeing, Mike Hammer–creating, detective-novel-writing Mickey Spillane and some much tougher women, all battling the spread of commercial development.

When Mickey Spillane married Jane at the old and legendary restaurant **Oliver's Lodge,** his words were, "I do; let's eat."

More than likely, none of the wedding guests, at least none who call "the Inlet" home, thought that at all strange, probably including the bride. Murrells Inlet

An aerial of Murrells Inlet, home of crime novelist Mickey Spillane.

always has been, and still mostly is, about seafood: the skill, hard work, pleasure, and secret recipes of cooking it, and the slow, grinning pleasure of eating seafood prepared by masters.

There are about 30 restaurants in Murrells Inlet today: Mexican, Japanese, Italian, Cajun, and seafood. Oliver's (843-651-2963), a boarding house for weekenders who went charter fishing with Capt. Mack Oliver, used to be the only restaurant. Except for a screen porch built during the 1960s, Oliver's hasn't changed. The long, old, swaybacked joggling board first used for crossing ditches on rice plantations is still a seat on the porch for diners waiting to be seated inside. There have been a few other, probably inevitable, changes at the Inlet.

The Murrells Inlet Historic District, locally known as Little Marion, isn't there anymore. Dozens of families from the farm town of **Marion**, about 60 miles inland on U.S. 501, once summered at the Inlet and built their cottages in the same neighborhood. Jane Spillane's was one of them.

There were about 20 white clapboard summer cottages with large screen porches in the neighborhood, most of them overlooking the tidal creeks and saltwater

While the boom of North Myrtle Beach has attracted the young at heart . . .

marshes that gave the Inlet its name and led to the creation of a fleet of commercial and charter fishing boats.

Hurricane Hugo damaged or destroyed most of the old summer places, and when the neighborhood was rebuilt, fancier, bigger, and pricier homes replaced those in Little Marion. The only old summer cottage left is the Bates house. The Marionites, the kitchen crew at Oliver's, among others, used to go right into the Inlet's tidal creeks for fresh oysters and clams, and there were cinder-block oyster bars along the highway, which served nothing but oysters, shrimp, and crackers. The oyster shacks are gone now, and yellow pollution-warning signs dot the old oyster beds, victims of growth in and around the Inlet.

On the other hand, the Inlet still has plenty of stubborn, salty, independent, and unincorporated residents determined to keep at least some of the old ways. In 1991, for example, a proposal was made to merge Murrells Inlet with Garden City and Surfside Beach, just to the north, into a single, artificial place to be named South Myrtle Beach. The plan had a precedent in North Myrtle Beach. Before the big boom, there was no such place as North Myrtle Beach; there were Cherry

. . . residents of southern Myrtle Beach prefer more reflective pastimes.

Grove, OD, Crescent, Atlantic, and Windy Hill beaches along the north end of the Strand. When people went there, they went to a place with one of those names. After the boom, a referendum put them all inside an artificial place named North Myrtle Beach.

Jane Spillane, Maxine Oliver Hawkins (who owned Oliver's Lodge), and Genevieve "Sister" Peterkin (a retired librarian who grew up in the Inlet and daughter-in-law of the novelist Julia Peterkin and author of her own book, *Heaven Is a Beautiful Place*) drafted a petition against the merger. The three women got 1,400 signatures of property owners agreeing with them, and that was the end of that.

■ STATE PARKS

In the development boom that washed over the Grand Strand, two oases of relative solitude and natural beauty were saved. Simply by entering either Myrtle Beach or Huntington Beach State Park, visitors get a respite from the traffic and noise of hectic beach life.

The Grand Strand, with the exception of some golf courses, is least crowded during the winter. Even in January and February, daytime high temperatures in the upper 60s (F) and low 70s are not uncommon. It's the kind of weather that lures the golfers, and the kind of weather that's perfect for scavenging on the beach and hiking the maritime forest at these two parks.

The 312-acre **Myrtle Beach State Park** (843-238-5325), on business U.S. 17 opposite the airport, includes about 100 acres of one of the last maritime forests along the Strand. There are thousands of birds in the wind-sculpted myrtle trees and a pristine beach. The first South Carolina state park, it has picnic tables, shelters, camping, playground equipment, cabins, a pool, a 750-foot pier (the Strand's oldest), and a store selling everything one needs for fishing.

Huntington Beach State Park (843-237-4440), about 15 miles south of Myrtle Beach on U.S. 17 below Murrells Inlet (across from Brookgreen Gardens), has 2,500 acres of salt marsh and tidal creeks with boardwalks to fish or catch crab. The Mullett Pond attracts alligators, herons, egrets, gallinules, and grebes.

Archer Huntington and his wife, the sculptress Anna Hyatt Huntington, built their unusual, fortress-like home—**Atalaya,** the Spanish word for "watchtower"— on this land. It was constructed from 1931 to 1933 and had no detailed plans, although it is said Archer Huntington was inspired by a Moorish castle he saw in Spain. The result is inside square 200-foot walls facing the ocean.

Up close and personal with a cypress swamp alligator.

The large, open inner court is filled with palms and surrounded by 30 rooms of living quarters around three sides of the perimeter. The tower is the house's old cypress water tank. The Huntingtons last used their beach mansion in 1947, and its furnishings were removed years ago. Today, the unusual home has a ghostly presence and a deep quiet absorbing sounds of the surf.

The 3-mile beach at Huntington is a paradise for shorebird enthusiasts. Salt marsh, tidal water, woodlands, freshwater lagoon, maritime thickets, and sand dunes thick with sea oats attract a wide range of species, including terns, Wilson's plovers, and painted buntings. Spider crabs, razor clams, sponges, and sea cucumbers also wash ashore regularly.

■ GOLF

In 1927, when the Greenville textile magnate, Robert Woodside, was building the first grand resort hotel at Myrtle Beach, Robert White, the Scot who was the first PGA president, began building the first golf course on the Grand Strand. It was **Pine Lakes International** (803-449-6459) in Myrtle Beach.

For years, Pine Lakes was the only golf course on the Strand. By the 1960s, there were a half-dozen courses in the area, and then "Buster" Bryan built his two courses and marketed his "golfotel" packages. Today there are more than 100 golf courses in the 60-mile strip between Little River and Georgetown, the densest concentration of golf courses in the nation.

Myrtle Beach may have plenty of sunbathers, beach strollers, shoppers, fishermen, diners, and even country music fans, but, it seems, every one of them also plays golf.

Golf Digest has called South Carolina the top golfing destination in the country. In green fees alone, the Grand Strand courses collect more than $500 million, from more than 4 million individual rounds of golf. The entire state has more than 300 golf courses, which pump more than $1.5 billion into the economy, not counting the restaurants, hotels, motels, and other businesses supported by the golf industry.

Golf, and homes in golf course developments, are so popular in South Carolina that the single most valuable agricultural "crop" grown in the state is no longer tobacco: it's turf sod, for fairways, greens, and lawns. Annual revenues from growing sod in the state have approached $1 billion.

Along the Strand, especially from fall through spring, it's routine for a package-golfotel visitor to get a tee time and play 18 holes even before check-in. Then, for the next six days, that same golfer will get in 36 holes a day, often playing on a dozen different courses, then get in 18 more holes after check-out.

The Strand's courses range in quality from the average, small-town country club layout to some of the nation's most praised. (Most are open to the public through golfotel packages.) Some are luxurious, self-contained resorts and second-home developments such as **Ocean Creek** and **Kingston Plantation** in North Myrtle Beach.

Myrtle Beach has the highest ratio of golf courses to people in the nation.

COASTAL PLAIN

Northwest of the Sea Island beach resorts and sprawling tropical greenery of Charleston, Georgetown and the Grand Strand, the coastal plain spreads inland for a hundred miles into South Carolina. Two-thirds of the state lies within this Atlantic coastal plain, which rises so gently that when it ends at rapids on the Broad and Saluda rivers in Columbia, it still is only 135 feet above sea level.

This rolling terrain, created during millions of years by the advancing and retreating ocean, made the region ideal for agriculture, and the coastal plain became the farming heart of South Carolina, dotted with small towns and great barbecue.

The plain extends to the fall line that, in South Carolina, roughly follows the route of Interstate 20 from the Savannah River border with Georgia, then northeast through Columbia and Camden, then along U.S. 1 through Cheraw to North Carolina. Northwest of the line are the textile mill towns of the hilly Piedmont region.

Geologists divide the coastal plain into four regions as it spreads inland: the lower and upper pine belts, the red hills, and the sandhills. Those living on the coastal plain see it a bit differently.

Inland from the Grand Strand beaches, the locals call the northeastern section of the coastal plain the Pee Dee, after the Great Pee Dee River flowing down from Cheraw to Winyah Bay into the Atlantic. Soybean and flue-cured tobacco farming dominate the Pee Dee economy. The landscape of farms is punctuated by small curing sheds, and huge tobacco auction warehouses, many of which lie unused and empty.

At the Pee Dee end of the fall line, around Cheraw, huge hills of sand left by the ancient ocean create a mini-region as well as a microclimate known as the sandhills.

The stretch of the plain inland from Charleston along the Interstate 26 route to Columbia is old cotton country where plantations spread along the Santee and Cooper rivers during the early 1800s. Cotton still exists as a minor crop for the region, which present day is called Santee Cooper country, after the hydroelectricity project that created two freshwater reservoirs in the 1940s, Lake Marion and Lake Moultrie.

Reckless timbering and farming of the ancient Pee Dee sandhills led to the creation of such habitats as the Carolina Sandhills National Wildlife Refuge.

The coastal plain inland from the Sea Islands and Lowcountry plantations, running parallel to the Savannah River, is dominated first by tree farms, then pulpwood and lumber mills. The huge Savannah River Site, sprawling over more than 300 square miles on the Savannah River in Barnwell and Aiken counties, has fueled the economy since the 1950s, when the federal government built five huge nuclear reactors to produce the explosive fuels, tritium, and plutonium for hydrogen bombs. "The bomb plant," as it's locally known, is South Carolina's largest single private employer.

In Aiken, just inland from the plant, wealthy northerners built elegant horse farms, stables, and racing tracks as a winter colony in the early 1900s. This has led to a growing horse-breeding industry, including several Kentucky Derby winners.

Above the coastal plain, at the fall line, the region is known as the Midlands and includes Columbia, the state capital, and nearby Lake Murray.

Compared with the popularity of South Carolina's ocean resorts, plantation museums, and historic Charleston, the vast coastal plain might seem to be mainly farmland, or a thoroughfare to cross to get somewhere else. Travelers who take the time, and any two-lane highway crossing this plain, can find contemplative glimpses into a slowly vanishing small-town way of life, which still thrives in the shadow of the sexy beaches and Blue Ridge mountains. The curious also can find, in between forest and farm, the majesty of a bald cypress swamp and the mystery of the huge, unexplained depressions called Carolina Bays. (See "Carolina Bays and Sand Hills" section later in this chapter.)

Aiken's spring festival of thoroughbred, steeplechase, and sulky races (also known as harness races, where the driver sits on a wheeled cart, or sulky), as well as polo, draws tens of thousands. Bass fishing on Lakes Marion and Moultrie is famous nationwide among anglers. Columbia's Riverbanks Zoo and Botanical Garden is regarded as one of the nation's best, and the city's State Museum has many devotees. Among stock-car racing fans, there's no more historic track than Darlington Raceway.

Still, the region's principal charm may be found in ambling and stopping at a roadside stand selling fresh boiled peanuts or tree-ripened peaches, or at a farm-town barbecue shack, driving through a cotton or tobacco field in full flower, or dropping in on a fall county fair or small-town festival.

By late February all across the coastal plain, tractors are back on the country roads moving from field to field for plowing. There's rarely a freeze from early March to late November in this broad agricultural belt.

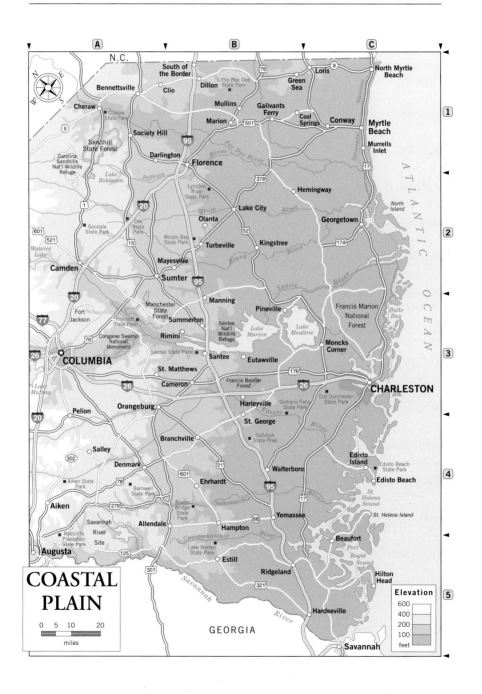

COASTAL PLAIN

0 5 10 20
miles

Tenant farming and sharecropping were the systems in which laborers, usually African-Americans, lived and worked on a farm in return for rudimentary housing, a small wage, or a small share of the profit on the crop. These systems virtually disappeared during the 1960s and 1970s, diminishing from 133,000 individual farms in the 1950s, with 12 million acres of crops, to only 25,000 farms with 1.7 million acres planted in 2002. Less than 2 percent of the state's population still lives and works on a farm. The income from agriculture in South Carolina has been only a small part of the state's economy for decades. As is the case with agriculture everywhere in the nation, the few family farms that survive today are usually the ones whose owners inherited their lands, adapted and diversified their skills, and expanded.

South Carolina farmers have tried a lot of unusual crops, hoping to remain on their land. Commercial catfish farming once was touted as a growth industry for the coastal plain's rural communities. Small-town investors, banks, and state and federal agencies lost millions on the venture, however, and the last commercial cat-

---

COASTAL PLAINS FESTIVALS

CATFISH

Hardeeville: Catfish Festival. Festivities include a dance, arts and crafts, live entertainment, boat races, and sports tournaments. On I-95 near the Savannah River. *September.*

Society Hill: Catfish Festival. A hometown event with children's games, fishing tournaments, arts and crafts, fried catfish, and catfish stew. On U.S. 401 and 52 north of Florence. *November.*

CHITLINS

Salley: Salley Chitlin' Strut. Featuring the deep-fried small intestines of pigs. At SC 39 and SC 394 in Aiken County. *November, Thanksgiving Saturday.*

GRITS

St. George: World Grits Festival. In addition to the Miss Grits beauty pageant, the festival has singing and dancing on Main Street, a carnival, and contests in grits eating. Northwest of Charleston at I-95 and U.S. 78. April.

PEACHES

Trenton: Ridge Peach Festival. Arts and crafts, a softball tournament, and peach desserts. *June.*

Gilbert: Lexington County Peach Festival. A festival of arts and crafts, live music, food concessions, and peach dishes and barbecue. Held at Gilbert Elementary School. *Fourth of July weekend.*

fish processor in the state, an Orangeburg firm, closed in 1993.

In the coastal plain, however, agriculture still remains a crucial part of the economy, even though almost every year another little farm town becomes virtually deserted. Economics aside, the traditions of farm life remain strong even in the cities, as the popularity of farm-town festivals among all South Carolinians shows.

■ FARM FESTIVALS

Watermelon is king in the small towns of Pageland, near North Carolina, and Hampton, in the pine belt near the Savannah River. Both towns hold watermelon festivals. Other farm towns sponsor peach festivals, tobacco days, and other special celebrations for crops that remain staples for many South Carolinians and other southerners.

Every April, the small town of St. George (population 2,000) in Santee Cooper country hosts more than 50,000 visitors for the World Grits Festival. Grits are

PEANUTS
Pelion: South Carolina Peanut Party. Four and a half tons of peanuts boiled in two days. Activities include the annual blessing of the peanut pots and crowning of the Peanut Princess. At U.S. 78 and SC 302. *August.*

POSSUMS
Barnwell: Possum Creep and July Blast. Eat real possum and coon and enjoy carnival rides, horse show, and other attractions. *July.*

RICE
Walterboro: Colleton County Rice Festival. The rice industry celebrates with dances, a parade, rice-cooking contests, and the "world's largest pot of rice." On SC 64 near I-95. *April.*

TOBACCO
Mullins: Golden Leaf Festival. Celebrating the tobacco industry with live entertainment, a husband-hollering contest, a Party after Dark, and other events. On SC 41 east of Florence. *September.*

WATERMELON
Pageland: Pageland Watermelon Festival. Thousands come to this festival for its clogging, arts and crafts, food, seed-spitting contests, rodeo, and more. On U.S. 601 and SC 9 near North Carolina border. *July.*
Hampton: Hampton County Watermelon Festival. A weeklong festival offering free watermelon, food, parades, dances, and races. On U.S. 278 near Savannah River. *June.*

grains of hulled corn ground into a coarse meal, cooked, and typically eaten hot with butter, salt, and pepper for breakfast. There are old-fashioned stone-ground grits cooked for an hour or more, quick grits cooked for a few minutes, and instant grits mixed with hot water. In addition to the Miss Grits beauty pageant, the festival has the usual singing and dancing on Main Street, a carnival, and grits-eating contests.

In the little Midlands town of Pelion, in Lexington County, about 15,000 visitors turn up each August for the annual Peanut Party. Nearly 4½ tons of peanuts are boiled over the course of two days, producing a slightly spongy nut, slick as a raw oyster and (once boiled) officially called a goober. Festival activities include the annual blessing of the peanut pots.

Every year in November, in the small Aiken County village of Salley, 50,000 people attend the Chitlin' Strut. Formally called chitterlings, these gastronomic delights are the deep-fried small intestines of a pig. The aroma of cooking chitlins has stopped many a newcomer dead in his tracks.

South Carolina's fall pecan crop contributes significantly to the state's family farms—almost all of which have a pecan grove. The state's total pecan crop is usually more than 5 million pounds. What began as a sideline on the Summerses' family Calhoun County farm during the Great Depression grew into the Golden Kernel Pecan Co., Inc., perhaps the state's biggest, certainly its oldest, pecan-shelling plant. The Summers family has been shelling and selling pecans since 1932, from groves in the small community of Cameron in Santee Cooper country.

Grits, goobers, and chitlin celebrations: Is this a great country, or what?

Tobacco, however, is still the most valuable crop for South Carolina's farmers, as it has been since 1956, when it surpassed cotton. Almost all the state's tobacco crop is grown in the Pee Dee counties of Horry, Florence, Williamsburg, and Darlington. Perhaps no two crops in the history of the nation have been so associated with human misery and controversy: cotton for its dependence on slavery and tobacco for its dependence on addicted consumers.

■ PEE DEE *map page 169, B/C-1/2*

The pungent, almost gamy aroma of tobacco —not tobacco smoke —wafts through the small farms of the Pee Dee from mid-summer to early fall as the crop is auctioned in warehouses from Conway to Darlington.

Skilled buyers from giant corporations, who judge with a flick of an eye or brush of a fingertip the worth of the broad leaves, pass between rows of the harvested crop inside long, humid warehouses. Just as imperceptibly, the buyers bid in response to a nearly unintelligible chant from an equally skilled and specialized tobacco auctioneer.

The scene is repeated from late July to mid-September at tobacco auction warehouses in Conway and Loris in Horry County, where 25 percent of South Carolina's tobacco is grown, and a bit farther west in Hemingway and Mullins, and in the U.S. 52 towns of Kingstree, Lake City, and Darlington. Most of the **tobacco warehouse auctions,** held from late July to mid-September, are open to the public. Check local newspapers and chambers of commerce for dates, times, and directions.

South Carolina never had the huge cigarette factories found in North Carolina and Virginia, but nearly 13,000 people are employed by the tobacco industry in the state, and the annual economic impact of tobacco in South Carolina is estimated at $500 million. While this pales in comparison to the billions brought in by tourists, it remains a sizeable part of the state economy.

In January, all across the Pee Dee's farm lands, the tiny seeds are sown in beds of what will soon become 4- or 5-foot-tall tobacco plants. In spring, the shoots are transplanted to the open fields. Trimmed and topped as the season passes, they are harvested from the bottom up at intervals through the summer, with the most valued leaves taken last from the top.

On some of the few small family farms still growing tobacco, the ripe leaves are tied onto sticks, then hung in a barn and cured for nearly a week as the farmer constantly monitors and adjusts the heat inside the barns with a system of flues— hence the term for cigarette tobacco, flue-cured.

Migrant laborers do most of the summer harvesting and, like most other agricultural and industrial laborers, face hazards peculiar to their crop, in this case cuts from the tobacco knives used to slice a leaf at its stem; impalement on sticks used to hang the tobacco in barns; falls from the barn rafters; and a little-known hazard called green tobacco sickness. Pure, concentrated nicotine is as poisonous as the venom of the deadliest snake. During harvest, field laborers often carry wet tobacco leaves under their arms, and the solubilized nicotine from the leaf is absorbed through the worker's skin. The resulting green tobacco sickness produces symptoms akin to a severe case of the flu.

A very fit and fast tobacco picker might make up to $20 an hour, but most make minimum wage, operating a mechanical harvester. The leaf-sticker machine has made it easier to sew leaves together to hang them on sticks. A setter, which is a machine pulled behind a tractor, has streamlined the transplanting and watering of seedlings. The biggest changes in recent years have included the introduction of a mechanical harvesting machine to pick the ripe leaves, and a new method of curing in large quantities. Twenty acres was once all a farm family could harvest. Now, three times that amount can be planted, though the profits are absorbed by the added costs of mechanization.

As a result, the small tobacco farmer is disappearing, and the surpluses caused by this new efficiency frequently cause the market price to drop. Still, a farmer can net between $800 and $1,000 an acre on tobacco, more than any other crop these farmers could grow. Tobacco growers were in trouble long before the public health warnings over cigarette smoking. Although the number of cigarette smokers is increasing worldwide, so is the number of countries producing cheap tobacco. More than half of South Carolina's crop is sold abroad, and that market is dwindling. Even U.S. cigarette makers are importing more foreign tobacco, mostly from Brazil.

The issues in the national debate over cigarette smoking, almost a social movement, are familiar to most readers—new taxes, labels warning that nicotine is addictive, smoking bans in most public places. In the fields and warehouses of the Pee Dee, where money from tobacco buys food, clothing, and shelter for thousands of South Carolinians, that debate is big news almost every day.

As Marion Fowler, 80-something patriarch of South Carolina's tobacco community and sales supervisor of the Lake City auction market, put to his fellows at a 1993 convention: "Tobacco is in trouble. I've been told by a top tobacco official that unless we can work out these problems, we might as well rent out our warehouses as skating rinks."

The tobacco economy, like those before it based on cotton and slavery, already knows that while it may continue to exist in some form, its heyday is over. In the fields of the Pee Dee, there's talk of learning how to grow asparagus, or maybe ornamental shrubbery, fresh flowers, and herbs for medicinal benefits.

Tobacco farming remains a mainstay of the economy of coastal-plain counties.

■ **CAROLINA BAYS AND SAND HILLS** *map page 169, A-1*

As tobacco, cotton, and other crops spread across the Pee Dee, farmers and, later, naturalists came across mysterious and huge elliptical depressions, some covering almost 2,000 acres. Every one of these egg-shaped formations lay on the land with one tip pointing northwest, the other southeast. Some of the depressions are dry, some are shallow lakes, and some are wet, dense swamps, but all have the same northwest–southeast alignment. They are found on the huge Atlantic coastal plain from New Jersey to Florida, but most of them, and the most defined ones, are found in the coastal plain of the Carolinas. At one time, 2,600 such depressions— called **Carolina Bays**—were documented in South Carolina's coastal plain, but agriculture, timbering, and development reduced that number to about 200 today. The most widely accepted theory for the existence of Carolina Bays is a meteorite shower that might have passed through the area millennia ago and impacted the coastal plain.

One of the largest bays has been preserved in a state park just east of I-95 and north of U.S. 378 near the Florence County town of Olanta. **Woods Bay State Park** (843-659-4445) is South Carolina's first all-nature state park, with no camping or playgrounds. There are picnic tables; a large aerial photograph of the 3-mile-long, mile-wide bay; canoe rentals and a canoe trail into the shallow black water of the swamp; and a 500-foot boardwalk reaching into the wetland.

Stone tools and bits of pottery from 10,000 years ago have been found on the rim of a Carolina Bay inside the huge federal reservation used by the Savannah River Site "bomb plant" in Aiken and Barnwell counties.

Another unusual feature of the Pee Dee terrain is the ancient sand hills, which rise several hundred feet above the northern edge of the Pee Dee, where the plain meets the fall line. These are the remains of sand dunes from when the ocean reached here 65 to 136 million years ago. The old dunes still exist all along the fall line from Fayetteville, North Carolina, south to Columbus, Georgia; they are best seen and most exposed along U.S. 1 for 30 miles south of Cheraw.

Reckless timbering and farming of the sand hills from 1900 to the 1930s left the dunes bare and eroded. The federal government bought nearly 90,000 acres of them during the 1930s as a relief program under the Resettlement Administration, relocating the landowners to more fertile farms elsewhere, then reforesting and restoring the land.

A summer microclimate makes winter an ideal time to visit the Carolina Sandhills Refuge.

Today, the **Carolina Sandhills National Wildlife Refuge** (843-335-8401) and the **Sand Hills State Forest** (843-498-6478) opposite each other on U.S. 1, are examples of a unique habitat and also of how social and ecological programs can succeed. Longleaf pines, although commercially logged, dominate the state forest. On the wildlife refuge the pines often give way to stretches of prickly pear, yucca, and Spanish bayonet.

Ducks and geese begin migratory stays here in late September, remaining through early April, and there are observation towers and a photo blind at two lakes on the refuge. The preserve also hosts one of the largest remaining populations of the relatively nondescript, but also endangered, red-cockaded woodpecker, which nests only in living pines suffering from red heart disease. Winter is the best time to visit the sand hills because they have a summer microclimate all their own. In daytime, the sand heats more rapidly than surrounding clay soils. Days are hot. At dusk and into the evening during the summer, the sand hills release their stored thermal energy into the atmosphere, producing more thunderstorms than nearby areas on either side.

■ **PEE DEE TOWNS** *map page 169, A/B-1*

The little towns of the Pee Dee are often thickly settled with well-kept antebellum and Victorian homes and historic districts. A 100-mile car trip off I-95 at Florence, then north on U.S. 52 to Cheraw, and a return via SC 9 to the interstate highway at Dillon offers a one-day overview of the 250-year-old agricultural society of the Pee Dee.

Florence, in the center of the Pee Dee and with a metro area population of 195,000, is the shopping, financial, and entertainment center of the region. Its growth began during the 1850s when three railroad lines converged on the settlement and made it a shipping hub to the cotton ports in Charleston and Wilmington, North Carolina. After Sherman burned Atlanta, nearly 18,000 Union prisoners from Andersonville, Georgia, were shipped to a makeshift prison here. Many of them perished in the poorly outfitted Florence Stockade, and they are buried as unknown soldiers in Florence National Cemetery. Here also is the grave of Florena Budwin, a Pennsylvania woman who disguised herself as a man in order to follow her husband, a Union captain. He died at Andersonville, and when she was transferred to Florence, the secret of her gender was uncovered by a Confederate doctor. She died in January 1865, the first female soldier buried in a national cemetery.

No other town in the Pee Dee has as many as 10,000 residents, a few have about 5,000, and most have fewer than 1,000, which is part of the Pee Dee's appeal. **Darlington** (population about 10,000) gets publicity for its twice-a-year, 500-mile stock-car races, but that is a fans' event. The famous raceway is bolstered by the largest collection of stock-car racers in the world inside the **Joe Weatherly Stock Car Museum and National Motorsports Press Association Hall of Fame** (803-395-8821). Both are off SC 34 in Darlington; for race times call 803-395-8821. The 60-acre **Williamson Park** on Spring Street in Darlington has a 5-mile boardwalk and trail through moss-draped swamplands planted in azaleas and camellias.

Just north of Dillon, on I-95 at the state line, a dubious notoriety beckons devotees of garish glitz to the hamlet of **South of the Border** (800-845-6011), which began in the 1950s as a motel named Pedro's on the old U.S. 301 route to Florida. Advertised on dozens of I-95 billboards in the old Burma Shave tradition (I never SAUSAGE a place! Keep yelling Kids! They'll Stop!), SOTB has a sombrero-shaped restaurant, adult bookstores, a golf course, an RV park, and an all-night wedding chapel that requires no blood test and attracts amorous couples throughout the South.

Fifteen miles north on U.S. 52, Society Hill (population 900) typifies the communities settled by Welsh Baptists during the colonial era in South Carolina. The little town, established in 1747 on a hill overlooking the Great Pee Dee River, is known for its **1822 library** (843-378-0026) and **1834 Trinity Church.**

Ten miles farther north, **Cheraw State Park** (843-537-9656) is one of the oldest and largest in South Carolina. It has an 18-hole golf course, fully furnished rental cabins, lakes for swimming, boating, and fishing, and campsites.

The historic town of **Cheraw** (population 6,000) is 5 miles beyond the park. Founded as a trading post around 1740, it became a commercial shipping center owing to its location at the head of navigable waters on the Great Pee Dee. The 1744 **Old St. David's Episcopal Church** (843-537-8425) was used as a Revolutionary War hospital, and the town once had a huge cotton market. Jazz trumpeter Dizzy Gillespie was born here in 1917 and attended Wesley United Methodist Church when he was a child. Today, Cheraw is known for its antiques market and a large downtown historic district of more than 50 antebellum mansions, gardens, and colonial buildings.

The old farm town of **Bennettsville** (population 10,000, founded 1819) is about a 15-mile drive south from Cheraw on SC 9. Once wealthy from cotton, the town is known today for its shaded neighborhoods of Victorian and antebellum homes.

The nearby village of **Clio** (population 882), founded in the early 19th century, reached its golden age when cotton was king and its barons built palaces here. Many of these mansions remain, as does **A. L. Calhoun's Store,** built in 1905 and seemingly frozen as it was in 1925, when the Depression first hit the Pee Dee.

■ SANTEE COOPER COUNTRY   *map page 169, B/C-3*

Cotton fields in full bloom are a rare sight today in this state; this crop is now produced in greater quantities by California and Texas. Patches of cotton are grown in most of the state, but most of the remains of the old cotton kingdom in South Carolina is in **Santee Cooper Country.** The region is a strip of the coastal plain along the northwesterly route of I-26 from north of Charleston to south of Columbia, including Orangeburg County, the state's top cotton producer.

Santee Cooper Country gets its name from a huge hydroelectricity project built by the U.S. Army Corps of Engineers. In 1939 the Corps of Engineers began building two dams on two of South Carolina's historic rivers just 20 miles apart, the Santee and the Cooper, in a swampy region 50 miles inland from the Atlantic coast, near the town of Moncks Corner.

Bass-fishing guide Erwin Wright (above) cruises an inlet of Lake Marion (left).

Santee Cooper, a state-owned electric utility, is the fourth-largest public power utility in the nation today. One of every three South Carolinians receives electricity either directly from Santee Cooper or from one of the 15 electric cooperatives that buy their power from the utility.

When the project was completed in 1941, it created two of the largest reservoirs in South Carolina. The southern one, **Lake Moultrie,** is at the headwaters of the Cooper River. The other, just north of Lake Moultrie and connected to it by a 6-mile canal, is **Lake Marion,** on the Santee River.

The clear, olive-colored waters of the lakes, sometimes blending into swamps along their shores, are famous for freshwater fishing, annually producing world-record catches. Because neither lake bottom was fully cleared of stumps and trees before the floodgates were closed and the reservoirs filled, Moultrie and Marion are havens for species such as striped bass, crappie, bream, white and largemouth bass, and catfish.

Lakeside communities such as Rimini, Santee, Pineville, Cross, and Bonneau, and sprawling 2,500-acre Santee State Park, specialize in supplying anglers.

Both lakes are relatively shallow, and neither ices over in winter, so, weather permitting, fishing is year-round. Moultrie, the smaller of the two at 60,400 acres, is also the more open, its waters 14 miles across at one point. The northern Lake Marion, 110,600 acres, narrows as it leads to the Wateree and Congaree rivers (which form the Santee River).

Experts say the best time for fishing the lakes' renowned striped bass is in spring, when the fish swim north from Moultrie, through the diversion canal to Marion, then up the Wateree and Congaree rivers. Live herring is the recommended bait. There are scores of experts, guides, fish camps, restaurants, and lodgings all around the lakes. One of the prime fishing havens is **Santee State Park** (803-854-2408) on Lake Marion's western shore just north of the I-95 bridge. The park has 30 cabins, some on land, others on piers over the lake; 150 campsites; fishing and pedal-boat rentals; and a swimming lake, boat ramp, tackle shop, hiking trails, tennis courts, and a restaurant.

Across Lake Marion and just south of the I-95 bridge is **Santee National Wildlife Refuge** (803-478-2217). The refuge, on the east bank of the lake, has a 1-mile, self-guided wildlife trail and from November through February is a vantage point from which to view wintering flocks of Canada geese and 17 other species of migratory waterfowl.

A cotton press squeezes oil from cotton seeds.

CAROLINA COTTON

In the springtime cotton is planted in rows, and by late summer the plants reach their mature height of about 3 feet. Then, at varying times from field to field, the plant flowers in an instant into a creamy, yellow blossom. The next day the flowers turn pink, and before the end of the third day, they fall to the ground, leaving a tiny green boll, or seed pod, which will grow to the size of a hen's egg. When ripe, it bursts open, revealing white fibers.

Early in the fall, the plants are defoliated, leaving only the boll and stem for harvesters to pick. The boll is two-thirds seed and one-third fiber (or lint), and the task is to separate the seeds of the boll from the fibers and spin the fibers into thread—a process that's been going on with various degrees of success since ancient times.

Cotton has been cultivated in southern Asia for 2,000 years, was known to the ancient Greeks, and by the time of Columbus's voyage to America was well established among indigenous cultures from the West Indies to Mexico to Peru and Brazil. When a new spinning jenny and power loom came into use in England between 1767 and 1790 the Industrial Revolution was roaring to life, and a great maritime nation such as England had the ships to import raw cotton, process it quickly and efficiently, then market it around the world. This capability in turn created a huge new demand for raw cotton, a need happily filled by farmers from the American South.

It was in the South that another new invention made the cotton easier to process. Before downy white cotton fibers can be sold and spun into thread, they have to be cleaned, and as seeds comprise two-thirds of the cotton boll, this can be a time-consuming process. In early days, large numbers of slaves were used to separate the fibers from the seeds by hand. Then in 1793, Eli Whitney invented his cotton gin— a revolving, toothed cylinder that caught the fibers and pulled them though a grate with openings too small for the seeds to pass through.

If this process has by now been further refined, you'll nevertheless find the country roads of South Carolina every fall, full of tall, wire-sided and -topped cages and flatbed trucks heading to the scores of cotton gins. There, the cleaned fibers are compressed into huge bales weighing 500 pounds, wrapped in coarse burlap, bound with steel strips, and shipped, eventually, to mills.

Modern cotton gins often allow casual visitors (just stop and ask) to watch the seeds and fibers being separated. Every pound of cotton ginned also results in 2 pounds of cotton seed, and this, too, is valuable. When squeezed under a hydraulic press at processing plants, the seed yields an oil that is refined and used in cooking, in making oleomargarine and lard, and in making soaps. The husks also are used as a rich food for farm animals and as a fertilizer.

■ SANTEE COTTON COUNTRY

Cotton and slavery raced inland from their origins on the Sea Islands, where the silky, longer-fibered cotton was cultivated, and from the coastal river plantations. For more than a century before the dams were built and the lakes created, cotton spread though the region, on plantations along the Santee, Congaree, Wateree, Pocotaligo, Black, and Edisto rivers.

With the cotton also came communities and growth.

Branchville (at U.S. 78 and U.S. 21), in the southern tip of Orangeburg County, grew during the 1830s around what is the oldest railroad junction in America. The town of 1,100 has a railroad museum and festival held the last weekend in September to celebrate the nation's first scheduled railroad. It began running Christmas Day 1830, between the cotton port of Charleston and the spreading cotton fields inland. The South Carolina Canal & Railroad Company's first locomotive, *The Best Friend of Charleston,* blew up one year later when its fireman, annoyed with the hissing steam from the safety valve, closed it. He blew up with the engine. Sherman and his army marched through here in 1865 and destroyed the junction, but the depot has a nice museum about its history.

Orangeburg, settled during the 1730s by German immigrants from Pennsylvania who named it after William, Prince of Orange, boomed as a cotton market and commercial center on the North Edisto River; Orangeburg County today is the state's top cotton producer. Now a town of about 14,000, Orangeburg is a beautiful town with huge oaks between lovely historic homes. Orangeburg also holds one of the oldest September county fairs and has the **Edisto Memorial Gardens** (803-533-6020), a 150-acre testing ground in the All American Rose selection process. This is also where 500 Confederate troops camped to defend the bridge against the Union army advance, although they eventually retreated. Along with roses, there are masses of azaleas, camellias, wisteria, dogwoods, and crabapples.

Also in Orangeburg is Claflin College (founded in 1869 by Methodists) and South Carolina State University, which was founded in 1896 as the Colored Normal, Agricultural, and Industrial College. Today, SCSU includes the state's largest planetarium and an art museum with African and African-American works. The university is a bright spot in the otherwise dismal history of higher education involving African-Americans in South Carolina.

Orangeburg is also the site of the 1968 massacre by state troopers and National Guardsmen that wounded many and claimed the lives of three African-Americans during a civil rights protest in front of a "whites-only" bowling alley.

Dogwoods and azaleas in full bloom at the Edisto Memorial Gardens.

Sumter (population 45,000), at the headwaters of the Pocotaligo River and halfway between the cotton plantations along the Black and Wateree rivers, was a major cotton center. The 150-acre **Swan Lake Iris Gardens** (803-436-2640) has seven species of swans and 25 types of iris. In spring, its dark swamp-water lake is surrounded by vivid Dutch and Japanese iris. Cotton fortunes built the 1845 Victorian mansion called the **Williams-Brice House,** part of the Sumter County Museum complex (122 North Washington Street; 803-775-0908), as well as the antebellum home of the late artist Elizabeth White. The palatial 1890s stone **Sumter Opera House** (803-436-2616) is another landmark of the boom era.

Mary McLeod Bethune, who founded what became Bethune-Cookman College in Daytona Beach, Florida, in 1904 and was its president for 38 years before becoming an advisor to President Franklin D. Roosevelt, was born and raised in the small (population 700) cotton-farm town of Mayesville by the Black River in Sumter County.

Brigadier General Thomas Sumter, nicknamed the Gamecock for his harassment of British forces during the Revolution, was the namesake for the city of Sumter.

Driving from one to another of these Santee Cooper Country towns, you'll occasionally see long-abandoned tenant farmers' shacks standing forlornly in fields, ghostly reminders of how freed slaves and poor whites lived for almost a century after the Civil War. These two- or three-room houses were primitive, without water, sewer, or electricity.

Some tenant farmers worked for a small salary, but most labored in exchange for their shack, a garden spot, and a small percentage of the profit on the crop they harvested—cotton. The tenant, also called a sharecropper, was dependent upon the landowner for a livelihood, and the landowner dependent upon the tenant for labor. The system began to collapse after World War II, when many tenants began moving to northern cities in search of better-paying work.

■ SUMMERTON AND SCHOOL DESEGREGATION

During the 1950s, as new kinds of farm machinery spread through Santee Cooper Country's cotton farms, tens of thousands of African-Americans still living in the region found themselves out of work. Their children's segregated schools were so inferior to white public schools that they barely functioned—meaning the children would have no education and no jobs, either. And yet from this dire predicament arose one of the least known but most historic legal rulings in the history of both South Carolina and the nation.

On the north side of Lake Marion near Summerton (take U.S. 15 to St. Paul, then go north 1 mile on Road 373) in Clarendon County is the **Liberty Hill AME Church** (803-478-4812), built in 1905. Parents began meeting and organizing there to discuss desegregation and eventually contacted the South Carolina branch of the NAACP. Nineteen members of the Liberty Hill AME congregation, all of them parents, became plaintiffs in a suit first known as ***Briggs et. al. v. Elliot and the Summerton Public School System.*** The parents contended that so long as the public schools were segregated by race, their children's education would suffer— that, in fact, separate schools would always be unequal and must be declared unconstitutional.

The suit was heard in federal district court in Charleston in 1952. Their lawyer from the NAACP was Thurgood Marshall, who would go on in 1967 to become the first African-American appointed to sit on the Supreme Court.

The Summerton/Clarendon County case was merged with similar appeals from other states to become *Brown v. Board of Education,* and in 1954, the Supreme Court outlawed segregated schools.

Thirty miles east of Liberty Hill AME, in the cotton and tobacco town of **Kingstree** on U.S. 52 in Williamsburg County, granite monuments to Marshall and to Dr. Martin Luther King Jr. were dedicated on the county courthouse grounds in 1993. The county's population is 60 percent black, and in recent years its black residents gained political control, including offices such as county-school superintendent. However, the desperately poor county's taxes are paid mostly by its white residents, who remain the largest employers and landowners and who send their children to virtually all-white private schools. As elsewhere in the state, the county school district is almost 90 percent black and has little support from whites on matters such as bond issues to build new schools.

The Liberty Hill AME parents who brought suit in 1952 were grandparents by the time Clarendon County schools finally desegregated during the 1970s. When that occurred, whites abandoned the public school system in Clarendon, and by 1994 the historic school district had a 98 percent black enrollment, with the state's lowest test scores and the highest number of students from impoverished families.

The Clarendon, Williamsburg, Sumter, and Orangeburg counties of the Santee Cooper Country have among the highest unemployment rates (around 10 percent) in the state, and a high percentage of their citizens receive federal food stamps for the poor. The same story, about jobs, food stamps, schools, and race relations, exists all across the agricultural coastal plain.

African-Americans hold elected and appointed offices throughout South Carolina, from mayors of small farm towns to chief justice of the state supreme court to members of the state legislature. South Carolina's first black congressman since Reconstruction was elected in 1992 from the Pee Dee. Yet in every small town across the coastal plain, small groups of young, middle-aged, and elderly black men, poorly educated and unemployed, spend their days idling in parking lots of crossroads country stores.

■ Swamps: A Wet Wilderness

South Carolina encompasses more swampland than any state except Louisiana, and almost all of it is within the coastal plain. The Great Swamp, which once spread across much of the Lowcountry, was eventually drained for farming and exists now in countless patches of smaller swampland throughout the area.

Of these hundreds of small swamps, some are barely noticed, such as Pudding Swamp in the Pee Dee along U.S. 378 west of Turbeville. Yet each has its glories, such as the cathedral majesty of the bald cypress, kin to the redwood and sequoia, in the internationally renowned Congaree Swamp National Monument south of Columbia. Salkehatchie Swamp is where the Coosa Indians once lived (near Yemassee in the southern tip of the state); at Wambaw Swamp on the lower Santee River the early French Huguenots settled; and there's also Four Holes Swamp, Pee Dee Swamp, Wateree Swamp, and swamps whose names are only known by the people who live nearby.

Francis Beidler Forest is home to the largest remaining virgin stand of bald cypress and tupelo gum trees in the world.

There are shallow-water swamps of shrub-like willows, alder, oak, maple, and water hickory, and there are deep-water swamps of bald cypress, tupelo gum, and the epiphytic Spanish moss.

Francis Beidler Forest and Congaree Swamp National Monument are two of the most splendid and readily accessible parks preserving the subtle grandeur and the haunting beauty of wet wilderness. Both parks are most comfortably visited from late fall to early spring, when bird visibility is high and insect populations are low.

■ FRANCIS BEIDLER FOREST *map page 169, B-3*

The **Four Holes Swamp,** fed by springs and rainfall, meanders for more than 60 miles, from Lake Marion near the village of **Cameron** (U.S. 176 and SC 33) to the Edisto River near **Givhans Ferry State Park** (SC 27 and SC 61; 843-873-0692). Since Four Holes depends mostly upon rainfall, its water levels fluctuate with the seasons. In winter and spring, the swamp is a shallow river, and in summer and fall it shrinks to a series of creeks and ponds.

Within this swampland, the 5,800 acres of the Francis Beidler Forest contain the largest remaining virgin stand of bald cypress and tupelo gum trees in the world. Many of the cypress sentinels are 1,000 years old or older.

A visitors center, staff naturalists, and a mile-and-a-half boardwalk are open Tuesday through Saturday, 9 AM to 5 PM. There is no camping, nor food facilities, and canoe trips, night walks, and other explorations of the preserve are available only by reservation and in season.

The National Audubon Society manages the Beidler Forest, which is named for the wealthy lumberman and conservationist who preserved it from logging. Unconventional for his time, Francis Beidler allowed much of his timber to stay untouched. After his death in 1924, his family continued to preserve the area, and during the late 1960s, with the liquidation of the estate, local conservationists and the Nature Conservancy acquired the land as a sanctuary.

Francis Beidler Forest is in Four Holes Swamp, just off I-26 near Harleyville, 40 miles northwest of Charleston. For information, call 843-462-2150.

■ CONGAREE SWAMP NATIONAL MONUMENT *map page 169, A-3*

Congaree Swamp National Monument, 20 miles southeast of Columbia (on SC 48) and just north of Lake Marion on the Congaree River, is more a floodplain than a swamp. Its 22,000 acres include six bald cypresses believed to be the largest in the nation, in what is the largest tract of old-growth bottomland hardwoods.

Kayaking in the Congaree Swamp.

More than 90 species of trees have been identified in the Congaree Swamp, and half the preserve has never been logged. A boardwalk, five hiking trails ranging from 1 to 10 miles, and canoeing routes make the Congaree accessible to visitors, and more than 94,000 a year, including scientists from around the world, tour the unique ecosystem. In 1983, the United Nations designated the swamp an International Biosphere Reserve. For information, call 803-776-4396.

■ **SAVANNAH RIVER CORRIDOR** *map page 169, A-4/5*

South Carolina's diversity reveals itself most dramatically along the 100 miles paralleling the historic **Savannah River,** from the thick pine forests of Jasper County in the southern tip of the state to the mansions and stables built by Vanderbilts, Astors, Whitneys, and Hitchcocks in the fall-line town of Aiken.

Sleepy railroad hamlets follow the rails in a straight line through the pines. Grocers sell less and less feed, seed, and groceries to a dwindling number of customers. Locals find work at the sawmill and hope maybe a sock plant (yes, as in socks for your feet) will come along.

SUMMERS OUT ON THE PORCH

That was the summer it was so hot the katydids failed to sing and everyone spent their evenings out on the porch with large glasses of ice tea and damp hand towels to cool the back of the neck. Alma wouldn't even start cooking until after the sun had gone down. Twilight came on early, though, a long-drawn-out dimming of the heat and glare that made everything soft and magical, brought out the first fireflies, and added a cool enchantment to the metallic echoes of the slide guitar playing on Alma's kitchen radio. Granny would plant herself in the porch rocker, leaving Alma's girls to pick through snap beans, hope for a rainstorm, and tease her into telling stories.

I always positioned myself behind Granny, up against the wall next to the screen door, where I could listen to Kitty Wells and George Jones, the whine of that guitar and what talk there was in the kitchen, as well as the sound of Aunt Alma's twin boys thumping their feet against the porch steps and the girls' giggles as their fingers slipped through the cool, dusty beans.

—Dorothy Allison, *Bastard out of Carolina*, 1992

At the end of the corridor, **Aiken County,** perhaps after Charleston the most historic part of South Carolina, seems simply to line up and present one jarring contrast after another: cotton-mill hands, the richest men in America, pit mines for kaolin clay, bucolic pastures for Kentucky Derby champions.

In the antebellum South of cotton and slavery, paddlewheel steamboats regularly navigated the Savannah River all along this corridor. There were a score or more steamboat landings they called upon, no more than riverine whistlestops. Not so much as a hamlet grew along the river between the paddlewheelers' two destinations, the seaport of Savannah and the inland port of Augusta, both in Georgia, although dams controlling the flood plain are now opening the valley to development.

Railroads, beginning with the oldest railroad in the nation, created almost every town in this corner of the state. They are not factory railroad towns, nor wheat and cattle railroad towns, but simply rural railroad towns that used the trains as truckers, and tourists use the interstate highways of today.

From an airplane, it seems as though the entire corridor is a forest, interrupted only occasionally by plowed fields, orchards, and a few commercial blocks.

The stars appear to whirl above a pine-tree plantation in this time-exposure photograph.

■ TREE FARMS

Timber and pulpwood stands—not so much forests as they are tree farms, planted in rows like cotton or tobacco plants—cover thousands of square miles across the coastal plain. Most of them are loblolly or longleaf pines. They grow quickly and resist disease.

The natural pine belt stretches from Horry County in the tobacco country of the Pee Dee, through the cotton fields of Santee Cooper Country, to the Savannah River. The belt covers nearly 60 percent of the entire state, but unlike in western states, only 5 percent of South Carolina's forests are federal lands. About 22 percent of the forest is owned by forest-industry corporations. Another 68 percent is owned by individuals, most of whom lease their land, or sell their tree crops, to corporate buyers.

In the Lowcountry counties of Jasper and Hampton, there was never much else to the economy but what came out of the pine forests, which was not a lot of money. However, for the past two decades, the nation's major source of lumber for construction and paper pulpwood has been shifting from the forests of the Pacific Northwest to the tree farms of the southeastern states. In South Carolina, tree farms are now a multibillion-dollar industry, and most of that industry is within the coastal plain.

Throughout the Lowcountry, small family farms have disappeared and have been replaced not by larger farms but by facilities for corporate tree harvesting. However, the industry does not require a lot of workers. Most of the profits come from selling the trees or their products, not from the residuals of local payrolls. Unless there is a sawmill, or a paper plant, the forest-products industry creates few jobs, and most of those pay little.

■ HUNTING PLANTATIONS

For a growing number, what's left is another niche in the outdoor-sports industry: hunting plantations.

Perhaps the densest deer-per-acre population in the nation is along the Savannah River Corridor of South Carolina, especially in the Lowcountry. The state also has the longest deer-hunting season in the nation as well as liberal bag limits. A 1991 survey by Clemson University estimated that recreational hunting adds about $240 million a year to the state's economy. In some counties, such as Jasper, hunting income has surpassed that of agriculture in the local economy.

One of the first to convert his farm and forest into a hunting plantation was Joe Bostick, whose 5,000-acre plantation is near the Hampton County town of **Estill** (U.S. 321 and SC 3). Bostick's forebears farmed the plantation from the time it was given to them by King George III in 1769. Falling livestock and crop prices during the 1970s led Bostick to consider other uses for his land, and a commercial hunting operation was the idea he settled upon.

Now, about 500 hunters a year pay to shoot deer, turkey, quail, and wild boar on Bostick's plantation. They pay roughly $500 a day to stay in the three-story plantation-style lodge he built in 1980, and they get not only hunting privileges but also servants and fine dining.

Hunting is an old, stylized, and almost formal tradition in South Carolina. Plantation families depended upon hunting for part of their food supply and made hunts into social gatherings. Before 1800, planters along the Santee and Cooper rivers had formed two of the oldest hunt clubs in the state—St. John's and St. Stephens. The St. John's by-laws required each member in turn to supply the seasonal or monthly club meeting with:

> A barbecued shoat or sheep, a ham or piece of salt beef, a turkey, two fowls or two ducks, two loaves of bread, and in the season, potatoes, a half bushel of rice, pepper, salt, mustard and vinegar, one bottle of rum, half gallon of brandy, and one dozen of good wine. Pipes and tobacco, or one hundred segars, one dozen tumblers and two dozen wine glasses.

The hunt clubs founded on old rice plantations during the 1910s and 1920s by wealthy northerners, as well as those established by South Carolinians, preserved their lands from development and saved thousands of acres of wildlife habitat. The ACE Basin project is an example.

■ **SAVANNAH RIVER SITE**   *map page 169, A-4/5*
In the Savannah River Corridor of the coastal plain, the pine forest often seems ubiquitous along any road going inland and north along I-95 from the small towns of Walterboro, Ridgeland, and Hardeeville. For long stretches of highway, pines, small farms, and fading, old farm towns present a life of apparent somnambulism. There is one highway route through the corridor, however, that is scenic and fascinating at every mile, a literal drive through history and current events.

From **Estill,** in Hampton County, drive north on SC 3 for about 30 miles through **Allendale County.** The highway has little traffic and plenty of small, prosperous farms and pastures and bucolic churches. A few decades ago, most of the coastal-plain farms still looked like these.

At the intersection of SC 3 and SC 125, turn left and follow 125 into and through the site of one of the most remarkable industrial facilities in the nation. This is the **Savannah River Site,** run by the U.S. Department of Energy, constructed in the early 1950s by the old Atomic Energy Commission, and covering more than 300 square miles in Barnwell and Aiken counties, from the Savannah River inland for 25 miles.

The "bomb plant," as it is known locally, produced tritium and plutonium for the nation's hydrogen bombs until the late 1980s, when the end of the Cold War curbed the demand for more of those two "bang" ingredients.

When it was built, a dozen little farm towns and scores of farms were moved, or razed, and within months, the economy and pace of life changed thoroughly in towns all around the plant, including Aiken, Barnwell, and North Augusta, where thousands of technicians, engineers, and scientists from around the nation came to live. The plant's future is unsettled. Its five giant, weapons-grade nuclear reactors and other processing facilities are too old to safely operate again without costly repairs, and there no longer is a market for their products. Uncounted millions of gallons of radioactive waste remain on the site, some deadly on exposure, others merely hazardous. No other spot in the nation seems willing to accept these wastes in "permanent" storage, and it is possible the vast site will become a nuclear waste dump, requiring close monitoring for thousands of years. The University of Georgia operates a lab and monitors the wildlife in the area, where turtles and alligators survive in an irradiated mutation.

■ **AIKEN COUNTY HISTORY** *map page 169, A-5*
The presence of the "bomb plant" is only one unusual element in the history of Aiken County. A dark side of that history, and a beautiful place to visit, is about 10 miles north of the Savannah River Site near the community of Beech Island. Turn right off SC 125 onto U.S. 278, and about 2 miles down that highway is **Redcliffe Plantation State Park** (803-827-1473).

The antebellum plantation mansion, with many of its original furnishings still on display, was completed in 1859 by James Henry Hammond, for whom the term "scoundrel" may have been coined.

EXTREMELY STYLISH

[Dear Mother]

I might almost have staid at Silverton, for anything that I saw of the Bride. We got to Redcliffe about half past ten o'c, and she came down stairs a few minutes before 1 o'c, after having been sent for repeatedly, to see some of the neighbors who had called to see her. When she finally appeared, she entered the room, led by the "Proud husband," gave us all a sweeping bow, and curtsy, said a very fashionable, clipped off "good morning," took her seat, next to Dr. Cook, and began with much manner, and emphasis to apologize for her delay in coming down, being at the moment when he called in the act of "disrobing." This form of expression, which I heard, without exaggeration, three times afterwards, seemed the only appropriate one, for the removal of such fine clothes as those she had on then, and as I heard had worn since she came. She was dressed in a white swiss muslin flounced, with a low neck and short sleeves, and a cape of the same, trimmed with the richest valenciennes three or four inches wide. She had on too the handsomest diamonds I think I ever saw and a belt which I am sure was solid gold with gold and enamelled knobs in front, added to this a crimson and gold net on her hair, and a crimson silk fan. She looked extremely stylish, but as you may suppose, utterly out of place and keeping with the time and place and people around her. She was perfectly easy and self-possessed, and has evidently lived in a certain gay fashionable watering-place society, in which they say she was a belle. I was agreeably surprised in her appearance, for except that she has bad teeth, I think she is decidedly fine looking. Gen. and Mrs Hammond seem very much pleased with her, and Mrs. Paul [Loula Comer Hammond] is perfectly carried away. Catty is by no means so enthusiastic. For myself, she did not impress me as having the right style or finish. Indeed she seemed to me rather a "flash article." This opinion however is to be received with allowance, as Mr. Hammond intimates with a degree of earnestness which mortifies me not a little that I am envious of the notice and attention she received, and you know that I am unfortunatley not superior to that weakness. I think tho' that I felt more, the superb indifference with which she treated me thro' the day. I am rather afraid, that she must have mistaken me for the Baby's nurse. . . .

—Emily C. Hammond to her mother, Julia A. Cumming, 1861

Elected to the U.S. House in 1835, then as governor in 1843, and in 1857 to the U.S. Senate, Hammond is best known for his 1858 Senate speech in which he warned the Northern states: "No, you dare not make war on cotton. No power on earth dares make war on it. Cotton is king." His lesser-known pronouncements included: "Slaves are the mudsills of society" and women were created "to breed . . . and serve as toys for the recreation of men."

Hammond made a name for himself after marrying a homely 16-year-old heiress to several plantations. Their marriage was rocky after Mrs. Hammond's four nieces returned home from a visit and told their father that Henry had fondled them to "all but the last degree." Mrs. Hammond again moved away to protest the presence of her husband's slave mistress, refusing to live at Redcliffe while the other woman was there. Hammond, like so many other planters with a second, black family, was in effect passionate about the continuing enslavement of his own offspring.

Hammond's mansion, restored during the 1940s and 1950s by a descendant, John Shaw Billings, then editor-director of Time, Inc., is often used for weddings and is rented by the state parks department for similar social events.

An even older part of South Carolina's history, the state's oldest Baptist church is about 5 miles from Hammond's old plantation. Founded by white settlers in 1750, it was turned over to slaves in 1773 and is still going strong. Through nearly 250 years, the congregation has been forced to move its church three times, spurring the start of other churches but retaining its history.

Silver Bluff Missionary Baptist Church (803-827-0706) is on the western (river) side of SC 125, in Beech Island, on U.S. 278.

The first large-scale cotton mill and mill town in the South are about 5 miles farther north in **Horse Creek Valley.** Most of the old cotton and textile mills that filled this valley between Aiken and Augusta, Georgia, closed during recent years. The only one in operation today is the one that began it all, historic Graniteville Mills, now **Avondale Mills Inc.,** in Graniteville (6 miles west of Aiken, off U.S. 1). The mill and its company-owned village were founded in 1845, and much of both remain in **Graniteville's National Historic District.** Here you can still find the 1846 canal, as well as the original 1849 mill and 26 original mill-hand houses— their early Gothic Revival exteriors virtually unaltered. Also here is the 1847 academy built for mill children, and the 1849 St. John's Methodist Church.

Graniteville was built by William Gregg, who came to South Carolina from Pennsylvania in 1824 at the age of 24 and quickly built a fortune as a jewelry craftsman and merchant in Charleston. Gregg was a pioneer in many ways, urging the development of cotton mills along the creeks and streams where the coastal plain meets the fall line (the swifter streams of the Piedmont region to the north, however, attracted most of the mill investors).

Gregg envisioned mills as a place of employment for poor whites, and unlike most of his contemporaries, he refused to employ children under age 12. He also enforced compulsory school attendance for his employees' children in the academy he built.

Graniteville Mills was acquired by Avondale Mills Inc. in 1996 and is still thriving—sales exceed $500 million per year, with 3,600 employees. Its principal product is indigo-dyed denim, used in blue jeans marketed under Levi Strauss, Lee, and other labels.

■ **AIKEN COLONY** *map page 169, A-4/5*
During the 1840s, Gregg owned about 5,000 acres on the large hill—**Kalmia Hill**—at what are now the western town limits of Aiken where U.S. 1 enters the town.

When the Charleston merchants and cotton brokers built their railroad across the coastal plain in 1833, they used it not only to facilitate cotton trade from Augusta and Savannah but also to provide a cool, dry escape from Charleston's summers of humidity and malaria. **Aiken,** established during the 1830s and named for the railroad's president, became their summer resort, and a colony of regulars developed. Gregg was among the first.

The South's defeat in the Civil War left the Charleston merchants too poor to summer in Aiken anymore, but during the 1880s the town began attracting a new winter colony of wealthy northerners.

Legend has it that a frail heiress with prominent relatives in New Orleans and New York began living in Aiken for health reasons, and she fell in love with the place. When Louise Eustis married the prominent and wealthy New York sportsman Thomas Hitchcock, she informed him they would be spending a lot of time in Aiken. The couple began bringing their crowd with them for the winters

Vanderbilts, Whitneys, Mellons, Astors, and others followed the Hitchcocks to Aiken every November and stayed through March. The town began calling itself the Newport of the South. By 1935, the winter colony had nearly 100 new mansions, with horse stables, training tracks, polo fields, steeplechase courses, and a golf course. After her husband, Tommy, died, Louise Hitchcock started a polo

The Highland Park Hotel in Aiken was one of the first grand resorts of the area when it was built in 1869.

school. The colony's heyday passed after World War II, although the estates and stables have been renovated in recent years by new waves of northerners.

During its height, there often were as many as 80 private Pullman cars sitting on the railroad siding in Aiken. A regular sleeper train made nightly departures from New York to Aiken during the season, sometimes adding as many as 50 extra cars and pulling a special freight of 60 cars to carry horses and tack.

The colony became so well known that no further explanation was necessary for a 1937 cartoon published by the *New Yorker* portraying a smartly dressed matron stepping off a train and sighing, "Aiken, my Aiken."

Streets were left unpaved (and many still are) for the comfort of horses' hooves. Broughams and Victorias with their matched teams were a familiar sight throughout town during the mild winters. One coach-and-four, bearing Joseph Wilshire, heir to the Fleishman yeast fortune, often rounded corners in the downtown shopping district while its liveried footman sounded a flourish on trumpets.

A 1898 inn, **The Willcox**, was made famous by the likes of Franklin D. Roosevelt, Winston Churchill, John Barrymore, and Fred Astaire. Closed for more

Two of the nation's most famed horse-racing and breeding grounds flourish in Aiken and Camden.

The Willcox can count Franklin Roosevelt and Winston Churchill among its many famous guests.

than 40 years, the inn reopened in 1985. For lodging or a meal, this is a good spot to stop and get the flavor of the old colony; 803-648-1898.

The town still thrills to the old colony gossip. There was Sabrina, cook for the Grace family (Bethlehem Steel) who insisted her string beans all be the same length and, naturally, not cut. It took **Fulmer's Market** three bushels to get one bushel she liked. There was Catherine, cook for the Iselin family (fine china) who insisted her leg of lamb orders be filled only with left legs. She said the right legs would be tough, since lambs would stand more of their weight on the right than the left.

The 177 mansions, estates, and "cottage" neighborhoods of the winter colony make up three National Historic Districts in Aiken. Their presence—even though nearly all the colony members themselves are long gone—gives the town a charm unlike any other in South Carolina.

What equestrians such as the Hitchcocks and the colony also gave to Aiken, and through it to other parts of South Carolina, is a thoroughbred industry valued today at about $300 million. Some of the most famous thoroughbred racing champions in history have trained in Aiken and still do, traditionally from the late fall to early spring, racing the colors of the nation's most famed stables.

The horses, stables, trainers, jockeys, and owners, from Kelso to Pleasant Colony, are commemorated, with their photographs, racing silks, and trophies, at the **Aiken Thoroughbred Hall of Fame**, open afternoons in the heart of the winter colony district on the grounds of the old **Iselin Estate** (803-642-7630).

The estate, donated to the town by the late Mrs. Iselin, includes 14 acres of gardens and ponds, including a "touch-and-scent" trail with plaques in Braille. Concerts and plays are given Monday evenings on the grounds during the summer. Next door, the **Carriage Museum** (803-642-7630) has a collection of vintage horse-drawn carriages. Several of the grand homes are now open to the public, such as the 1900 Rose Hill College, the 1931 Banksia, and the 1905 Rye Patch.

Although horses are trained in Aiken throughout the year, the principal season for the major stables is the same as the old social season for the colony: November through March. This is when you will find polo games most Sunday afternoons. Visitors are welcome to lean on the track railing early on weekday mornings and watch the training sprints and exercise rides.

A variety of equestrian events, from shows to drag hunts, enlivens **Hitchcock Woods** (803-642-0528), at 2,000 acres the largest urban nature preserve in the nation, near downtown Aiken. The woods have miles of public trails for hikes, strolls, or horseback riding (but not bicycles) and, on three weekends in March, the Aiken Triple Crown. Rokeby Stable's Sea Hero won the 1993 Kentucky Derby, R. J. Key Stable's American Winner won the 1993 Hambletonian, and Dogwood Stable's Summer Squall and Storm Song won the 1990 Preakness and the 1996 Breeder's Cup, respectively.

■ MIDLANDS

In 1786, South Carolina's feuding factions of coastal planters and merchants against Upcountry settlers chose a compromise site for relocating the state capital from Charleston. This was an unpopulated tract of 2 square miles at the confluence of the Broad and Saluda rivers, which together form the Congaree.

The location seemed ideal for pleasing both parties: almost exactly in the geographic center of South Carolina. As often is the case with any compromise, however, the result was problematic. The legislature had selected a place hardly anyone wanted to visit.

■ COLUMBIA *map page 169, A-3 and map page 205*
Until relatively recently, the primary entertainment in the capital city, immediately christened **Columbia,** was the annual session of the legislature itself. Built solely around the state bureaucracy and later, in 1801, home to the University of South Carolina, Columbia became a ghost town every weekend as its residents found more interesting places to spend their free time.

George Washington passed through Columbia in 1791, but his impressions are not recorded. The man who sold the property to the state to build its capital, Thomas Taylor, himself lamented: "They spoiled a damned fine plantation to make a damned poor town."

The city's remarkable moments came in February 1865, when Gen. William T. Sherman's Union troops burned 80 blocks of its downtown to the ground and shot up whatever was left. Six bronze stars on the Classical (1855) blue granite **State House** (803-734-2430) at Main Street and Gervais mark where shells made direct hits. After much publicity, the Confederate flag was removed from the dome in 2002 and is now displayed on the grounds near a statue of the late senator Strom Thurmond. A tour of this building, offered weekdays, reveals fine marble floors, balconies with brass railings, and mahogany woodwork, as well as a chance to hear about the building's history.

Columbia and the Midlands lack the architectural history of Charleston, but there are a few antebellum houses in downtown Columbia typical of those in the capital city before Sherman's troops burned it. Two of the houses were designed by Robert Mills, the first architect trained in America and, during the 1830s, the official architect of the U.S. government. Mills designed the Washington Monument in the nation's capi-

A view of Columbia looking down Main Street from the steps of the capitol, ca. 1870.

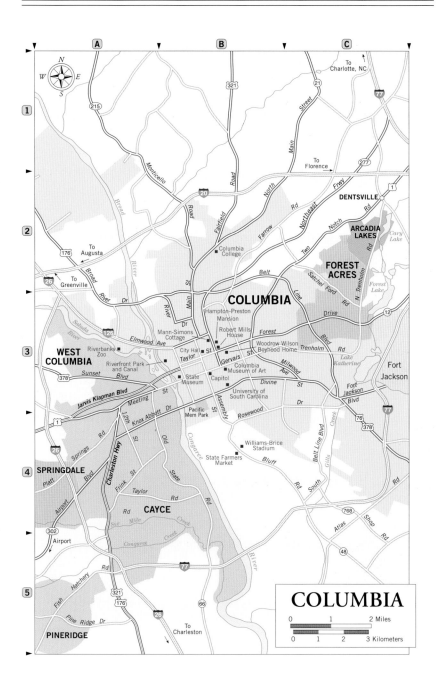

COLUMBIA

0   1   2 Miles

0   1   2   3 Kilometers

tal. His two Columbia houses are across the street from each other at 1615 and 1616 Blanding Street, between Henderson and Pickens streets. The 1818 **Hampton-Preston Mansion** (803-252-1770) was home to Gen. Wade Hampton of Revolutionary War fame, as well as his grandson, Gen. Wade Hampton III, who bankrolled his own Confederate militia and fought at Bull Run and later became the state's Reconstruction-era governor and U.S. senator. The house later became a convent, then a fashionable private college for young women. The **Robert Mills House** (803-252-1770), across the street at 1616 Blanding reflects Mills's neoclassical style.

The **Woodrow Wilson Boyhood Home** at 1705 Hampton Street (803-252-1770) was built by his parents and modeled after a Tuscan villa, and it contains some of the original furnishings.

The **Mann-Simons Cottage** (803-252-1770) is devoted to the black history of the area. At 1403 Richland Street between Marion and Bull streets, the house was bought in 1850 by Celia Mann, a Charleston slave who purchased her freedom

An interior view of the historic Robert Mills House

and walked to Columbia. Built in the early 1800s, it is now a historical heritage house, open Tuesday through Sunday.

The **South Carolina State Museum** (803-898-4921), on the Congaree River downtown, is a converted textile mill. Bricks for the five-story mill came from the nearby Guignard Brick Company, the oldest continually operating brickworks in the nation. The Columbia Mills Company ran its textile plant inside the building from 1894 until 1981. Its 1915-era spinning room, with the original spinning machines, is one of the museum's exhibits. The rest of the museum contains a wealth of eclectic artifacts from around the state, such as a homemade 1922 Anderson touring car, an *Apollo 16* spacesuit, an elaborate exhibit on antebellum slave life, and the world's largest exhibit about lasers.

The **Riverbanks Zoological Park and Botanical Gardens** (803-737-4664) on Wildlife Parkway/Greystone Boulevard contains thousands of acres and more than 2,000 animals in "natural" habitats and overlooks the Saluda River .

One of the most interesting places in the Midlands is the **State Farmers' Market.** South of downtown Columbia on Bluff Road (SC 48), across from the USC football stadium, the huge market, one of the largest in the Southeast, offers year-round access to a dizzying array of fresh fruit, vegetables, and other produce. It's open daily from 6 AM (803-253-4041).

Columbia is the site of several schools. The **University of South Carolina** was chartered in 1801 and opened with 2 professors and 5 students; today it has more than 25,000 students. Its historic area is the old **"Horseshoe"** of Georgian buildings set among magnolias and live oaks. The fall season stirs up football fever for the big Gamecocks-Cougars game, where longtime rivals USC and Clemson square off (and where Clemson almost always prevails). The college crowd keeps the Five Points neighborhood lively at night, at the bottom of Greene Street at Harden. This is an eclectic mix of coffee shops, book and music stores, restaurants, and nightclubs frequented by the university community. **Columbia College,** a women's school affiliated with the Methodist Church, and two private black schools—**Allen University** and **Benedict College**—add to the student life of the city.

Finlay Park (named for the late mayor Kirkman Finlay) gives downtown an aesthetic boost with its reflecting pools and walkways. The **Columbia Museum of Art** (803-779-2810) has the permanent Kress Collection paintings of the Italian Renaissance. **Main Street Jazz** is a popular spring jazz festival held outdoors, reflecting the community's growing interest in attracting tourists and promoting cultural activities.

■ **NEAR COLUMBIA** *map page 169, A-2/3*

The small towns and most farms in the two-county area known as the Midlands are primarily bedroom communities for state government employees, who commute to and from Columbia, expanding the circle of suburbs and subdivisions every year. Columbia (population 120,000) and surrounding Richland and Lexington counties (population 660,000) seem destined to remain largely the domain of their principal industry: state government.

Fort Jackson, one of the U.S. Army's largest bases (with a museum; 803-751-7419) and an infantry training center, blocks the suburban sprawl east of Columbia. As a result, the population, subdivisions, shopping centers, and office complexes spread north and west into Lexington County and toward Lake Murray.

Lake Murray was filled in 1930 and impounded by an earthen hydroelectric dam a mile and a half long and 208 feet high. It covers 78 square miles, with 525 miles of shoreline, 41 miles long and 14 miles across at its widest point. Boating, sailing, fishing, picnicking, camping, and swimming attract thousands to the lake, especially during summers. For details and directions on public facilities, including **Dreher Island State Park** near the center of the lake, visit the Lake Murray Country Visitors Center near the dam (I-26 north from Columbia to the Irmo exit and SC 60 west to its intersection with SC 6; 800-781-5940).

Fly fishermen, canoeists, and kayakers also frequent the 10-mile stretch of the **Saluda River** below the dam, running to the Broad River. The rapids range from easy to dangerous, and outfitters and guided trips are available.

Woodrow Wilson, 28th president of the United States, moved with his family from Augusta, Georgia to spend part of his teens at 1705 Hampton Street, later known as the Woodrow Wilson Boyhood Home.

THE PIEDMONT

A great crescent curves for hundreds of miles through the southeastern United States, from Virginia through the Carolinas and across northern Georgia and Alabama. The foothills of the Appalachians and the Blue Ridge mark its northwestern boundary. The fall line marks its southeastern boundary. The region in between is the Piedmont, a separate zone all its own of geology, terrain, and culture.

In South Carolina, the two frontiers of geology—foothills and fall lines—mark cultural divides between the agricultural, antebellum culture of the coastal plain and Sea Islands and a more hardscrabble, pioneering way of life.

The Piedmont's red clay soil was ill-suited to farming, but settlers persisted in tilling it for more than 150 years. Then, in the mid-1800s, a manufacturing boom spread across the Piedmont—in the form of cotton mills and company-owned mill towns—which quickly held the Piedmont in captivity just as cotton once controlled the coastal plain.

The people of this region never had the money or the time (nor the inclination, for that matter) to be as confident and arrogant as the old planters on the coast. But in one sense the table seems turned now, especially along South Carolina's 100-mile stretch of Interstate 85 as it runs through Gaffney, Spartanburg, Greenville, and Anderson. In these booming manufacturing areas, jobs pay wages that few other counties can match. People in the Piedmont make things: shock absorbers for cars in Anderson, silicon wafers in Spartanburg, roller bearings for cars and machinery in Gaffney. Yet there is more to the Piedmont than manufacturing. Historic towns such as Abbeville are worth any traveler's exploration, as are the four significant battle sites of the American Revolutionary War. Lush peach orchards line the byways of Edgefield County, and along the Savannah River a series of dams and reservoirs forms an inland "freshwater coast," fine for boating, camping, fishing, and swimming.

■ RED CLAY AND COTTON

Just as with the coastal plain, the history of this region is intertwined with geology and terrain. Merely by digging your fingers down into the soil anywhere in the Piedmont, you'll see you're in a region unlike the rocky foothills and mountains to

Lake Hartwell State Recreation Area is ideal for strolling, picnicking, and camping.

PLAIN FOLK

My kinfolks did not live in magnolia groves with tall white columns to hold up the front porches. We did not care for magnolias—they were swampy; and as for the white columns, we considered them pretentious. We did not call our farms plantations in the Upcountry, and we did not call ourselves old Southern planters—we were old Southern farmers. We were plain people, intending to be plain. We believed in plain clothes, plain cooking, plain houses, plain churches to attend preaching in on Sunday. We were Southerners, native-born and of the heart of the South, but we preferred the ways of Salem, Massachusetts, to those of Charleston, South Carolina. Charleston was a symbol to us—it represented luxury and easy soft living and all the evils of Egypt. Charleston believed in a code that shocked us. It was Cavalier from the start; we were Puritan.

—Ben Robertson, *Red Hills and Cotton,* 1942

the northwest or the dark loam of the coastal plain to the southeast. Here is a red-yellow clay, a soil produced by millions of years of rocks that weathered into a material called sapprolite. It often lies concentrated in deposits 100 feet thick and is mined for pottery. It was first used for this purpose by the Catawba tribe near the Piedmont town of Rock Hill; in the late 18th and early 19th centuries, pioneer settlers in the Edgefield area used the clay in the same manner. Today Edgefield and Catawba pottery are still highly valued.

Because of a warm, moist climate and relatively mild winters, bacteria thrive in the clay soil of the Piedmont, decomposing vegetation almost as fast as it falls to the ground. Very little humus (the organic part of the soil created by decomposition) accumulates, and without the acids produced by humus, iron oxides accumulate in the soil, making the land less fertile.

The region's hilly terrain also made farming on a large scale more difficult than on the flatlands of the coastal plain. Still, before and after the Civil War, farmers in the Piedmont persisted in planting cotton, primarily because they didn't know how to grow anything else, overworking an already poor soil in futile hopes of cotton fortunes.

By the 1880s, the Piedmont's croplands were virtually exhausted and eroding into huge gullies. (The exception to this is the peach-growing area along what is

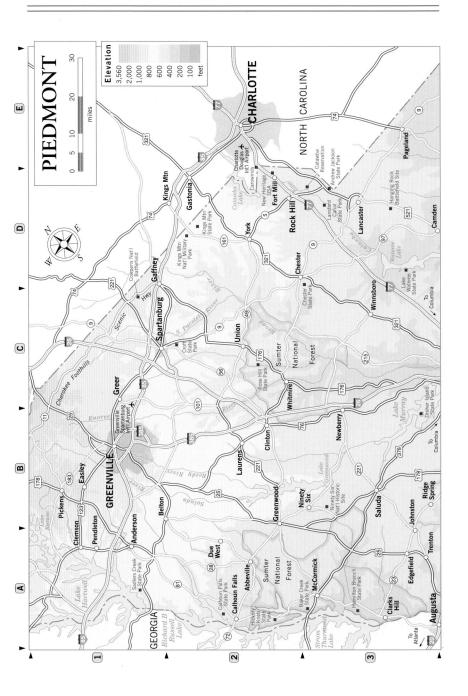

PIEDMONT

miles				
0	5	10	20	30

Elevation

3,560
2,000
1,000
800
600
400
200
100
feet

NORTH CAROLINA

GEORGIA

CHARLOTTE

Charlotte Douglas Int'l Airport
New Heritage USA
Carowinds
Fort Mill
Rock Hill
Lansford Canal State Park
Andrew Jackson State Park
Catawba Reservation
Lancaster
Hanging Rock Battlefield Site
Pageland
Camden
Lake Wateree State Park
Winnsboro
Chester State Park
Chester
To Columbia
Sumter National Forest
Union
Croft State Park
Spartanburg
Gaffney
Cowpens Nat'l Battlefield
Kings Mtn
Gastonia
Kings Mtn State Park
Kings Mtn Nat'l Military Park
York
Scenic Hwy
Greer
Greenville Spartanburg Int'l Airport
GREENVILLE
Easley
Pickens
Clemson
Pendleton
Anderson
Belton
Sadlers Creek State Park
Lake Hartwell
Due West
Calhoun Falls State Park
Calhoun Falls
Hickory Knob State Park
Abbeville
Sumter National Forest
McCormick
Baker Creek State Park
Clarks Hill
Hamilton Branch State Park
Strom Thurmond Lake
To Atlanta
Augusta
Edgefield
Trenton
Johnston
Ridge Spring
Saluda
Newberry
To Columbia
Dreher Island State Park
Lake Murray
Clinton
Laurens
Ninety Six
Ninety Six Nat'l Historic Site
Greenwood
Lake Greenwood
Whitmire
Rose Hill State Park
Chester State Park
Cherokee Foothills
Enoree
Reedy River
Saluda River
Enoree River
S. Pacolet River
Broad River
Catawba River
Wateree River
Lake Keowee
Richard B Russell Lake

Cherokee Foothills

known as the Ridge.) At the same time, South Carolina's economy, like that of all the former Confederate states, remained in ruins after the Civil War. During this period, the state's political and business leaders began to envision economic salvation from one untapped asset of the Piedmont: textile mills powered by the rushing rivers and waterfalls.

■ TEXTILE HISTORY

In scores of places all across the Piedmont, the region's major streams and rivers descend rapidly. The power of this falling water was ideal to run machinery, first with waterwheels, later with small dams and hydroelectric plants.

A campaign began to build cotton mills on those streams and rivers, and nearly every town in the Piedmont sought its own mill. In 1880, there were 14 textile mills in South Carolina, employing about 2,000 people. By 1910, there were 147 mills employing 45,000, and by 1931 the state had 239 mills with 73,000 workers. The sum total population of the mill villages was 190,000. Thousands of families from across the Piedmont and the Blue Ridge foothills in the northwest left their small farms. Their workplaces became the heat and noise of the mills while they lived in company-owned housing and bought groceries on credit at the company store.

Most of the mills were built by New England companies seeking cheap labor. In 1930, South Carolina textile workers were paid the lowest wages in the industry.

The mills, and later the apparel plants, controlled the Piedmont's economy and way of life until well into the 1970s. Through all those decades, mills and mill villages also remained the domain of white South Carolinians. In an unspoken, unofficial, well-known tacit agreement, mill hands regularly voted against allowing unions into their plants, and mill owners reciprocated by promising to keep the plants and company towns all-white.

Today, almost all the state's textile mills remain non-union, but the company town became obsolete during the 1970s, when most mills sold their houses and stores. The slow statewide desegregation of schools, public accommodations, and workplaces in that decade finally opened mill jobs to African-Americans.

Textile-mill employment in South Carolina peaked in 1973 at about 160,000 workers, almost all of them in the Piedmont. Since then, the industry's work force in the state has dropped to fewer than 90,000 and continues to fall as competition from overseas mills and automation within the textile industry take their tolls.

A child at work in a South Carolina cotton mill, circa 1908.

Wages in the state's textile mills are now the highest within the southern textile industry, averaging about $10 an hour, but still relatively low when compared with wages in most other manufacturing jobs. Despite the industry's declining status, textiles continue to dominate South Carolina's manufacturing economy, remaining the largest segment of industry in the state. About 22 percent of the state's manufacturing work force is employed in a textile mill, another 10 percent works in an apparel or fabric plant, and most of those jobs remain in the Piedmont.

What the cotton mills created in the Piedmont, beginning in the 1880s, was not only hundreds of mills and thousands of mill hands but also an industrial and manufacturing environment wholly different from life in the rest of South Carolina.

■ THE RIDGE   *map page 213, A-3*

There is a stretch of rolling hills and tiny towns in Edgefield County, on the southwestern edge of the Piedmont, an area no more than 5 miles wide and 12 miles long, that regularly produces more peaches per acre than anywhere else in the nation. In April, when pink peach blossoms cover those hills, there are few roads anywhere in South Carolina as stunning as U.S. 121 between Trenton and Johnston or SC 23 between Johnston and Ridge Spring.

South Carolina's peach harvest is second in size only to California's. Few people are aware that South Carolina actually outproduces the much larger Peach State of Georgia. While peaches are grown in most parts of South Carolina, the Piedmont dominates the commercial harvest.

Spartanburg County, on the northern border of the Piedmont, led the state in peach production until several years of unusually cold and long winters (as well as encroaching industrial development) cut the size of its orchards and put Edgefield County in the lead.

There are nearly a million peach trees in Edgefield County alone, all part of an expansive district of peach orchards known as the Ridge, reaching from Edgefield into Lexington County along U.S. 25, SC 23, and U.S. 1. Small towns along the Ridge host street festivals celebrating the fruit and its blossom—Johnston in April, Trenton in June, Gilbert in July.

From June to September, roadside peach stands pop up at every intersection in the Ridge. Thousands of migrant workers, from Mexico, Haiti, and other Central American or Caribbean countries, pour into the district to harvest the crop. They are among about 14,000 migrants who travel through South Carolina each year, harvesting peaches and apples in the Piedmont and Blue Ridge as well as tomatoes in the Sea Islands, tobacco in the Pee Dee, and watermelons in the coastal plain.

Edgefield County has been producing peaches commercially since shortly before the Civil War. It has been the home of South Carolina political leaders for just as long: 10 governors and 5 lieutenant governors of the state, including "Pitchfork" Ben Tillman and Strom Thurmond.

The entire small town of **Edgefield,** the county seat along U.S. 25 (population about 3,000), is listed on the National Register of Historic Places. Laid out around the courthouse square, the town has about 40 structures from the 19th century, mostly frame homes with center entrances and fan lights. Some are open to the public, such as Magnolia Dale on Norris Street (803-637-2233) and Oakley Park on Columbia Road (803-637-4027).

For longer than any other in U.S. history, Edgefield's thick deposits of clay have been a source of raw material for pottery. Archaeologists date Edgefield clay pottery found along the Savannah River to 2500 BC, among the earliest pottery vessels known in North America. Shortly after 1800, potters began establishing small

Stephen Ferrell helps preserve a longtime craft at Old Edgefield Pottery.

businesses in Edgefield County to supply pioneers moving here with kitchen necessities such as storage jars, pitchers, pans, and bowls. By 1850, five potters employing 35 people were operating in the area. The invention of the Mason screwtop glass jar in 1858 made most pottery obsolete. By then, however, Edgefield's potters were making pieces now collected by museums, such as "face vessels" made by slaves (with faces modeled into the jug) as well as other pieces with verses and scenes.

■ OLD NINETY-SIX DISTRICT *map page 213, B-2/3*

What didn't vanish from Piedmont agriculture in the wake of the cotton mill boom of the 1880s did not survive a second wave of expansion during the 1920s. On the 40-mile stretch of U.S. 25 route north from Edgefield to Greenwood, there remains not a single hamlet or farm. There are dairy pastures and small cattle ranches here and there, and long stretches of thick trees as the highway cuts through Sumter National Forest, but nothing agricultural beyond an occasional patch of corn or grain. An even more scenic, east–west route through this section of the Piedmont (although equally barren) is U.S. 378 from Columbia to McCormick, Strom Thurmond Lake, and Hickory Knob State Resort Park. In this 2½-hour drive you will encounter only one town, Saluda.

The demise of all the small farms has created at least one bonanza. Most of the old furniture, furnishings, tools, and implements from the bygone farm families were put into storage as the farms disappeared, and over the last two decades the items have been brought out again and put on sale. Consequently, antiques shops and collectibles emporiums are thriving in the Piedmont today, especially in Abbeville, McCormick, and other towns in a four-county part of the western Piedmont just north of Edgefield and the Ridge.

The four counties—McCormick, Greenwood, Laurens, and Abbeville—were part of what was the "Old Ninety-Six District." The area takes its name from an 18th-century British fort that was 96 miles south of the old Cherokee capital, Keowee, in the Blue Ridge. At that time, this was the western frontier of the colony. When the colony became a state, with districts created by the legislature, the colonial fort and village around the Old Ninety-Six became the district seat of government.

Today's town of **Ninety Six** is a small mill village 10 miles east of Greenwood on SC 34. Two miles south of town on SC 248 is the old star-shaped fort, site of South Carolina's first battle of the Revolutionary War, a historic site operated by the National Park Service, with a visitors center and interpretive trail (803-543-4068).

The towns of the Old Ninety-Six District, like those throughout the Piedmont, don't reflect antebellum architecture or sentiment. Most seem relatively modern, with redbrick storefronts and Victorian houses. Irish, Scottish, and German pioneers established these towns during the early decades of the 19th century, and they had little in common with the Barbadian, English, and Huguenot gentry who settled on the coast. Examples of these towns are Clinton (population 9,500), home of Presbyterian College; Due West (population 1,250), home of Erskine College; and Greenwood (population 22,000), home of Lander College.

The famous mail-order seed-catalog firm Park Seed Co., founded in 1868, and its test gardens, open to the public, are 7 miles north of Greenwood on SC 254. The gardens are at their most brilliant during the summer months. Thousands attend its two-week Festival of Flowers each summer. For festival information, call the Greenwood Area Chamber of Commerce; 864-223-8411.

■ **ABBEVILLE** *map page 213, A-2*
Despite the fact that the Piedmont's architectural styles are quite different from those of the gentrified South, and that its manufacturing industries created a different culture, some of the most significant moments of antebellum and Confederate history took place here, especially in the small town of Abbeville, on SC 72 about 15 miles west of Greenwood.

Abbeville may be the jewel of the Piedmont. With some 300 Victorian homes to take in, it's definitely one of the best places in South Carolina for strolling. The town's large historic district spreads for several blocks in all directions from the restored town square, where the streets have been resurfaced with red brick. A visitors center on the south side of the square provides brochures and maps for walking tours; call 864-459-4600.

On the east side, the **Abbeville Opera House** (864-459-2157) was restored to Victorian elegance in 1968. When the ornate theater opened in 1908, Abbeville was a railroad stopover for theater companies en route between New York and Atlanta, and one-night performances continued until the late 1940s. The Ziegfeld Follies, Jimmy Durante, Fanny Brice, and Sarah Bernhardt were among the performers here, and it continues to stage professional productions year-round. There are free tours daily, except during rehearsal times.

On the southeast corner of the square, renovated and refurbished in the same Victorian style as the opera house, is the **Belmont Inn** (864-459-9625), with its elegant lobby, wide porches, and excellent French restaurant.

Abbeville, with its abundance of historic homes, may be the jewel of the Piedmont.

Restaurants, bookstores, and antiques shops line all four sides of the square and Trinity Street at the northwest corner. One block down Trinity Street is the 125-foot pink-spired **Trinity Episcopal Church** (864-459-5186), built in 1859 and one of a score of structures in the historic district listed on the National Register of Historic Places.

Abbeville calls itself "the birthplace and deathbed of the Confederacy." In the middle of the square, a monument to the Confederacy explains, "The first mass meeting for secession was held at Abbeville, November 22, 1860. The last cabinet meeting (of the Confederate government) held at Abbeville May 2, 1865." John C. Calhoun, the South's leading antebellum politician, was born near Abbeville in 1782, had his law offices on the town square from 1807 through 1817, and was first elected to Congress from Abbeville.

■ INLAND COAST *map page 213, A-1/2*

Ice Age glaciers never reached as far south as South Carolina, and as a result there are no large natural lakes in the state. Along the Savannah River, on the western border of the Piedmont, however, are several reservoirs formed by dams built by the Army Corps of Engineers. They turn the Savannah River into a virtually continuous lake, from the fall line at Edgefield County all the way into the Blue Ridge foothills.

Campsites, marinas, and state parks draw millions of visitors to the Savannah River reservoirs each year. From south to north on the river, there is Strom Thurmond Lake (also called Clarks Hill), Russell Lake, and **Lake Hartwell**. On the Savannah River at I-85 in the heart of the Piedmont's industrial and manufacturing boom, Hartwell is a troubled reservoir. PCBs (poly-chlorinated biphenyls, shown to cause cancer in laboratory animals) traced to a capacitor manufacturer's discharges from the mid-1950s until 1977 contaminated an upper branch of Hartwell known as the Twelve Mile River. Federal and state agencies have contained the pollution, and the only significant health risk to humans would seem to come from eating fish caught in this upper branch of the reservoir.

Downriver from Hartwell is the smallest of the three Savannah River reservoirs, **Richard B. Russell Lake** (706-213-3400), named for the late, powerful, longtime senator from Georgia. It also is the least used, which makes it very popular with bass fishermen and small-boat sailors. The old mill town of **Calhoun Falls,** 30 miles west of Abbeville at SC 72 and 81, is the base camp for supplies. Relatively new **Calhoun Falls State Park** (864-447-8267) off SC 81 2 miles north of town and on the lakeside, has campsites, RV hookups, and a small marina and shop— the only one on the lake.

Downriver from Russell is the largest and most popular Army Corps of Engineers reservoir east of the Mississippi River. Its name is yet another wonderful story of southern politics and southern roots.

■ THURMOND LAKE *map page 213, A-2/3*

During the early 1950s, when the reservoir was filled, it was **Clarks Hill Dam and Lake,** named for a small South Carolina town nearby. During the 1980s, after having schools, roads, office buildings, and monuments named for and erected to him in virtually every part of South Carolina, it was rechristened after Sen. J. Strom Thurmond and is now known as the **J. Strom Thurmond Dam and Lake** (864-333-1100), more commonly referred to as Thurmond Lake.

The locals in Clarks Hill, Modoc, and Plum Branch, most of whom voted for Thurmond, remain outraged to this day. Billboards protesting what happened years ago continue to appear, saying, "Keep Clarks Hill." (As some say: It is unwise to mess around with a South Carolinian's dog, pickup, or the names he's used to.) In neighboring Georgia, everyone simply still calls it Clarks Hill Lake, including state highway maps.

The lake itself, with 1,200 miles of shoreline and 70,000 acres of water, is so large that a boat can get caught in a major squall on one side while others are becalmed at the other end.

Nearly all the South Carolina shoreline of Thurmond Lake is either within Sumter National Forest or in one of three state parks.

Hamilton Branch State Recreation Area (U.S. 221 and SC 28; 864-333-2223) and **Baker Creek State Park** (U.S. 378; 864-443-2457), both near McCormick, have campsites, water and electrical hookups, hot showers, and rest rooms. Hickory Knob is more of a self-contained resort than a state park.

Hickory Knob Resort State Park (6 miles west of McCormick on U.S. 378; 864-391-2450) has an 18-hole championship golf course and clubhouse on the lake; a skeet-shooting range; a swimming pool; tennis, basketball, and volleyball courts; nature trails and programs; guided bus tours to nearby attractions such as Abbeville; a boat ramp and docks as well as rental boats; a restaurant and convention facilities; and campsites as well as fully furnished cabins and motel rooms with cable TV and phones.

■ REVOLUTIONARY WAR SITES

One month after the Revolutionary War battle at Bunker Hill, in 1775, until the British surrender at Yorktown, Virginia, in 1781, virtually the entire state of South Carolina became a battleground. The state was the site of the key battles of the southern campaign of the war, in particular the one battle most historians consider the turning point of the American victory.

There are roadside historical markers at many of the 137 battlefield sites in South Carolina, and four of them, all in the Piedmont, are national historic sites. These are Ninety Six, Camden, Kings Mountain, and Cowpens.

Volunteers in period dress replicate 1700's day-to-day activities at the Ninety Six National Historic Site.

■ **NINETY SIX** *map page 213, B-3*

The first significant battle of the Revolution in South Carolina began November 19, 1775. About 560 rebel patriots behind a crude stockade of straw bales, fence rails, and animal hides at the old colonial fort of Ninety Six were attacked and defeated by a Tory force three times larger than their own, although there was not a British officer on the field of battle.

Ninety Six became a key British stronghold in the Piedmont, where Tory sympathy was widespread. In May 1781, loyalist colonel John Harris Cruger and his forces defended the Tory stronghold against Gen. Nathanael Greene and 1,000 patriots. Greene's losses were twice those suffered by Cruger, but the patriots managed to cut off the Tory water supply and to cause a great deal of damage with fire arrows. The assault led to the British abandonment of their last upcountry fort. On Route 248, the Ninety Six National Historic Site is open daily; call 864-543-4068.

The Battle of Camden.

Revolutionary War in South Carolina

South Carolina experienced some of the fiercest fighting of the Revolutionary War. Of its 137 battles, only 103 were reinforced by other colonies.

1775   April 19, Revolutionary War begins at Lexington and Concord Mass.

November 19, about 560 patriots at the old fort of Ninety Six are attacked and defeated by loyalists.

1776   In June, British fleet of 11 warships under Admiral Parker is repulsed at Charles Town by Colonel Moultrie from fort at Sullivan's Island.

On July 4 Declaration of Independence signed in Philadelphia by delegates of the last Revolutionary convention.

1778   British turn to a southern campaign. Savannah, Georgia, falls.

France recognizes the United States of America.

1780   April 14, British victorious in battle at old Moncks Corner.

Nearly 11,000 British troops lay siege to Charles Town, which surrenders on May 12.

June 1, Lord Cornwallis takes Camden, the oldest inland city in the state.

Americans win two battles at Hanging Rock, July 30 and August 6.

October 7, Americans defeat 225 British soldiers in a one-hour battle at Kings Mountain. Considered the turning point in the war.

Huguenot planter Francis Marion becomes known as the Swamp Fox for his brilliant guerrilla raids and ability to hide his forces in the swamps.

1781   January 17, American defeat British at a cattle drover's shelter called the Cowpens.

April 25, British win at Hobkirk's Hill near Camden.

May 12, Americans capture the British Post at Motte's.

September, Battle of Eutaw Springs (now Eutawville) ends in a draw.

October 19, Lord Cornwallis surrenders British army to Gen. George Washington at Yorktown, Virginia.

1782   In December, British forces withdraw from Charles Town.

1783   Peace of Paris; Britain recognizes the United States of America.

■ CAMDEN   *map page 213, D-3*

By 1778, the war in the North had become a stalemate, and the British turned to a southern campaign, hoping to control the southern colonies before returning north to victory. The strategy began well. Savannah fell to the British in 1778. In 1780, nearly 11,000 British troops laid siege to Charles Town, which surrendered May 12 of that year.

On June 1, 1780, Lord Charles Cornwallis took Camden, the oldest inland city in the state, established in 1732 near the Wateree River (at one time known as River Watery) on the southern rim of the Piedmont (U.S. 1 and U.S. 521, 2 miles north of I-20 and 32 miles northeast of Columbia). For 11 months, Camden was the principal supply post for British operations in the South. The town was heavily fortified and surrounded with a stockade and redoubts. The old fort and village are part of the 92-acre **Historic Camden Revolutionary War Site** (803-432-9841), affiliated with the National Park Service, on U.S. 521 just south of the city.

Then, in October 1780, the British southern strategy began to crumble.

Cornwallis had headed into North Carolina, leaving a force of 1,100 to scour the South Carolina Piedmont. Instead, that force found itself attacked by backwoods patriots.

■ KINGS MOUNTAIN AND COWPENS

A Tory militia force of over 1,000 men led by Maj. Patrick Ferguson took a defensive stance at Kings Mountain on October 7, 1780, surrounded by about 900 patriots. In a one-hour battle, 225 British were killed and the remainder wounded or captured.

The Kings Mountain battle is considered the turning point in the war because Cornwallis was forced to split his forces, leaving some in South Carolina. On January 17, 1781, much of that force was defeated by patriot militia in another key battle at a cattle drover's pasture called the Cowpens.

The meadow's terrain, gradually sloping up to a rise 70 feet above the surrounding forest, was effectively used by Gen. Daniel Morgan to defeat Gen. Banastre Tarleton and his loyalist troops. Carefully positioned lines of riflemen at different elevations on the slope shot at advancing loyalists, who charged into the firing until reserve cavalrymen refused to follow. The battle was an important victory for the American patriots after their defeat at Camden the previous summer.

Today, **Cowpens National Battlefield** (864-461-2828), about 30 miles west of **Kings Mountain National Military Park** (864-936-7921) on SC 11 at SC 110, has a visitors center with exhibits, picnic areas, a walking trail, and a marked road tour. The Kings Mountain National Military Park offers similar facilities (16 miles northwest of York on SC 161, just off I-85 near the North Carolina border). Nearby is **Kings Mountain State Park** (803-222-3209) with campsites and a lake for fishing and swimming.

■ OLDE ENGLISH DISTRICT

When the Revolutionary War began, the eastern Piedmont, from Camden north to Rock Hill, was a hotbed of Tory sympathizers. This was due in part to the settlers' feeling that if they had a real enemy, it was the planter-merchant gentry of Charleston and the coastal islands, who refused to share political power with the Upcountry.

A somewhat cohesive wave of pioneers from the Pennsylvania colony settled most of this region during the early and mid-18th century. They gave their settlements such names as York, Lancaster, and Chester, after towns left behind in Pennsylvania, which had themselves been named after towns in England. As a result, in a bit of a stretch, South Carolina tourism promoters call the eastern Piedmont the Olde English District.

Those early pioneers were as much interested in cottage industry as they were in cotton farming. They manufactured things—tools, farm implements—much as the other pioneers, as well as the Catawba, manufactured and sold pottery.

When the "New South" industrialism began in the 1880s, the eastern Piedmont, already accustomed to mechanization, was one of the first areas to build cotton mills. Today, it remains dominated by textile and chemical fiber plants. DuPont's huge fiber plant at Camden and the largest textile mill in the South—Springs Industries' Lancaster plant—are examples.

Camden (population 7,500) is better known to most South Carolinians not for its Revolutionary War history but for its **Carolina Cup**—a day of steeplechase and flat racing, held each spring around Easter and hailed as "the world's largest outdoor cocktail party." Crowds of 55,000 or more, most of the women in spring finery, jam **Springdale Race Course** (803-432-6513). Tailgate picnics may include china, silver, crystal, and linen. Couples often get married during the annual Saturday event, one of the South's most prestigious steeplechases. The **Colonial Cup**, another steeplechase, is held here in late fall.

The Colonial Cup, a prestigious steeplechase, comes to Camden in late fall.

Camden does not have the mansions, estates, and winter-colony historic districts of South Carolina's other "horse" town, Aiken. But nearly 300 thoroughbred jumpers and 300 thoroughbred flat racers train from fall through spring at Springdale Race Course and nearby Wrenfield stables. The Jell-O magnate, Ernest L. Woodward, and his friend Harry D. Kirkover began Camden's wintertime steeplechase fraternity during the 1920s. Mrs. Marion du Pont Scott expanded it during the 1930s and, upon her death, donated the Springdale course to the state. It now houses the **National Steeplechase Museum** (803-432-6513).

The WPA's 1941 guide to South Carolina observes that Camden was once known for its duels, and gentlemen flocked to the city seeking instruction in the ritual's code of honor. The state's last legal duel occurred here in 1880, when Col. William S. Shannon and Col. E. B. C. Cash fought (apparently in an inheritance dispute). Colonel Shannon was mortally wounded, and his death resulted in the adoption of the state's anti-dueling law.

Even for those who don't follow the horses, Camden remains a charming town to visit, with some fine homes, beautiful old gardens, and antiques stores.

In the Piedmont, even if you don't follow the horses, they just may follow you.

Pontiac's Freedom Weekend Aloft, held each year in Anderson County, sends balloonists into the gray skies over neighboring Greenville County.

■ EASTERN PIEDMONT *map page 213, D-2/3*

For the Catawba, the usual route through the eastern Piedmont was via the Catawba-Wateree river system. For modern motorists, especially truckers, the usual route today is I-77, the busy connection between Charlotte and Columbia.

For the curious, slow-paced traveler, however, there is a less-traveled route: SC 97, which branches off U.S. 601 just north of Camden. This scenic back road passes by Wateree Lake, a Duke Power Company reservoir popular with small-boat sailors, water-skiers, and fishermen. Several marinas are along the highway. The route crosses the Catawba River at the mill town of Great Falls, and 6 miles west is I-77.

An alternate route north is U.S. 21 from Columbia to Charlotte, along the river through the Catawba Reservation, then Rock Hill. Along that road is **Landsford Canal State Park** (803-789-5800), one of the most scenic picnic spots in the eastern Piedmont.

The architect Robert Mills designed a series of four canals on the Catawba-Wateree system during the 1820s, to facilitate shipping on the Santee and Cooper rivers from the Piedmont to Charleston and the Atlantic coast. The canals never quite worked properly, and railroads quickly made them obsolete. But Landsford State Park includes the best-preserved section of the old canals, as well as a museum and interpretive center. The park's 222 acres include a nature trail along the canal. The trail leads to river shoals with one of the world's largest collections of spider lilies (which bloom in May) as well as great fishing for striped bass and bream.

The **Catawba Reservation** (803-328-2427), and Catawba pottery exhibits and sales, is at the intersection of U.S. 21 and SC 5, a few miles south of Rock Hill. On I-77 is **Paramount's Carowinds** (800-888-4386), a roller-coaster and water-ride complex that straddles the state line 13 miles north of Rock Hill.

■ I-85 CORRIDOR *map page 213*

The economic engine behind the booming Piedmont economy is visible to anyone who drives on I-85 during rush hour. As you cross the northwestern corner of South Carolina, the 100 miles between the North Carolina and Georgia state lines is plant-to-plant with industrial development, the majority of them recently opened by foreign corporations.

It wasn't always like this. In the 1950s, when I-85 was being built, there were only two major news stories each year: whether the textile mills would permit summer vacations and how the peach crop was doing.

By the 1970s, towns and cities along I-85 (roughly following the northwestern edge of the Piedmont) were facing economic hardship. Spartanburg County's famous peach crop, once the state's biggest, with 40 packing plants, was greatly diminished. An unusual series of harsh weather contributed to the decline, but so did the rising real estate prices paid for peach groves by industrial, commercial, and residential developers.

The area's textile plants had long been its only major employers, and they were cutting back or moving overseas. Things began to improve with the arrival of foreign-based companies such as Rieter, a Swiss manufacturer of textile machinery, which built its plant in 1962. Now, there are so many foreign corporations with plants in Spartanburg county—and about 12,000 foreign citizens (primarily

Germans)—that little Cowpens National Battlefield, 17 miles north of Spartanburg, provides brochures in English and German.

In Spartanburg County alone, more than 20 German, Swiss, and Austrian manufacturing companies can be seen from the interstate. A mammoth BMW plant, the German automaker's first outside Germany, began production in the 1990s. It's also visible from I-85.

Just out of view from I-85 are more than 60 other foreign-owned plants, more than 40 of them German-owned plants in Spartanburg County. Many of them are auto suppliers who followed BMW into South Carolina. Germany has had the highest rate of foreign investment per capita in the state for more than a decade, and there are nearly 500 foreign-based companies employing about 85,000 people in South Carolina, from the Swiss-based Hoffmann-LaRoche pharmaceuticals plant at Florence to the Japanese-owned Fuji Photo film plant in Greenwood to the Italian-based Union Switch & Signal plants in Columbia and Batesburg.

And that's just in Spartanburg County. The boom encompasses the entire I-85 corridor from Gaffney to Anderson. In Spartanburg, the **Westgate Mall** (864-574-

Ground-breaking ceremony at the BMW plant near Spartanburg.

Riding Home

I rode my bicycle home from school. All looked normal. I sniffed: high spring, Carolina, health and prosperity. People were shopping like crazy in stores along the highway. Plants were growing in the median, big sturdy weeds that looked a lot like carrots and celery, with thick stalks and ferny leaves dense enough to hide the underlying road trash. Traffic was a carefree stream of cars. The afternoon was average and happy, to the eye of a casual observer. . . .

Out in the developments, some of the new roads curved back upon themselves, and I sometimes lost my sense of direction trying to get somewhere; or I might be riding along and all of a sudden the smooth asphalt turns to soft dirt and I'm in the country, with wooden houses balanced on concrete blocks, and the tragic crowing of roosters. . . .

It was as if new places had been slapped down over the old ones, but some of the old was still showing through. I tried not to lose myself in those pockets. It could sometimes be too much for me, a house at the edge of a field, the rim of pines, and the smoke. It wrenched my heart. There was too much emotion for me in the country.

—Josephine Humphreys, *Rich in Love*, 1987

7573), expanded from 78 stores to 128, and today it's the only mall in the Carolinas with six department stores. I-85 is being expanded from four to eight lanes, as projections estimate daily traffic to reach 120,000 vehicles by 2020. Unless you live, work, or have business on I-85, or you're traveling between 10 PM and 6 AM, find another route—perhaps SC 11, a longer but more scenic route that is comparatively free of traffic jams.

Industrial development experts usually credit two key reasons for the state's appeal to new industry, especially foreign-based industry. Beginning in 1961, South Carolina opened 16 technical education campuses across the state, promising new industry that it would train new employees specifically for their plants. The program has been so successful it is a model for similar programs in other states. The second reason is South Carolina's traditional anti-union population and laws. It is a "right-to-work" state: no worker can be openly compelled to join a union—even if the union represents the majority of workers in a plant. The state has less than 3 percent of its workplaces union-organized, the second-lowest percentage in the nation. BMW opposes organizing efforts by the United Auto Workers, just as the state's textile industry long has opposed unions—almost always successfully.

For all the foreign-owned plants and industrial diversification in the Piedmont, especially the I-85 corridor, textile and textile-related employment remains dominant in the state.

■ **PENDLETON**   *map page 213, A/B-1 and map page 237, B/C-3*

Fifteen miles north of the I-85 corridor, on U.S. 76, is the small town of Pendleton, a welcome relief after the manufacturing plants and commuter traffic along the interstate. The entire town and its surroundings are listed on the National Register of Historic Places and compose one of the largest historic districts in the nation. The 1770s town was named after Judge Henry Pendleton, whose Virginia militiamen helped defend South Carolina. It was once an important trade center and still has more than 45 historic buildings, some of which are open to the public. Among them are the **Farmers' Society Hall** (864-646-3782), the oldest such meeting hall in continuous use in the United States; **St. Paul's Episcopal Church** (800-862-1795), built in 1822; and **Hunter's Store** (864-646-3782) on the town green, also the tour center for the historic district.

B L U E   R I D G E

In the wondrous way the natural world works, the tiny reproductive spores of the Tunbridge fern from the rain forest of South America were carried by wind and water north across the equator, across the Caribbean Sea, and into the Gulf Stream. The great current transported the tiny cells farther north along the Atlantic Ocean coast of the southeastern United States. Somewhere off that coast, perhaps in winter when northeasterly storms sweep over the coast and all the way to the mountains of South Carolina, the Tunbridge fern spores sailed aloft from the Gulf Stream and carried far inland.

They landed in the mists of Eastatoe Gorge, at the end of a long valley near Sassafras Mountain, at 3,560 feet the highest point in the state. There, the Tunbridge fern thrives. It seems improbable, but so far as is known, that fern grows nowhere else on earth but in the South American rain forest and in Eastatoe Gorge.

The Tunbridge fern and the Eastatoe Gorge are among the subtle, remote charms of South Carolina's Blue Ridge, the southern end of the mountain chain that begins in Virginia and is the "front range" of the southern Appalachians.

Soc'em Dog, Screaming Left Turn, and Jawbone—fearsome rapids on one of the nation's most famous whitewater rivers, the Chattooga (of *Deliverance* movie fame)—are among the Blue Ridge's wild wonders.

Remote streams for fly fishing; deep, clear lakes renowned for trout; an 85-mile, eight-day mountain hiking trail; amateur Saturday-night bluegrass music jams at country stores; hillsides thick with apple orchards; and six of South Carolina's best state parks are all within 45 miles of each other, making this old homeland of the Cherokee Nation one of South Carolina's most splendid corners.

The Blue Ridge covers only the northern sections of Oconee, Pickens, and Greenville counties within South Carolina. Its boundaries are set by the state's borders with Georgia and North Carolina on one side and on the other by the Cherokee Foothills Scenic Highway, SC I 1, from the foothills town of Walhalla northeast to the intersection of SC 11 and U.S. 25 north of Greenville.

Within this small area is the greatest annual rainfall in the eastern United States. Six rivers drain from its low mountains: the Chattooga, Eastatoe, Thompson, Horsepasture, Middle Saluda, and Toxaway. Actually, the deep, cold, clear waters of Lake Jocassee, (created by a hydroelectric dam in 1973) inundated the Toxaway

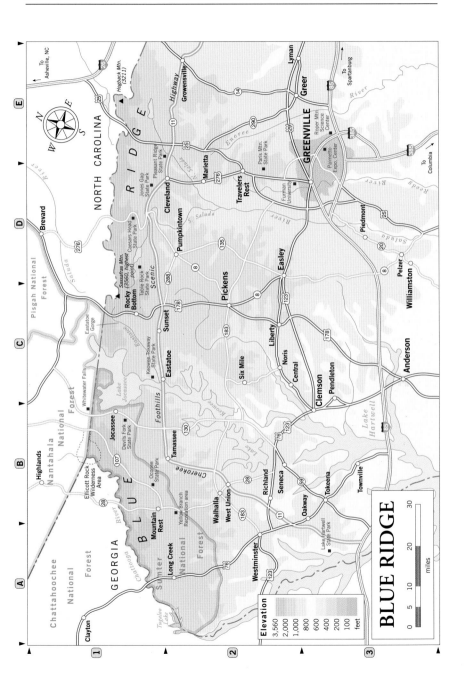

and Horsepasture rivers within South Carolina, as well as portions of the Thompson and Whitewater.

Just up the Whitewater River from Lake Jocassee, and straddling the border of North and South Carolina, are the highest series of waterfalls in eastern North America. Whitewater Falls drops a total of about 900 feet.

Most of the Blue Ridge is within Sumter National Forest. Oaks dominate the mountain and ridge tops, pines the lower and the southern slopes. Carolina laurel, kalmia, rhododendron, large hemlocks, tulip poplars, hickory, black gum, beech, white ash, and sweet-gum trees make this a varied forest. Chestnut trees once grew here, too, but a blight in the 1900s wiped out most of them. The dogwoods are struggling against another blight, a fungus that has spread down here from forests of the Northeast.

■ MOUNTAIN FOLKS

South Carolina's Blue Ridge once was home for the Lower Cherokee Nation, which established a town and capital on the banks of the Keowee River. Neither the river, the capital town, nor the Cherokees are here anymore. The Cherokees began retreating deeper into the northwest Appalachian Mountains during the 1780s, as broken treaties and constant warfare with invading white settlers forced the Native Americans to flee their homeland. By the 1820s, only the names the Cherokee gave to rivers were left—Keowee, Toxaway, Jocassee, Seneca, Tokeena, Tamassee, and Eastatoe.

The Cherokee capital, also named Keowee, was just south of what today is **Keowee Toxaway State Park** (864-868-2605), on SC 11. The town and the entire Keowee River are submerged under Lake Keowee, a reservoir filled in the late 1960s to provide cooling water for Duke Power Company's Oconee Power Plant.

As the Cherokee left, the Scots-Irish arrived, and their descendants remain in the Blue Ridge today, fighting a losing battle of their own against another wave of invaders—wealthy resort developers and retirees seeking Blue Ridge beauty while driving up property taxes.

The Scots-Irish came to America by the hundreds of thousands throughout the 18th century. They came from northern Ireland's Ulster province, fleeing drought and war. When they arrived at ports such as Philadelphia, they kept on going, through more populous Pennsylvania, Maryland, Virginia, and most of North Carolina, until reaching the dark mountain hollows and river bottoms of the Blue Ridge.

This 1937 photograph from the files of the WPA shows an Appalachian mother of 14 children and 56 grandchildren.

For nearly two centuries, the Scots-Irish and their descendants preferred living in relative isolation. They survived by hunting, raising livestock, and growing corn, cabbage, and apples. There was a time when they also made applejack and "white lightning," or moonshine—illegal, untaxed whiskey—and, every so often, you hear about an operational local still.

Cultural changes across the Blue Ridge didn't begin until the 20th century, and even then the changes were few. First, during the 1900s and 1910s, the timber and lumber industry grew. Roads were built, sawmills constructed, new towns established, railroad tracks laid down. Centuries-old forests were leveled, and where the ridge of mountainside was clear cut, erosion soon followed. During the 1930s, another transformation arrived—electricity from the Rural Electrification Administration.

Beginning in the 1970s, two centuries after the Scots-Irish arrived, other migrants began moving here. Vacation homes, resort developments, dams, and reservoirs—pleasant as they are—have been built where mountain rivers once ran.

NATIVE AMERICANS

Beyond archaeological remnants and the small tribe of Catawba near Rock Hill in the northeastern Piedmont, there is little left of the estimated 15,000 Native Americans who lived in South Carolina in 1600.

There is evidence of an aboriginal presence going back at least 12,000 years. By the early 1600s, there were 46 separate tribes in the state, the largest being the Cherokee and Catawba. Along the coastal rivers and on the Sea Islands were a dozen or more small tribes, distinct cultures all their own. European, mostly English translations of their tribal names remain in those places now: Edisto Island, Kiawah Island, the Stono River, the Ashepoo and Combahee rivers, the town of Yemassee.

Traveling primarily by canoe, small tribes summered on the coastal islands, catching fish, harvesting oysters, and growing corn, peas, and beans. They wintered as far as 80 miles inland on the coastal plain, gathering nuts and wild fruit and hunting game, especially deer.

Up the rivers of the eastern coastal plain, along the Pee Dee, Waccamaw, Lynches, Black, Sampit, Pocotaligo, and Wateree rivers, lived a dozen or more tribes of Siouan heritage, known to be excellent hunters and warriors. Along the Savannah River were a half dozen more tribes, such as Apalachee, Yuchi, and fierce Yemassee. The Midlands and western Piedmont were dominated by the powerful Cherokee, the Catawba River in the eastern Piedmont by the Catawba.

All these tribes were village dwellers with diversified crops as their primary source of food and game as their second. They lived in huts of cypress or cedar bark, often inside log palisades. The Cherokee built houses, sometimes two stories high, of post and clay and roofed with narrow boards. According to one 17th-century English frontier trader, John Lawson: "I have never felt any ill, unsavory smell in their cabins, whereas, should we live in our houses as they do, we should be poisoned with our own nastiness, which confirms these Indians to be, as they really are, some of the sweetest people in the world."

The Native Americans were susceptible to diseases brought by Europeans, especially smallpox. An epidemic of smallpox in 1738 killed half of the Catawba and Cherokee, and in the end, illness killed more Native Americans than did all their wars combined.

By the 1670s, most of the coastal tribes had retreated inland. In 1684, they signed a treaty surrendering claim to their lands—all except the Yemassee. This tribe, known among the other tribes as fiercely independent, lived mostly in the swamps and forests inland from Beaufort. After years of being swindled, enslaved, and killed by white traders who were financed by Charleston merchants, the Yemassee attacked with devastating suddenness on Good Friday, April 15, 1715. They hit plantations and settlements around Beaufort, killing about 100 settlers, then moved rapidly north to attack plantations on the Combahee, Edisto, and Stono rivers. The Yemassee came within a few miles of Charleston, raiding plantations along the Ashley, Cooper, and Santee rivers.

White refugees and their African slaves escaped into Charleston seeking protection. The war did not end until early in 1716, when the Cherokee agreed to counterattack from the north (the Yemassee, a Creek tribe, were traditional enemies of the Cherokee). This relieved pressure on Charleston, and a militia force attacked the Yemassee. The Yemassee retreated across the Savannah River into Georgia and eventually into Spanish Florida, where the tribe became extinct, assimilated with remnants of another Creek tribe, the Miccosukee. They were eventually designated as Seminole Indians of Florida.

The war almost broke the South Carolina colony. Buildings and fences were burned and livestock was killed or stolen. Crops went unplanted for years.

Benjamin Hawkins and the Creek Indians, *painted by an unidentified artist, depicts the early settler bartering for foodstuffs in the 18th century.*

The Cherokee, whose southern capital was at Keowee on the Keowee River (near what today is Clemson), never occupied the western Piedmont, but they held great influence there. Accommodating the steady advance of white settlers, in 1755 they ceded to the British colony all but the northwestern tip of South Carolina, reserving for themselves their Keowee capital and today's Anderson, Oconee, Pickens, and Greenville counties, as well as tracts in Georgia and North Carolina. In return, the British were allowed to build forts in the Piedmont, such as the fort at Ninety Six.

The peace ended and the treaty was broken when the Cherokee War was launched in November 1757, after four Cherokee were murdered by whites near Saluda. Cherokee reprisals and raids continued until 1760, when an army of 1,200 Highlander and Royal Scots arrived from Canada, marched up from Charles Town to Keowee, and eliminated what had been the Lower Cherokee Nation. In 1761, another force of 2,600 British troops, colonial militia, and warriors from native enemies, the Chickasaw and Catawba, forced the Cherokee into the mountains of the Blue Ridge. In 1761 the Cherokee Nation sued for peace, and the long war ended.

Immediately after the treaty was signed, however, white settlers began moving into Cherokee lands. The Cherokee signed treaty after treaty ceding vast tracts, in hopes of preserving part of their homeland for themselves. Warfare again broke out in the Blue Ridge and Appalachians, from Georgia up through the Carolinas into Virginia, Kentucky, and Tennessee. Massive colonial armies scoured the entire Cherokee Nation during 1776, and in 1777, the Cherokee finally surrendered all their lands in South Carolina and all their lands east of the Blue Ridge in every southern colony.

In 1838, most members of the Cherokee Nation remaining in the southern Appalachians were forcibly marched west to Indian Territory on the arid Oklahoma plains. Thousands died en route in the infamous tragedy known as the Trail of Tears. As a recognizable tribe, only the Catawba remained in South Carolina, and by the time the Cherokee left, they, too, were rapidly dwindling and had lost their status with the government as an independent tribe.

Today, the Catawba have regained federal status as a tribe and have reestablished a reservation near Rock Hill. The reservation operates a community and cultural center where Catawba pottery is sold, and an annual tribal festival is held in November.

■ CHEROKEE FOOTHILLS HIGHWAY *map page 237*

The Cherokee Foothills Scenic Highway (SC Highway 11) is the only road traversing the Blue Ridge in South Carolina. Despite its "scenic" name, it is not as spectacular as the Blue Ridge Parkway of North Carolina and Virginia. Autumn leaves and spring blossoms make sections of SC 11 a beautiful drive, while other parts of the 130-mile-long two-lane road offer vistas of mobile homes, small factories, and convenience stores.

■ SHOOTING THE CHATTOOGA   *map page 237, A/B-1*

The Cherokee Indians named the Chattooga "Pouring White Rocks," and you can glide in a raft downstream over deep, quiet pools beneath steep ridges of impenetrable forest rising on both sides.

The Chattooga suddenly becomes a powerful current that allows no stopping, tossing rafters toward "the Ledge," a 6-foot sheer drop onto boulders over which, hopefully, you will sail clear. Canoeing, kayaking, and rafting the wild sections of the Chattooga once killed many an ill-equipped boater inspired by the movie *Deliverance* (based upon the novel by poet James Dickey), After the movie was released in 1972, river-rafters went from 800 per year to 22,000. The Scots-Irish locals, already offended by what they considered an insulting portrayal in *Deliverance,* were angered at having their baptisms, picnics, and fishing trips disrupted by the arrival of visitors.

The U.S. Congress stepped in when, in 1974, it named the Chattooga one of the nation's rivers protected by the Wild and Scenic Rivers Act. The Forest Service was given jurisdiction over regulation of river use and the land on both sides of the Chattooga.

Under this federal protection, the Chattooga corridor is divided into sections: 68 percent classified "wild," with only foot or boat travel allowed; 5 percent scenic, with vehicles allowed to cross only by bridges; and 27 percent classified "recreational" and accessible by car on only five roads. Hiking trails and primitive campsites are on both sides of the "wild and scenic" corridor. Fishing (brook, brown, and rainbow trout and redeye bass) and hunting in season (deer, wild turkey, quail, and grouse) are also allowed.

The Chattooga is much more than wild water. The 50-mile river originates as a trickle of runoff in the mountains between Highlands and Cashiers, in North Carolina and, 10 miles later, acts as the border between Georgia and South Carolina for 40 miles. At Tugaloo Lake, the Tugaloo River replaces the Chattooga as the state border for a short stretch to Lake Hartwell and the Savannah River. The Chattooga descends nearly half a mile in that length, from 3,360 feet in North Carolina to 891 feet at Tugaloo reservoir. That's an average of almost 50 feet

An irresistible lure for kayakers is shooting the Chattooga...

per mile, a sharper drop than the average on the Colorado River. It crashes through rock plumes and over boulders, a challenge many kayakers, canoeists, and rafters cannot resist. Its rapids run the entire "class" list, from I to VI, and the final 7 miles below Earl's Ford—where Jawbone, Decapitation Rock, and others lie in wait—are restricted to professional raft guides and the most skilled kayakers.

The Chattooga is also pristine, its mountain climate heady in forest aromas of pine. This also means it is a paradise for retirement and vacation homes and resorts. A mere quarter mile of buffer on either side cannot entirely protect the Chattooga corridor. As a result, the Forest Service, urged by the Wilderness Society and other environmental and conservation groups, continues to buy, bit by bit, parcels of prime real estate beyond the corridor, from landowners threatened by development and willing to sell.

The best driving route to the river from South Carolina passes through Westminster on U.S. 76, through the heart of Blue Ridge apple orchard country. Roadside stands sell apple juice, cider, and butter, and, of course, apples all along the way. The small town of Long Creek is the "apple capital" of South Carolina, host of the South Carolina Apple Festival in mid-September. The orchards bloom in early April, and harvesting begins in September.

...whose class list runs from I to VI.

This road leads to the U.S. 76 bridge over the Chattooga. On the right, just before the bridge, is a large parking area. An easy 15-minute walk leads to picnic sites overlooking one of the most spectacular and dangerous of the river's rapids, Bull Sluice Falls, a 14-foot, three-level drop rarely ventured in a canoe but a favorite of kayakers.

Kayak aficionados will want to explore **Perception, Inc.** (800-595-2925), the world's largest manufacturer of whitewater and touring kayaks, just below the Blue Ridge in the Piedmont town of Easley, 15 miles west of Greenville on SC 8 and U.S. 123.

■ THE FOREST   *map page 237, A/B-1/2*

One day in 1990, Hunter Sams, a Blue Ridge native of Long Creek, shinnied up a towering white pine in the Sumter National Forest and perched there for five days. Sams was protesting a Forest Service timber sale in the Chattooga River basin. Sams' theatrics struck a sympathetic chord among politicians and led to a three-state alliance, the Chattooga River Coalition, with supporters in both Carolinas and Georgia. The coalition persuaded the Forest Service to embark on an unprecedented step in forest management history. In short form, the Forest Service and its researchers defined the complex ecological relationships inside the forest. Defining this ecosystem involved three national forests in the Chattooga Basin: the Chattahoochee in Georgia, the Nantahala in North Carolina, and the Sumter in South Carolina's Blue Ridge. Hundreds of forest users took part, from the Forest Service, state and county agencies, Trout Unlimited, the Chattooga River Coalition, outfitters and guides, local businesses, private landowners, and lumber and timber interests.

The Chattooga watershed covers 122,000 acres of national forests and the convergence of two rich and different ecosystems: the Piedmont and the southeastern escarpment of the Blue Ridge Mountains. Although the region was heavily logged earlier in the 20th century, the forests have recovered enough to be classified again as maturing forest, well on the way back to their pristine condition.

The Forest Service still manages the Sumter and other national forests with an emphasis on timber production (which, by law, it is mandated to do), but travel and tourism now produce more jobs. A Wilderness Society study in 1994 found that service-related jobs in the southern Appalachians, including the Blue Ridge, grew from 43 percent of all jobs in 1970 to 55 percent of all jobs in 1990. Timber employment in the area, meanwhile, accounted for less than 5 percent of all jobs.

The wonders of the Sumter National Forest can perhaps best be enjoyed with a stay at **Oconee State Park** (864-638-5353), in the heart of Blue Ridge. Oconee was one of South Carolina's first state parks, built during the 1930s by young men lucky to find food, shelter, and a few dollars with jobs in the Depression-era Civilian Conservation Corps (CCC).

Their handiwork remains today in the park's 19 rental cabins; each has a fireplace and is fully furnished, heated, air-conditioned, and supplied with linens and necessary cooking and eating utensils. The CCC's bathhouse, stone picnic shelter, log picnic shelter, and a waterwheel built to provide electricity are other examples of the use of native materials and local resources at the park.

Visitors enjoy a 20-acre lake, rental fishing boats and canoes, lake swimming, and picnic areas. Many use Oconee State Park as a base camp for trips on the Chattooga River or setting out on the 85-mile Foothills trail, which winds along the Blue Ridge border with North Carolina and ends at Table Rock State Park. Take note: "Foothills" is a misnomer. This is rugged, steep mountain country in a forest wilderness.

Crossing through icy mountain streams and forests of hemlock, some 4 feet thick, the Foothills trail passes Whitewater Falls and some 80 primitive campsites. Hikers can join the trail from four other road heads or two boat access points on Lake Jocassee.

Stumphouse Tunnel Park (864-638-4343) and Issaqueena Falls are about 6 miles northwest of Walhalla, on the right side of SC 28. A short, steep path leads from the park's parking area to the bottom of the 100-foot falls, named for a legendary Indian maiden. No locomotive ever passed through the 1,600-foot tunnel (now sealed), built in hopes of linking the port of Charleston with cities in the Midwest. Its builders went bankrupt in the 1850s. There are picnic facilities and hiking trails at the park. A half-mile farther up SC 28, in the Yellow Branch recreation area, Yellow Branch Falls cascade 60 feet over a series of ledges.

■ LAKE JOCASSEE

When Duke Power Company dammed the Keowee River just north of SC 11 near Salem in the 1960s, it created South Carolina's most beautiful reservoir, Lake Jocassee. Duke Power then built a park on the lake, Devils Fork, with villas quite unlike any in the state. The setting, backed by the Blue Ridge Mountains, includes several waterfalls pouring directly into the lake, remarkably clear and as deep as 440 feet in places. Brown and rainbow trout raised in **Walhalla National Fish Hatchery** (on SC 107 north of Oconee State Park and open to the public; 864-638-2866) are stocked in the lake annually.

Duke Power built the park and the state now manages it. There are 59 campsites on the 620 acres, each equipped with water and electricity for RVs, plus picnic tables and outdoor grills, and a separate area for walk-in tent camping, as well as swimming and a public-access boat ramp.

The prize accommodations, however, rhapsodized in travel magazines so much that reservations are necessary at least a year in advance, are the 20 mountain villas. The villas overlook the Lake Jocassee from a stand of mixed evergreens and hardwoods, and they are luxurious. All have cathedral ceilings, stone fireplaces, central heat and air, screened porches, and fully equipped kitchens for cooking your fresh catch of the day.

Jocassee has become famous for its trout and white bass. Record catches include a 17-pound, 8-ounce brown trout; a 2-pound, 5-ounce brook trout; and a 4-pound, 13-ounce white bass.

The second highest dam in the eastern United States at 385 feet (Fontana Dam in North Carolina is the highest at 480 feet), Jocassee Dam backs the reservoir into gorges and coves of the Blue Ridge Mountains. Fish grow at phenomenal rates in the cold, oxygen-rich depths. Nine-inch rainbow trout stocked in January average 17 inches by October. Keowee Toxaway State Park is just across the valley from Jocassee and Devils Fork, also on SC 11. It protects the headwaters of Duke Power's other reservoir, **Lake Keowee,** just downstream from Jocassee. The park has RV sites, tent camping sites, and picnic areas. A few miles before SC 11 reaches Jocassee and Keowee, turn north on SC 130, and in about 10 miles (watch for the sign at the state line) is **Whitewater Falls** (828-526-3765). The falls descend over six sets of cascades and are technically two falls: Upper Whitewater Falls in North Carolina, with a 411-foot drop; and on the South Carolina side, Lower Whitewater Falls, with a 400-foot drop.

■ EASTERN BLUE RIDGE PARKS *map page 237, C/D-1*

The Blue Ridge range reaches its southern end at an abrupt precipice 20 miles northwest of Greenville, in the Mountain Bridge Wilderness Area. The drop of about 2,000 feet from the mountains to the Piedmont foothills along this escarpment offers scenic vistas of distant horizons.

The state's tallest mountain, Sassafras (3,560 feet), rises just west of the wilderness preserve. Its most famous natural landmark, Caesar's Head (3,266 feet), looms within the preserve, as does what many consider to be the state's most spectacular waterfall, 400-foot **Raven Cliff Falls** (864-836-6115). A network of hiking trails, ranging in challenge levels and including portions of the National Trails System, traverses the mountains.

The lair of the Tunbridge fern is within one of South Carolina's most undeveloped, unspoiled, and least-known valleys, the **Eastatoe.** The valley extends west from U.S. 178 along the first creek north of Rocky Bottom, and there are no road signs marking it. A 1½-lane paved road parallels Eastatoe River (more accurately a large creek) down the middle of the valley, past a few houses and vegetable gardens, to **Eastatoe Gorge.** Fly fishermen often prowl the 7 miles of creek before the gorge, hoping for rainbow trout. At the end of the paved road, a strenuous hike

Along the wild and beautiful rivers of the Blue Ridge Mountains are many waterfalls, including Whitewater Falls, which empties into Lake Jocassee.

A misty mountain morning frames two horses and Lake Jocassee.

through places where the gorge walls come within a few feet of each other leads to a whitewater mist, the Tunbridge fern, and 11 species of rare moss, including one found nowhere else on earth.

Sassafras Mountain is visible farther north and to the east of U.S. 178. There are no access roads or parks at the mountain.

Three state parks in this eastern part of the Blue Ridge offer a mountain experience of wilderness, waterfalls, primitive trailside camping, and summit climbs to two Blue Ridge mountains.

Table Rock State Park (on SC 11 about 4 miles east of U.S. 178; 864-878-9813) is the oldest and most popular state park in the Blue Ridge. Built in the 1930s by the Civilian Conservation Corps, it was placed on the National Register of Historic Places in 1989. Table Rock has 14 rustic cabins with fireplaces, 100 campsites, a restaurant with dining patio, a 36-acre lake for swimming (with rental canoes, pedal boats, and fishing boats), and a 10-mile network of hiking trails. One trail leads to the 3,425-foot summit of Pinnacle Mountain and is an access to the Foothills Trail. Another leads to the 3,157-foot summit of Table Rock.

Mountain Bridge Recreation and Wilderness Area (864-836-6115) is just east of Table Rock and includes Caesar's Head and Jones Gap state parks, two of South Carolina's best fly-fishing streams, Raven Cliff Falls, and a challenging network of mountain trails.

Caesar's Head State Park (864-836-6115), with its rocky promontories and lookout tower, is popular among birders who—for a change—can look *down* upon hawks, ravens, and turkey vultures flying in the valley. From mid- to late September, great numbers of migrating broad-winged hawks pass by, drawing hundreds of binocular- and camera-toting visitors. The migratory period continues into November as osprey, sharp-shinned hawks, red-tailed hawks, peregrine falcons, and other species pass by Caesar's Head.

The same overlooks drawing birders also attract amateur and professional photographers. Visibility, however, is sometimes obscured by fog or haze. Caesar's Head is a day-use park, although trailside camping is permitted. One of the park's trails is a moderately strenuous, 2.2-mile hike to an overlook at Raven Cliff Falls.

Jones Gap State Park (864-836-3647), 6 miles east of Caesar's Head on SC 11 and U.S. 276, is within a pristine Blue Ridge valley known for its diverse plant life, hiking trails, and the Middle Saluda River, the state's first Scenic River. More than 400 species of plants have been found in the valley, including rare or endangered species and state-record-size trees.

Primitive trailside camping is permitted along the 5-mile Jones Gap Trail, which threads its way along the Middle Saluda, connecting with the 3-mile Cold Spring Branch Trail, which, in turn, leads to Caesar's Head. Both the Middle Saluda and Cold Spring Branch are noted for rainbow, brook, and brown trout.

The network of trails across South Carolina's Blue Ridge is much like the labyrinth of tidal creeks and rivers across the marshes of the state's Sea Island coast—inspiring and often humbling, two diverse refuges of wilderness only an hour's drive from major metropolitan areas.

One result of South Carolina's growing interest in nature-based tourism is the **Palmetto Trail.** A mountains-to-sea path for hikers, bikers, and campers, the Palmetto Trail connects McClellanville in the Lowcountry to the state parks at the North Carolina–Georgia border. The trail, which will run more than 425 miles, is being built one leg at a time and is more than halfway completed.

PRACTICAL INFORMATION

■ AREA CODES

The major area codes for South Carolina are 843 for Charleston, Pee Dee, and the Lowcountry; 803 for Columbia and the Midlands; and 864 for the Upcountry. South Carolina is in the Eastern Standard Time zone.

■ CLIMATE

In winter, temperatures generally average in the low 40s inland to the 60s along the coast. Summer temperatures are modified by mountains in some areas, by water in others; they usually range from the high 70s to the mid-90s, sometimes reaching into the 100s. Spring is probably the most attractive season in this part of the country, and the blooming season is when the state is most visited. Peach blossoms are followed throughout the season by blooming azaleas, wisteria, and dogwood from April into May and by apple blossoms, oleander, and crepe myrtle in the summer. Fall and winter bring glorious camellias, and the mild weather makes for great golfing and fishing year-round.

■ GETTING THERE AND AROUND

■ BY AIR

Charleston International Airport (CHS), on Interstate 526 8 miles north of downtown, is served by many national airlines. *843-767-7009; www.chs-airport.com.*

Columbia Metropolitan Airport (CAE) in the Midlands is convenient to I-26 and I-77 at 3000 Aviation Way in West Columbia and is served by many major airlines. *803-822-5000; www.columbiaairport.com.*

Greenville-Spartanburg International Airport (GSP) is halfway between Greenville and Spartanburg at Exit 57 off I-85 and is serviced by more than a dozen major airlines *864-877-7426; www.gsairport.com.*

Myrtle Beach International Airport (MYR) has many daily flights on major airlines; it's just off the Highway 17 overpass at SC 501. *843-448-1589; www. myrtlebeachairport.com.*

Two out-of-state airports are on the borders of South Carolina and can be accessed easily by car from anywhere in the state: **Savannah/Hilton Head International Airport** in Georgia (912-964-0514; www.savannahairport.com) and **Charlotte International Airport** in North Carolina (704-359-4013; www.charlotteairport.com).

■ BY CAR

The north–south routes include Interstate 95 along the Eastern Seaboard, Interstate 77 down from the Great Lakes, and Interstate 85, which passes through the upstate for just a few miles between North Carolina and Atlanta. Two other interstates crisscross South Carolina: I-20 runs from Florence past Aiken, to the southwest, and I-26 leads all the way from Greenville southeast to Charleston. Automobile is the best way to see the sights in this state, and two-lane back roads throughout the state are often the best way to encounter cotton fields, vegetable stands, and barbecue diners in small towns.

■ BY TRAIN

Amtrak provides service on its trains that run between New York and Florida, servicing Camden, Charleston, Clemson, Columbia, Denmark, Dillon, Florence, Greenville, Kingstree, Spartanburg, and Yemassee. *800-872-7245; www.amtrak.com.*

■ BY BUS

Greyhound/Trailways offers many routes throughout South Carolina. *800-231-2222; www.greyhound.com.*

■ FOOD

Dining in South Carolina is always a pleasant surprise to visitors. Particularly pleasurable are oysters, crab, and shrimp plucked out of the water only hours before they're served and locally grown tomatoes, collards, corn, peaches, and strawberries. South Carolinians take great pride in using these fresh local ingredients to make original recipes as well as contemporary renditions of old-time favorites, such as shrimp and grits, Hoppin' John, hush puppies, and she-crab soup.

CHARLESTON SHE-CRAB SOUP

The recipe calls for a *she*-crab, as opposed to a *he*-crab, because traditionally it included roe. It is illegal now to catch female crabs in the spring, when they have roe, but it is possible to buy crab roe. Most restaurants use cooked egg yolks instead.

1/4 lb. butter	Mace, salt, pepper to taste
1 Tbs. flour	Few drops onion juice
1 qt. milk	1/2 tsp. Worcestershire sauce
2 cups white crabmeat	4 Tbs. dry sherry
1/4 cup roe or 2 cooked egg yolks	1/2 cup cream, whipped

Melt butter and blend in flour. Add milk, crabmeat, roe, and all seasonings, except sherry. Cook slowly 20 min. over hot water. Pour ½ Tbs. warmed sherry into individual bowls. Add soup. Top each bowl with a serving of whipped cream (milk or half-and-half can be substituted). Serve piping hot.

There are many casual roadside spots with tasty barbecue from a "secret home-made" recipe. Every southern state seems to have its own barbecue specialty. In South Carolina, you can find all kinds of ribs and chops, but the state is most famous for a tangy pulled pork in a distinctive mustard-based barbecue sauce.

The seafood comes in seasons: shrimp season begins in May and lasts through December. Wintertime is oyster season, when locals will boil up vats in their backyard and toss hot clusters of oysters on a wooden table for you to open yourselves, with the help of your own rubber glove and a rusty knife. Lunch might be a locals' favorite known as pimiento cheese, which can be bought at the deli of any supermarket—smashed cheddar spiced with red peppers and spread on very white bread. Ham and biscuits are never out of season, especially with a cold gin and tonic.

Restaurants in Charleston can be more expensive than others in the state, but you can still find great food at lower prices in small towns and family-owned restaurants. Following are some perennial and award-winning favorites of South Carolinians.

■ FAVORITE RESTAURANTS

Anson. An elegant, local-owned favorite of Charlestonians for unforgettable crispy flounder. *12 Andon St., Charleston; 843-577-0551.*

Charlie's L'Etoile Verte. A superb French bistro with seafood and a famous Cobb salad. *1000 Plantation Center, Hilton Head Island; 843-785-9277.*

1109 South Main Restaurant. Fresh seafood in a lovely Greek Revival mansion. *1109 S. Main St., Anderson; 864-225-1109.*

Gullyfield Restaurant. A landmark eatery famous for its lobster pie. *Kings Hwy., Myrtle Beach; 843-449-3111.*

Hudson's. Casual spot serves seafood from its own family-owned fishing boats. *The Landing, Hilton Head Island; 843-681-2772.*

Jasmine Porch at The Sanctuary. The newest culinary experience in the new beachside luxury resort. *Kiawah Island; 843-768-6000.*

Jestine's Kitchen. Southern comfort food, including fried chicken, spicy collards, and red beans and rice. *251 Meeting St., Charleston; 843-722-7224.*

Lilfred's. Gourmet dining in the middle of the Midlands, serving seafood, steaks, and game. *11 Main St. on Hwy. 521 between Sumter and Camden; 803-432-7063.*

Magnolia's. Chef Donald Barickman invented nouvelle southern cuisine in this pretty downtown favorite. *185 E. Bay St., Charleston; 843-577-7771.*

The Old Post Office. Wonderful preparations of shrimp, filet mignon, flounder, and quail. *1442 Hwy. 174, Edisto Island; 843-869-2339.*

Oliver's Lodge. The oldest seafood restaurant in town serves sophisticated seafood with modest prices. *4204 Business Hwy. 17, Murrells Inlet; 843-651-2963.*

Peninsula Grill. Chef Robert Carter has won many awards and local acclaim for his chops, and seafood. Inside the elegant Planters Inn. *Meeting St. at Market St., Charleston; 843-723-0700.*

River Room. Lovely dining room and fresh seafood, overlooking the Sampit River. *801 Front St., Georgetown; 843-527-4110.*

Saluda's. A fine restaurant in Columbia's Five Points District. *751 Saluda Ave. Columbia; 803-799-9500.*

Track Kitchen. A local favorite of the horsey set, serving breakfast and lunch. *420 Meade Ave., Aiken; 803-641-9628.*

Woodlands Resort & Inn. People drive from Charleston for the food at this opulent resort just 25 miles from the harbor town. *125 Parsons Rd., Summerville; 843-875-2600.*

■ LODGING

The Sea Islands and coastal resorts, including Charleston and Hilton Head, have deluxe hotels with deluxe prices. The islands also have many rentable private vacation homes and villas, listed on dozens of Web sites. These range from simple bungalows to grand oceanfront mansions and are a good option if you plan to stay a week or longer. The entire state has major chain motels, and many towns have delightful hotels and B&Bs.

■ RESERVATIONS SERVICES

Historic Charleston Bed & Breakfast represents 60-plus private homes and carriage houses in the historic district. *57 Broad St., Charleston, SC 29401; 843-722-6606 or 800-743-3583; www.historiccharlestonbedandbreakfast.com.*

Hospitality Association of South Carolina. *3612 Landmark Dr., Columbia, SC 29201; 803-765-9000; www.schospitality.org.*

South Carolina Bed & Breakfast Association. *Box 1275, Sumter, SC 29150-1275; 888-599-1234; www.bbonline.com/sc/scbba.*

■ FAVORITE LODGINGS

Charleston Place Hotel. A deluxe hotel in the heart of town, with an award-winning grill and full-service spa. *205 Meeting St., Charleston; 843-722-4900; www.charlestonplace.com.*

Chesterfield Inn. A small inn with verandas and ocean views. *700 N. Ocean Blvd., Myrtle Beach; 843-448-3177.*

John Rutledge House Inn. Built in the 1700s by the statesman who signed the Declaration of Independence. *116 Broad St. Charleston; 843-723-7999.*

Kiawah Island Resort. Choose from the sumptuous new beachfront hotel, the Sanctuary, or rent a cottage by the week and enjoy the 12-mile beach, marsh kayaking, and superb golf. *12 Kiawah Beach Dr., Kiawah Island; 843-768-2121; www.kiawahresort.com*

Litchfield Plantation. A luxurious 1750 plantation house in an unparalleled setting. *River Road, Pawleys Island; 843-237-9322.*

Rhett House Inn. A luxurious Greek Revival mansion with gracious service, in the heart of historic Beaufort. *1009 Craven St., Beaufort; 843-524-9030.*

Sea Pines Plantation. The original Sea Island resort has been renovated and still offers the best of amenities. *Hilton Head Island; 843-842-1894 or 800-845-6131.*

Myrtle Beach, circa 1940.

The Willcox. This old hotel with pegged oak floors and a beautiful lobby has hosted Winston Churchill, FDR, and many others in its long history. *100 Colleton Ave., Aiken; 803-648-1898.*

Woodlands Resort & Inn. A 42-acre estate with superb food and golf and tennis, only 25 miles from Charleston. *125 Parsons Rd., Summerville; 843-875-2600 or 800-774-9999.*

■ HOTEL AND MOTEL CHAINS

Best Western. *800-528-1234;* www.bestwestern.com.

Days Inn. *800-325-2525;* www.daysinn.com.

Doubletree. *800-222-8733;* www.hilton.com.

Hilton Hotels. 800-445-8667; www.hilton.com.

Holiday Inn. 800-465-4329; www.6c.com.

Marriott Hotels. 800-228-9290; www.marriott.com.

Quality Inns. 800-228-5151; www.qualityinn.com.

Radisson. 800-333-3333; www.radisson.com.

Ramada Inns. 800-272-6232; www.ramada.com.

Sheraton. 800-325-3535; www.sheraton.com.

Westin Hotels. 800-228-3000; www.westin.com.

■ CAMPING

The South Carolina state park service has family campgrounds (some with hot showers and power hookups) for tents, trailers, and RVs. These are listed at www. discoversouthcarolina.com.

■ GOLF COURSES

South Carolina's collection of golf courses is among the best in the nation. From rolling hills of former plantations to the challenges of seaside links, the courses are open year round. Many of the private courses are open to members of out-of-state golf clubs. Here are just a few of the recognized favorites.

Bay Tree Golf Plantation. *Myrtle Beach; 843-249-1487 or 800-845-6191.*

The Dunes Golf and Beach Club. *Myrtle Beach; 843-449-5236.*

Haig Point. A locals' favorite. *Daufuskie Island; 800-922-3635.*

Heather Glen Golf Links. *North Myrtle Beach; 843-249-9000.*

Heritage Club. *Pawley's Island; 843-236-9318.*

Hilton Head National Golf Club. An established, classic challenge. *843-842-5900.*

Indian Wells. *Garden City; 803-651-1505.*

Island West Golf Club. *Hilton Head; 843-842-2401.*

Kiawah Island Golf Resort. Five award-winning courses, many on the ocean. *800-576-1570; www.kiawahresort.com.*

The Legends. *Myrtle Beach; 800-299-6187.*

Sea Pines Plantation. *Hilton Head; 843-842-1894 or 800-845-6131.*

Tidewater Golf Club. *North Myrtle Beach; 843-249-3829 or 800-446-5363.*

Wild Dunes Resort. *Isle of Palms (just north of Charleston) 888-778-1876.*

■ USEFUL WEB SITES

Offbeat sources for events and sites in South Carolina can be found on Web sites of alternative weeklies such as the *Columbia Free Times* (www.free-times.com) and the *Charleston City Paper* (www.charlestoncitypaper.com). Another good source for state activities and tourism news is www.charleston.net. South Carolina's official Web site, www.discoversouthcarolina.com, is a wonderful source with basic contact information for many of the state's sights and attractions.

■ Festivals and Events

■ January

Charleston: Lowcountry Oyster Festival. Steamed oysters, live music, an oyster-shucking contest, children's events. *843-853-8000.*

Cowpens: Battle of Cowpens Reenactment. Annual reenactment of this Revolutionary War battle at the Cowpens National Battlefield. *864-461-2828.*

Orangeburg: Grand American Coon Hunt. The largest American field trial for coon dogs. *800-545-6153.*

■ February

Charleston: Southeastern Wildlife Exposition. Wildlife paintings, sculptures, auctions, at more than 15 venues downtown. *843-853-8000.*

■ March

Aiken: Aiken Triple Crown. Three weekends in March showcase fine horse racing as young thoroughbreds trained in Aiken race for the first time. *803-641-1111.*

Beaufort: Spring Tour of Homes. Mansion and garden tours of downtown Beaufort and Lowcountry plantations. *843-524-3163.*

Charleston: Festival of Houses and Gardens. Historic Charleston Foundation tours of treasured homes and gardens, which are especially beautiful during this season. Continues through April. *843-723-1623.*

Darlington: The NASCAR Winston Cup Series Transouth Financial 400. The best NASCAR, Indy, and other road-racing drivers compete for championship. *843-395-8892.*

Myrtle Beach: Canadian-American Days Festival. In honor of Canadians on spring break. Sporting events, concerts, and St. Patrick's Day parade. *843-626-7444.*

■ April

Allendale: Allendale County Spring Cooter Fest. In honor of the town's favorite turtle species; events include a turtle race, music, and beauty contest. *803-584-0082.*

Camden: Carolina Cup. Thoroughbred steeplechases and flat racing. Held at the Springdale Race Course. *803-432-6513.*

Charleston: Family Circle Cup. Ladies' professional tennis tournament featuring the top-ranked players from around the world, at a new stadium on Daniel Island. *843-856-7900.*

Charleston: Lowcountry Cajun Festival. Spicy Louisiana and Lowcountry cooking draws big crowds to James Island County Park. Also crawfish races, crawfish-eating contest, Cajun and zydeco music. *843-762-2172.*

Columbia: Taste of Columbia. Popular food festival held at Riverbanks Zoo and Garden. *803-779-8717.*

Hilton Head Island: MCI Heritage. PGA professional golf tournament. *843-671-2448.*

Manning: Striped Bass Festival. Celebrating spring and the legendary striped bass with a parade, crafts, catfish wrestling, and boat poker run. *803-435-8477.*

St. George: World Grits Festival. Features the Miss Grits beauty pageant, a carnival, and grits-eating contests. *803-563-9091.*

Summerville: Flowertown Festival. Flower show, arts and crafts, food, and entertainment in downtown Azalea Park. *843-871-9622.*

Walterboro: Colleton County Rice Festival. Parade, fireworks, rice-cooking contests, and the "world's largest pot of rice." *843-549-1079.*

■ MAY

Anderson: Freedom Weekend Aloft. The state's largest hot-air balloon event. *864-232-3700.*

Beaufort: Gullah Festival. Highlights the fine arts, customs, language, and dress of Lowcountry African-Americans. *843-524-3163.*

Charleston: Spoleto Festival USA. Runs through early June. World-renowned chamber music concerts, international opera and ballet, as well as a concurrent **Piccolo Spoleto Festival,** with hundreds of shows, among them theatrical plays, spirituals concerts, and live jazz. *843-722-2764; www.spoletousa.org or www.piccolospoleto.com.*

Columbia: Mayfest. The capital city's largest arts and entertainment festival, with a southern-food plaza and children's fun fair. *803-343-8750.*

Whimsically invigorating the Piccolo Spoleto Festival is an Atlanta band, The Seed & Feed Marching Abominable.

■ **JUNE**

Greenwood: South Carolina Festival of Flowers. Garden tours, events, music, house tours. *864-223-8411.*

Hampton: Hampton County Watermelon Festival. A weeklong festival with parades, races, and dances. *803-943-3784.*

Myrtle Beach Sun Fun Festival. A sandcastle-building contest among other summer kickoff activities. *843-626-7444.*

Trenton: Ridge Peach Festival. Arts and crafts, a softball tournament, and peach desserts. *803-275-2538.*

■ **JULY**

McConnells: Revolutionary War Battle Reenactment. Watch a reenactment of the 1780 Battle of Huck's Defeat near historic Brattonsville. *803-684-2327.*

Pageland: Pageland Watermelon Festival. Features clogging, arts and crafts, watermelon-eating and seed-spitting contests, and a rodeo. *843-672-6400.*

■ **AUGUST**

Pelion: South Carolina Peanut Party. Activities include the annual blessing of the peanut pots. *803-894-3535.*

■ **SEPTEMBER**

Charleston: Moja Arts Festival. African-American and Caribbean cultures of the Lowcountry showcased with lectures, art exhibits, performances, tours, and jazz concerts. *803-724-7308.*

Charleston: The Preservation Society of Charleston's Annual Fall Candelight Tour of Homes & Gardens. *800-968-8175.*

Mullins: South Carolina Golden Leaf Festival. Celebrating the tobacco industry with live entertainment, a husband-hollering contest, and a Party after Dark. *843-464-5200.*

■ **OCTOBER**

Charleston: Coastal Carolina Fair. 10-day county fair with rides, animals, shows, and food. *843-572-3161.*

Georgetown: Ghost Tour. A self-guided tour and carnival sponsored by the "ghost capital of the world." *843-546-8436.*

Georgetown: Wooden Boat Challenge. Wooden-boat builders from across the state compete in a contest along historic Front Street at the harbor walk. *843-527-4110.*

Myrtle Beach, Valhalla, Spartanburg: Oktoberfest. Oompah music, bratwurst, and beer. *843-626-7444.*

■ **NOVEMBER**

Camden: Colonial Cup. Championship steeplechase. *803-432-6513.*

Camden: South Carolina Revolutionary War Field Days. 600 reenactors perform daily, along with special activities and food. *803-432-9841.*

Rock Hill: South Carolina Yap Ye Iswa (Day of the Catawba) Tribal Festival. Pottery, crafts, drummers, performances, food. *803-328-2427.*

St. Helena Island: Penn Center Heritage Celebration. Celebrates Sea Island history and culture with crafts, educational exhibits, traditional spirituals, and food. *843-838-2432.*

Salley: Chitlin' Strut. Deep-fried pig intestines, hog-calling contests, and country music. *803-258-3485.*

Society Hill: The Catfish Festival. Fried catfish and catfish stew, as well as children's games, fishing tournaments, and all-day entertainment. *843-378-4681.*

■ **DECEMBER**

Charleston: Christmas at Middleton Place. Tours of the house museum, decorated with traditional holiday greenery. Family yuletide in the stable yards and other events. *843-556-6020.*

Columbia: The Lights Before Christmas. Riverbanks Zoo and Garden becomes a winter wonderland. *803-779-8717.*

RECOMMENDED READING

◼ FICTION

Allison, Dorothy. *Bastard out of Carolina.* New York: Penguin, 1992. A mesmerizing story of a young girl in Greenville County caught between her stepfather's violence and her love for her mother.

Baldwin, William. *The Hard to Catch Mercy.* Charleston: History Press, 1993. Humorous tale about outlandish, down-and-out characters in South Carolina's Lowcountry during the early 20th century.

Conroy, Pat. Mr. Conroy has authored several best-selling works of fiction that center on characters from South Carolina's Lowcountry. Best known, and developed into a major motion picture, is *The Prince of Tides,* about a football coach who travels to Manhattan and befriends his disturbed sister's psychiatrist, thus reviving childhood family traumas. Other books by Mr. Conroy with Lowcountry characters include *Beach Music* and his first book, the memoir *The Water Is Wide.* All published by Bantam Books, New York.

Frank, Dorothea Benton. *Sullivan's Island.* New York: Jove, 2000. A woman returns to the beachfront house where she grew up, to contemplate her future as well as her troubled past.

Humphreys, Josephine. *Rich in Love.* New York: Penguin, 1987. The story of a Gullah woman in South Carolina.

Peterkin, Julia. *Scarlet Sister Mary.* Athens: Univ. of Georgia Press, 1928. The Pulitzer Prize–winning life story of Mary, a Gullah woman on a South Carolina coastal plantation.

Sanders, Dori. *Clover.* New York: Ballantine Books, 1991. Touching story about a young black girl's relationship with her white stepmother.

■ History and Culture

Edgar, Walter B. *South Carolina, A History.* Columbia: Univ. of South Carolina Press, 1999. This 714-page masterwork is the daddy of all South Carolina history books, as much admired for its thoroughness as for its ease of reading.

Rogers, George C., Jr. *Charleston in the Age of Pinckneys.* Columbia: Univ. of South Carolina Press, 1980. A history of a prominent Charleston family throughout the 18th and 19th centuries.

Rutledge, Archibald. "Plantation Lights and Shadows" in *The Carolina Lowcountry.* New York: Macmillan Co., 1931. Life and culture of the Lowcountry, with essays by DuBose Heyward, Josephine Pinckney, and others.

Twining, Mary A., and Keith E. Baird. *Sea Island Roots: African Presence in the Carolinas and Georgia.* Trenton, N.J.: Africa World Press, 1991. A collection of essays and personal reminiscences about the life and culture of the Gullah.

Woodward, C. Vann. *Mary Chesnut's Civil War.* New Haven: Yale Univ. Press, 1983. The Pulitzer Prize–winning history of the daughter of a South Carolina senator and wife of a Jefferson Davis military aide, during the years 1861–1865.

■ Memoirs and Diaries

Ball, Edward. *Slaves in the Family.* New York: Ballantine, 1998. The National Book Award winner about one South Carolinian's search for the black descendants of his ancestors.

Bolton, Ruthie. *Gal: A True Life.* New York: Onyx, 1995. The best-selling memoir of a poor girl growing up in 1960s Charleston.

Daise, Ronald. *Reminiscences of Sea Island Heritage: Legacy of Freedmen on St. Helena Island.* Orangeburg, S.C.: Sandlapper Publishing, 1986. A beautiful collection of historic photographs of and interviews with the Gullah people of St. Helena Island.

Higginson, Thomas Wentworth. *Army Life in a Black Regiment.* New York: Penguin Classics, 1971. In this work originally published in 1870, a white Union officer records his experience as the officer in command of the First Southern Carolina Volunteers, the first all-black military unit of any kind mustered into the Union forces.

Whaley, Emily, with William Baldwin. *Mrs. Whaley and Her Charleston Garden.* New York: Fireside, 1998. A lively memoir from the late grande dame of Charleston gardening.

■ GUIDEBOOKS

Baldwin, William. *Lowcountry Daytrips.* Greensboro, N.C.: Legacy Publications, 1993. A detailed driver's guide to notable historic sites along the coast.

Edgar, Walter B., editor. *South Carolina: The WPA Guide to the Palmetto State.* Columbia: Univ. of South Carolina Press, 1988 (originally published in 1941). This classic guide to the state was part of the highly acclaimed Federal Writers Project of the 1930s and 1940s and remains an indispensable text.

INDEX

COMPASS AMERICAN GUIDES

This book is available for special discounts for bulk purchases for sales promotions or premiums. Special editions, including personalized covers, excerpts of existing books, and corporate imprints, can be created in large quantities for special needs. For more information, write to Special Markets/Premium Sales, 1745 Broadway, MD 6-2, New York, New York 10019, or e-mail specialmarkets@randomhouse.com.

COMPASS AMERICAN GUIDES

Critics, booksellers, and travelers all agree: you're lost without a Compass.

"This splendid series provides exactly the sort of historical and cultural detail about North American destinations that curious-minded travelers need."
—*Washington Post*

"This is a series that constantly stuns us . . . no guide with photos this good should have writing this good. But it does." —*New York Daily News*

"Of the many guidebooks on the market, few are as visually stimulating, as thoroughly researched, or as lively written as the Compass American Guide series."
—*Chicago Tribune*

"Good to read ahead of time, then take along so you don't miss anything."
—*San Diego Magazine*

"Magnificent photography. First rate."—*Money*

"Written by longtime residents of each destination . . . these handsome and literate guides are strong on history and culture, and illustrated with gorgeous photos."
—*San Francisco Chronicle*

"The color photographs sparkle, the archival illustrations illuminate windows to the past, and the writing is usually of the utmost caliber." —*Michigan Tribune*

"Class acts, worth reading and shelving for keeps even if you're not a traveler. "
—*New Orleans Times-Picayune*

"Beautiful photographs and literate writing are the hallmarks of the Compass guides." —*Nashville Tennessean*

"History, geography, and wanderlust converge in these well-conceived books."
—*Raleigh News & Observer*

"Oh, my goodness! What a gorgeous series this is."—*Booklist*

ACKNOWLEDGMENTS

■ FROM THE PUBLISHER

Compass American Guides would like to thank the following individuals or institutions for the use of their illustrations or photographs:

All photographs in this book are by Eric Horan unless noted below.

History & Culture:
Page 14, South Caroliniana Library, University of South Carolina
Page 17, South Caroliniana Library, University of South Carolina
Page 18, Library of Congress Geography and Map Division
Page 20, South Caroliniana Library, University of South Carolina
Page 22, Library of Congress Prints and Photographs Division
Page 24, Greenville County Museum of Art
Page 25, South Caroliniana Library, University of South Carolina
Page 29, Greenville County Museum of Art
Page 31, South Carolina Historical Society, Charleston
Pages 32-33, Greenville County Museum of Art
Page 39, South Carolina Historical Society, Charleston
Page 43, Carolina Boykin Spaniel Retriever Club

Sea Islands:
Page 50, South Caroliniana Library, University of South Carolina
Page 57, Kiawah Island Golf Resort
Page 68, Penn School Collection, St. Helena Island
Page 74, South Carolina Department of Parks, Recreation, and Tourism
Page 75, Kiawah Island Golf Resort

Coastal Plantations:
Page 81, South Caroliniana Library, University of South Carolina
Page 82, South Caroliniana Library, University of South Carolina
Page 90, South Carolina Historical Society, Charleston
Page 99, South Carolina Historical Society, Charleston

Page 101, South Carolina Historical Society, Charleston
Page 102, Greenville County Museum of Art

Charleston:
Page 108, Library of Congress Prints and Photographs Division
Page 111, South Caroliniana Library, University of South Carolina
Page 113, South Caroliniana Library, University of South Carolina
Page 117, South Caroliniana Library, University of South Carolina
Page 122, South Caroliniana Library, University of South Carolina
Page 125, South Carolina Historical Society, Charleston
Page 138, South Carolina Historical Society, Charleston

Myrtle Beach:
Page 147, South Carolina Historical Society, Charleston
Page 148-49, South Carolina Department of Parks, Recreation, and Tourism

Coastal Plain:
Page 182, South Caroliniana Library, University of South Carolina
Page 186, South Caroliniana Library, University of South Carolina
Page 200, South Carolina Historical Society, Charleston
Page 204, South Carolina Historical Society, Charleston

The Piedmont:
Page 215, Photography Collection, Miriam and Ira D. Wallach Division of Art, Prints and Photographs, The New York Public Library, Astor, Lenox and Tilden Foundations
Page 217, South Carolina Department of Parks, Recreation, and Tourism
Page 224, South Caroliniana Library, University of South Carolina
Page 231, David Crosby

Blue Ridge:
Page 239, South Caroliniana Library, University of South Carolina
Page 241, Greenville County Museum of Art

Practical Information:
Page 257, South Caroliniana Library, University of South Carolina, photograph by Carlisle Roberts (WPA-PL-HC-MB-14)

■ ABOUT THE AUTHORS

Henry Leifermann grew up in South Carolina and attended the University of South Carolina. He has worked as a reporter for *The State* in Columbia, as well as for UPI, Newsweek, and the *New York Times* Sunday travel section. He is the author of *Crystal Lee,* which was later adapted for the Academy Award–winning film *Norma Rae.*

Jane O'Boyle is a writer who lives on Clark Sound. A former book publishing executive, she is the author of several books and is a columnist for *Charleston* magazine.

■ ABOUT THE PHOTOGRAPHER

Eric Horan is a freelance photographer based in Hilton Head, South Carolina. He has been recognized in state, national, and international competitions, including Sierra Club and *South Carolina Wildlife Magazine.* His work has appeared in *Time, Fortune, Business Week, Tennis,* and the *New York Times* travel section.